# Integrated management tools in the heritage of South-East Europe

Directorate of Culture and Cultural and Natural Heritage
Regional Co-operation Division

Council of Europe Publishing

Cover and text: Documents and Publications Production Department, Council of Europe

Cover photos:
*Albania* – The Church of the Holy Virgin Mary Monastery, Goranxi, Dropulli region (Council of Europe)
*Bosnia and Herzegovina* – Old town of Stolac (Council of Europe)
*Bulgaria* – Hydro-electric power plant "Pancharevo", Kokaliane (Council of Europe)
*Croatia* – Urban ensemble, Lubenice, Island of Cres (Council of Europe)
*Montenegro* – Church of St Nicholas, Nikoljac (Council of Europe)
*Romania* – "Biserica Doamnei" ("The Church of the Princess") (Council of Europe)
*Serbia* – Smederevo Fortress (Council of Europe)
*"The former Yugoslav Republic of Macedonia"* – The Archaeological Site of Heraclea Linkestis, Bitola (Council of Europe)

Council of Europe Publishing
F-67075 Strasbourg Cedex
http://book.coe.int

ISBN 978-92-871-6264-9
© Council of Europe, January 2008
Printed at the Council of Europe

# Integrated management tools in the heritage of South-East Europe

Directorate of Culture and Cultural and Natural Heritage
Regional Co-operation Division

# Colophon

Director of the Publication: Robert Palmer (Director of Culture & Cultural and Natural Heritage, DGIV)

Co-ordination: Mikhäel de Thyse (Regional Co-operation Division, DGIV)

Editor: Robert Pickard (Expert consultant, Co-ordinator of the Legislative Support Task Force)

Text: Part 1 of this publication sets out a series of National Reports and identifies the names of the various contibutors of these reports.

The expert presentations in Parts 2 to 5 of this publication were authored by Juris Dambis (Latvia), Graham Fairclough (United Kingdom), Todor Krestev (Bulgaria), Friedrich Lüth (Germany), Robert Pickard (United Kingdom), Geneviève Pinçon (France), Jacques-Emmanuel Remy (France), Tatjana Rener (Slovenia) and Ann-Mari Westerlind (Sweden).

The Conclusion in Part 6 was prepared by Robert Pickard.

# Contents

**Bulgaria**

**Croatia**

**Montenegro**

**Romania**

**Serbia**

**"The former Yugoslav Republic of Macedonia"**

# PART 2

## CHARACTERISATION AND DOCUMENTATION SYSTEMS

# PART 3

## ENVIRONMENTAL ASSESSMENT

# PART 4

## SPATIAL AND URBAN PLANNING SCHEMES AND REGULATIONS

# PART 5

## AUTHORISATION, CONSULTATION, SUPERVISION AND PENALTY PROCEDURES

**PART 6**

# Foreword

As a part of its contribution to ensuring democratic stability in South-East Europe, the Council of Europe proposed to Albania, Bosnia and Herzegovina, Bulgaria, Croatia, Kosovo/UNMIK, Montenegro, Romania, Serbia and the "former Yugoslav Republic of Macedonia" the Regional Programme for Cultural and Natural Heritage in South-East Europe. The programme is conceived as a specific contribution to the development of democratic, peaceful and open societies in South-East Europe, in which the active participation of all citizens is promoted irrespective of religion, language, gender or ethnicity.

The Regional Programme includes three main complementary components: an Institutional Capacity-Building Plan, an Integrated Rehabilitation Project Plan and the proposed development of Local Development Pilot Projects.

The Institutional Capacity-Building Plan concentrates on the provision of policy and legal advice, with the aim of establishing appropriate legislative frameworks, administrative reforms and national and local cultural heritage policies. It also considers the development of management tools and human resource development in relation to the provision and use of inventories and documentation, institutional co-ordination, integrated heritage conservation and enhancement, urban and land use planning decisions, and provision of realistic strategies for development.

Within the context of this plan, a series of international debates has been organised by the Council of Europe in association with different host countries. This book is the second to be published as a result of these multilateral activities and it addresses issues in relation to the development and use of integrated management tools, through the presentation of national reports, comparative summaries and expert presentations.

# Introduction

Since 2003, the Regional Programme for Cultural and Natural Heritage in South-East Europe (RPSEE) has been one of the main activities of the Technical Co-operation and Consultancy Programme (Directorate of Culture and Cultural and Natural Heritage, DG IV) of the Council of Europe. It focuses on Albania, Bosnia and Herzegovina, Bulgaria, Croatia, Kosovo/UNMIK, Montenegro, Romania, Serbia and "the former Yugoslav Republic of Macedonia".

The first part of the regional programme is the Institutional Capacity-Building Plan, which is a forum for exchanging experience and best practice between all the participating countries and experts from other Council member states. It encourages analysis and discussion, and it provides a common conceptual basis for the other two strands, the Integrated Rehabilitation Projects and Local Development Pilot Projects, which are geared more towards action on the ground.

The main challenge facing the south-east European countries is the adoption of a legal framework conducive to the emergence of new cultural and natural heritage management methods in line with the concepts of integrated conservation and sustainable development.

The issue of legislative reforms in the field of cultural heritage was the first theme of the multilateral debates, which aimed to review the progress of legislative reforms under way in the participating countries and to identify the key issues of common interest to be dealt with by the regional programme in future years. The debate continued in order to help the participating countries to build up or improve their integrated management tools for cultural and natural heritage.

It was aimed specifically at officials from the Ministries of Culture, the Environment and Regional/Spatial Planning responsible for implementing integrated management tools, in particular the countries' representatives on the Council of Europe's steering committees in the policy sectors concerned, namely CDPAT (cultural heritage), CODBP (environment) and CEMAT (regional/spatial planning). This cross-sectoral approach was both a "first" and a key opportunity for technical, political and institutional co-operation at the Council of Europe in the cultural and natural heritage field.

The experts of the Technical Co-operation and Consultancy Programme's Legislative Support Task Force put forward four topics corresponding to the main integrated heritage management tools:

1. documentation systems for cultural and natural heritage;

2. environmental assessments for major development projects and plans;

3. spatial and urban planning plans/regulations;

4. permits, supervision and penalties concerning heritage conservation work.

Representatives of the ministries concerned presented summaries of the situation regarding each of the above topics in their countries. Part 1 contains the full text of these national reports. They are the result of a questionnaire sent out by the Legislative Support Task Force on the basis of in-depth knowledge of the situation on the ground. It is reprinted in an appendix to this publication.

Parts 2 to 5 concentrate on the four topics in turn, with a comparative summary of the situation in each country, followed by expert presentations on the particular theme. Part 2 gives examples of good practice in characterisation and documentation systems from France, Germany, Latvia and the United Kingdom. Part 3 has examples of environmental impact assessment of landscape in Sweden and heritage and tourism on the southern coast of Albania. Part 4 considers examples of planning and development schemes and integrated conservation issues from Bulgaria, Latvia and Slovenia. Part 5 looks at processes and procedures for consultation, applications for consents and permit controls, the supervision of works and the application of sanctions in Germany, England and Ireland.

Part 6 of the publication is a conclusion, which recapitulates the main issues discussed and the recommendations proposed.

# PART 1

## NATIONAL REPORTS

# Albania

*Florent Çeliku, Arlinda Kondi Toçi, Ariana Koça and Shpresa Leka*

## 1. Documentation systems

The Ministry of Culture, Youth and Sports, the Academy of Sciences, the General Directorate of State Archives, the universities and local governing bodies, each in accordance with their respective fields of investigation, carry out searches, protection, preservation, restoration, treatment and study, as well as creating inventory and database entries, of cultural heritage objects.

The Ministry of Culture, Youth and Sports through the Cultural Heritage Department is responsible for the protection and restoration of monuments of culture. The Cultural Heritage Department is a policy-making unit which has under its jurisdiction the Institute of Monuments of Culture, the Centre for Computerised Inventory of Cultural Properties and the National Museums of Albania. The ministry collaborates with the Ministry for Territorial Planning and Tourism and the Ministry of the Environment over inter-related issues of heritage, environment, planning and similar matters.

### 1.1. Identification

The institution responsible for cataloguing cultural properties is the Albanian Centre for Computerised Cataloguing of Cultural Properties. It is under the jurisdiction of the Ministry of Culture. Cataloguing cultural properties is an ongoing process: so far, the centre has registered in its database the movable objects in the ownership of state institutions dependent on the Ministry of Culture, and the National Museums.

The Institute of Monuments of Culture is the state institution responsible for restoration and preservation of monuments of culture. The archive of this institute has full records of data relating to cultural monuments. Each monument has a file (hard copy) in which are shown its main characteristics, with description, plans, photos, elevation, dates of restoration of that monument, persons responsible for restoration and estimates of interventions. This institute is dependent on the Ministry of Culture, Youth and Sports of Albania and has eight branches in the main cities of Albania.

The Institute of Archaeology is the state institution responsible for archaeological excavation and restoration of archaeological objects. It is dependent on the Academy of Sciences, not the Ministry of Culture. The Institute of Archaeology collaborates efficiently (as provided by Law No. 9048, dated 7 April 2003 on Cultural Heritage) with the Institute of Monuments of Culture. The Institute of Archaeology has its own archives, where there are full records of archaeological excavations undertaken by this Institute and/or in collaboration with foreign experts. The documentation can be consulted upon official request to the institute.

The Institute of Archaeology and the Institute of Monuments of Culture are obliged (by the Law on Cultural Heritage) to give the necessary data to the centre compiling a computerised inventory of these objects.

Example: There are examples of good collaboration between the General Directorate of Forest and Pasture or GDFP (Ministry of Agriculture and Food) and the Department of Nature Protection (Ministry of the Environment) relating to protected areas. An example is the CDDA exercise, where the GDFP made available its database to the Directorate of Nature Protection Directorate. There are some difficulties to overcome in formal communication because of intellectual property rights and use of information for profit.

## 1.2. Characterisation

The necessary information related to a monument is found in the archives of the Institute of Monuments and in the Institute of Archaeology. The information is only about the monument or object itself and any interventions undertaken on it. So we have scope to elaborate the 'characterisation' package of heritage in Albania.

Documents illustrating the whole evolution of the context (in particular, environmental and planning) of certain monuments can be consulted in relevant responsible ministries.

Example 1: When the intervention to be undertaken concerns urban planning, and is at national level, the proposal for the intervention is subject to a meeting of the Council of Territorial Planning of the Republic of Albania. Before this meeting, the proposal is distributed to relevant ministries (Ministry of Culture, Ministry of Territorial Planning, Ministry of the Environment, Ministry of Justice, Ministry of Local Government and Decentralisation) who provide their professional expertise (supporting documentation, suggestions, approval or not) about this intervention in written form. They discuss it in the meeting of the Council of Territorial Planning, where each relevant ministry is represented by the minister. The Institute of Monuments of Culture is represented in this body as the Technical Secretariat. The opinions of relevant ministries are attached to the project decision of the Council of Ministers, which, by written approval of the ministers, signs it.

Example 2: Information related to the environment is held in the Ministry of the Environment, at the Ministry of Agriculture and Food, which operates at central level. An example of information taken into account when environmental planning documents are prepared is in the case of the Management Plan of Divjaka–Karavasta Lagoon or Dajti National Park, where heritage, culture and settlements are considered together with landscape character, geomorphology, climate, water resources, agriculture, forestry, mineral and energy resources.

Example 3: If there is a proposal by a donor to contribute financially for the restoration of a specific monument, the proposal is submitted to the Ministry of Culture and the Institute of Monuments of Culture. The feasibility study, with supporting documentation and relevant estimates, is drawn up by specialists at the Institute of Monuments of Culture. The feasibility study is put before the National Council of Restoration (a decision-making body), the members of which, after consulting and evaluating the study, approve it, if it is in accordance with the laws and regulations. After approval, procedures for tender continue. If the proposal for intervention concerns the monument itself and the surrounding area, it becomes subject to an agreement signed by the interested parties. An example is the agreement signed recently by UNOPS and the University of Parma on one side, and the Ministry of Culture, Institute of Archaeology and Municipality of Durres on the other, concerning the valorisation of the Amphitheatre of Durres.

## 1.3. Database and computerised mapping

The Institute of Cultural Monuments, the National Centre of Cultural Properties' Inventory, the Institute of Archaeology, the Institute of Folk Culture and the General Directorate of the State Archives, following scientific criteria, ascertain the values of the tangible and intangible cultural heritage (already declared as such), which are the property of any physical or legal person, and assemble their certification. These objects must be recorded in the National Centre of Cultural Property Inventory, which issues the certification passport of the object based on the above mentioned data. Every change in ownership of the objects should be registered in the National Centre of Cultural Property Inventory.

The National Centre of Cultural Property Inventory has already begun compiling the necessary data for immovable objects. The centre has two main databases: one for objects in the ownership of state authorities or individuals, and one for lost cultural heritage objects. An electronic card is compiled for each object, which contains relevant data for that object, such as: characteristics and description, date of creation, photographs, place and address, construction, date of interventions for restoration undertaken up to the time of registration, ownership, current location, author of the object and plans. The centre is collaborating with central and local institutions to collect the necessary data. The database is not yet available for public use; it can be consulted only at the centre itself.

There have been efforts to construct other databases, such as a Common Database on Designated Areas (CDDA) or for flora, fauna, soils and forests, water and air quality (with statistics, text and illustrations, in Word and Excel software) using the raw monitoring data of research institutions, but these are not linked with GIS, and neither integrated nor co-ordinated. This information is supplied to the Centre of Information in the Ministry of the Environment (Communication and Foreign Relations Directorate), which can make it available to the public. There is also a webpage of the Ministry of the Environment (www.moe.gov.al) and data are made available to the public through the clearing-house mechanism of biodiversity (http://nfp-al.eionet.eu.int:8180). The Environmental Legislation and Planning CARDS project, funded by the EU, is working on building a modern information system with a database and computerised mapping.

There is an ACESS database on Albanian protected areas, which was constructed in 2004 on the Common Database on Designated Areas (CDDA), which reports to the European Environmental Agency (EEA) and is renewed every year. It contains the names of protected areas, World Conservation Union (IUCN) category, surface, partial co-ordinates and date of designation. This database is managed by the Directorate of Nature Protection in the Ministry of the Environment.

The Law on Protected Areas (Law No. 8906), dated 6 June 2002, ensures the protection of natural resources and biodiversity, by designating protected areas. The categories of protected area according to this law and IUCN are:

1. Natural reserve/scientific reserve (strictly considered as such)

2. National Park

3. National Monument

4. Natural managed reserve/ area of managed habitats and species

5. Protected landscape

6. Protected area of managed resources/protected area with multi-purpose use

The protected areas are mainly designated for natural environmental protection, but some of them interlink with the cultural environment (archaeological sites, caves, churches) as in Butrinti National Park.

Example: Few of the protected areas have GIS mapping or scanned JPG plans, the main exceptions being those recently designated, like the Narta-Vjosa protected landscape.

Most protected areas are owned by the General Directorate of Forestry and Pasture, which manages them (and their database). There are initiatives of local government, in districts like that of Tirana, that with the help of scientific advice are producing catalogues, databases and maps of natural monuments (including caves, which are important for the natural and cultural heritage of Albania – for example, the Black Cave in Tirana).

Other databases relating to natural heritage are inventories for flora and fauna in coastal lagoons, soil indicators, irrigation water quality, soil erosion, the health of forests, and water and air quality. The latter are monitored by research institutions, funded by the Ministry of the Environment since 2000. This information is made public every two years through the State of the Environment Report. Other information comes from state-funded projects on environmental aspects of certain areas.

## 2. Integrated management studies, plans and regulations

### 2.1. Environment

According to the Law on Environment Impact Assessment (Law No. 8990), dated 23 January 2003, Albanian experts carry out two types of environmental study, depending on a project's size and environmental impact: profound and summary studies.

Activities that undergo a profound process of environmental impact assessment (EIA) are:

Foundries or factories

Production of base organic chemicals

Production of base inorganic chemicals

Plants for intensive rearing of poultry, pigs and sheep

Industrial plants

Treatment and processing aiming at production of food

Activities that undergo a summary process of EIA are:

Agriculture, forestry and aquatic life

Projects for rehabilitation of rural areas

Projects for using non-agricultural land or half-natural areas for intensive agriculture

Projects on water management for agricultural needs, including projects of irrigation and drainage of the land

Reforestation and deforestation with the intention of changing the land use

Intensive fish farms

Mining industry

Energy industry

Production and processing of metals

Chemical industry

Food industry

Leather, wood and paper industry

Rubber industry

EIA may also be conducted for:

### Infrastructure projects

Urban development, including construction of shopping centres and vehicle parking places

Construction of railways, inter-modal facilities and transport terminals

Construction of airports, roads, ports and port installations, including fishing ports

Construction of canals

Other installations designed to hold water or to conserve it for the long term

Trams, elevators and underground railways used only or mainly for passengers

### Pollution and waste projects

Installations used for waste elimination

Plants for treatment of polluted waters

Installations for collection of waste

### Tourism and leisure

Cable cars, transport using overhead wiring and developments including these

Tourist ports

Tourist villages and hotel complexes outside urban areas and developments including these

Camp sites and camping areas

Amusement parks

### Strategic environmental assessment (SEA)

In addition to the assessment of particular projects in terms of their impact on the environment, a form of strategic environmental assessment is carried out in relation to potential impacts of proposed plans and programmes in relation to:

Strategies and action plans for energy, mines, industry, transport, agriculture, forests, natural resources, mining property management and waste management

Territorial adjustment to national and regional plans of urban and rural centres, industrial areas, coastal areas, tourist areas, protected areas, areas of high pollution and damage-sensitive areas

The state body, natural or juridical person that submits a proposal shall compile a strategic environmental assessment and ask for its evaluation by the Minister of the Environment prior to endorsement by relevant organs. The assessment is presented in an Environmental Declaration, which is subsequently published.

Impact analysis is undertaken for EIA and SEA in relation to:

Impacts on human health, fauna and flora, land, water and air, climate and land-scape, and cultural and historical heritage

Nature of impact (direct, indirect, permanent, temporary, positive, negative)

Measures for the alleviation of the impact on the environment

Impacts of a cross-border nature

Environmental Impact Reports are compiled by licensed natural and juridical persons selected, contracted and paid by the proposer. The compilers of the report shall be liable for the accuracy of data and recommendations in accordance with the laws in force.

### Public consultation

The project and the report of impact assessment on the environment are subject to a public consultation where representatives of the ministry that licenses the project and any territory adjustment, tourist bodies, local government bodies, specialised institutions, interested parties, environmental non-profit-making organisations and the proposer participate.

The consultation should be organised and directed by the local government body for the area where the project will be implemented, which, within five days of receipt of the consultation request from the Minister of the Environment, should:

– notify the public and environmental non-profit-making organisations and put at their disposal the impact assessment on the environment for a period of one month, and

– in collaboration with the Ministry of the Environment and the proposer, set the debate day, notify participants ten days in advance and, within the one-month deadline, organise the open debate with all the interested parties.

If at the conclusion of the debate the participating parties do not submit their opinions to the Ministry of the Environment, the commission of request review should continue with the procedures.

The interested public and environmental non-profit-making organisations should partici-pate in all phases of the impact assessment on the environment, including the decision-making. The Minister of the Environment should determine with separate normative acts the duties of environmental organs in order to guarantee participation of the public and of environmental non-profit-making organisations in this process.

Consultation in relation to an object with architectural, historical or cultural value is compulsory, a legal obligation deriving from the Law on Culture Heritage and the Law on Urban Planning. These consultations ought to be expressed in an official way by legal documents. The consultations are made at the level of field experts, carrying out the necessary revisions on specific projects; furthermore, consultations are also made at the level of the Institute of Cultural Monuments and the Regional Office for the Protection of Cultural Monuments. After these consultations, the Scientific Council of the Institute of Cultural Monuments analyses the project and makes the relevant scientific and technical recommendations for the National Council of Defence and Monument Restoration. In cases of archaeological zones or discoveries, the same procedure is followed for the specialised institutions of archaeology.

If an interested party or environmental non-profit-making organisation observes irregularities in the process of impact assessment on the environment, they should require the Minister of the Environment to partially or entirely review the process of impact assessment on the environment and the Minister should reply within twenty days from receipt of the request.

According to Law No. 8906 for Protected Areas, dated 6 June 2002, the declaration of a protected area and its buffer zone should be made by a decision of the Council of Ministers on the proposal of the Minister of the Environment upon receipt of opinion from local government bodies, specialised institutions, non-profit-making organisations and private owners (if their estates are included in the protected area).

According to a Decision of the Council of Ministers No. 267 dated 24 April 2003, Concerning Procedures Regulating Proposal and Declaration of Protected and Buffer Zones, any state structure or institution, central or local, physical or legal person, non-profit-making organisation and/or community has the right to submit to the Ministry of the Environment proposals for protected zones, for changes in or withdrawal of protected area status, the expansion or contraction of boundaries and the internal zoning of such areas. When declaring a protected area, consideration should be given to the network of protected areas contained in the strategy and the action plan on biodiversity. Before publishing the plan on protected areas, a one-month lead time should be assigned for suggestions and objections that may be submitted to the Ministry of the Environment. Upon expiration of the lead time, provided there have been no suggestions and/or objections, the plan is considered valid. Based on this plan, the ministry starts procedures for the preparation and presentation of draft decisions to declare the protected areas.

## 2.2. Spatial and urban planning

Law No. 8405, dated 17 September 1998, on Urban Planning expresses and defines the general rules of construction placement and architecture in the entire territory of the Republic of Albania. The preparation process of the law has taken into account the economic and social development, present and future of the country, at national and local level, the protection of the environment, preservation and display of urban planning, architectural and archaeological value, and the protection of legal interests concerning private property.

Urban discipline is implemented through Territorial Planning, Urban Planning and the defined norms and regulations.

Spatial Planning is guided by the following principles:

Sustainable development of the area

Conservation of general and special values of the area

Improvement of the quality of life

Reducing the impact of human settlements on the natural and environmental systems

Benefiting, conserving, evaluating and improving the existing environmental, architectural, cultural and social qualities, as well as avoiding unfavourable land use

Predicting likely development, in case alternative possibilities already exist or might emerge from reorganisation or re-evaluation

Spatial planning in Albania is applied to the main territories on the basis of the area monitored by each district administration, and is organised through the Regional Studies.

A Regional Urban Study covers the territory of a district, of specific districts and communes, of different water catchment areas, or a territory that presents a certain set of problems (environment, conservation, drainage, tourism etc.), such as trans-border territories.

The highest state organ for approval of urban planning studies is the Council of Territorial Adjustment of the Republic of Albania (CTARA), which is a decision-making body and functions close to the Council of Ministers chaired by the Prime Minister. The technical secretariat of CTARA functions in the relevant ministry (Territorial Adjustment and Tourism). Subordinate to this ministry is the Institute of Studies and Urban Planning, which is the state organ at national level that elaborates the studies and urban construction plans defined in the Urban Planning Regulation.

The specialising urban planning units at local government level are:

The Council of Territorial Regulation, for regional, municipal and commune councils (CTR)

The Urban Planning Unit (director, section or bureau) of the region, municipality or commune

CTARA also approves the following documents:

1. Strategic plans;

2. Master plans of areas larger than 10 hectares and master plans for the development of tourist areas;

3. General adjustment plans, for developments bordering the boundaries or edge of the built-up area of administrative centres of a district and other towns with a population over 10 000;

4. Operational plans;

5. Urban planning studies of centres of towns with a population of over 50 000 and partial urban planning studies within towns larger than 15 hectares;

6. Land-use plans.

In preparing regional studies, master plans of territorial development, adjustment plans and partial studies, areas are assessed and their environmental values, ecological systems, national parks, and flora and fauna reservations determined, according to classification and criteria for their preservation, protection and development, under separate provisions.

Sites, existing constructions and complexes of archaeological, museum and historical value must be considered in urban planning studies, with a view to ensuring their protection according to the requirements of specialised institutions.

Example: Any type of construction within 200 metres of the border of an archaeological site under protection is prohibited.

It is obligatory for any construction in museum cities, on their protected sites, near separate monuments or on sites around them, to be built in accordance with the definitions of this law, in accordance with the prior opinion of the relevant institutions.

With regard to the administration of museum cities, the Law on Cultural Heritage provides that: "the City's Museums, historical centres, ensembles and archaeological parks are preserved in their complexity as historical, archaeological, monumental, urban ensembles, and to that end, new constructions which affect the existing heritage are prohibited". Also, according to this law architectural objects can be reused without having a negative impact on the current condition of the monument.

The law provides that, for each monument, a surrounding area (protected area) should be established by the Institute of Monuments of Culture, in which every intervention should be made only upon approval of the Institute of Monuments of Culture and the Institute of Archaeology. Regional spatial planning takes into consideration the existence of objects with values conditioning the preservation of protective spaces for a certain distance from the objects declared "cultural monuments" or architectural ensembles.

In some cases, architectural and urban ensembles are being re-evaluated and are to be changed into attractive travel destinations. In this direction, there is too much work to be done because in many cases funds are needed in order to achieve their revitalisation. The preservation, protection and development of structures, architectural and urban planning objects of special value are reflected in the urban planning studies approved by the Council of Territorial Adjustment.

The Institute of Monuments of Culture plays an active role in this Council, expressing professional expertise in the proposed intervention. The first step is the drafting of a Project Council of Ministers' Decision, which expresses the measures for the intervention. The draft is distributed to line ministries (central government) and local government, who give their approval about the proposal. The draft decisions are studied by the respective juridical departments and the relevant experts in the field. If there is a disagreement, a working group is established to work out the different suggestions and to come up with one decision. The decision is discussed in the above mentioned Council, which approves it, and the decision of the Council of Ministers is signed by the Prime Minister.

*St John Prodrom Church,*
*Voskopoja (Council of Europe)*

## 1. Strategic plans

Law No. 8991 dated 23 January 2003, concerning some additional changes to Law No. 8405 dated 17 September 1998 on Urban Planning, considers also a "Strategic plan", which is a progressive participatory process that, through a medium-term plan, ensures the interplay of all factors affecting the attainment of strategic goals set by the ultimate decision-makers at local government level. The strategic plan combines physical, financial and institutional aspects. The thrust of strategic plans is management of the residential area as a whole, or at least of its main elements: housing, land, infrastructure, generation of financial resources and general administration integrating these elements.

Likewise, the development of cities is monitored by a Strategic Plan, which through a medium-term plan attempts to achieve strategic objectives established by the local authorities. This strategic plan combines the physical, financial, and institutional aspects of development of the city. The strategic plan is targeted at the city management as a whole or at least its essential elements: residence, land, infrastructure, generation of financial resources and general administration, often aiming at their integration.

According to a decision of the Council of Ministers No. 267 dated 24.04.2003, concerning Procedures Regulating Proposal and Declaration of Protected and Buffer Zones, the Ministry of the Environment compiles the plans for the declaration of protected zones. The plans should define the zones to be placed under protection, with conditions, boundaries and proposed scale of protection in each case. The plan is compiled in conjunction with the Ministry of Agriculture and Food, the Ministry of Territorial Regulation and Tourism, the respective local governments, scientific research institutes and environmental non-profit organisations. In the case of one zone declared protected, the ministry should define primarily its status, boundaries and internal zoning, as well as its surrounding buffer zones, the administration staff and line of dependence, opportunities for utilisation and exploitation of the zone, revenue that may be created and manner of utilisation of such revenue based on regional developmental studies.

## 2. Master Plans

The Master Plan represents a specific urban plan, which predicts development in the physical context of the territory. It is supported by regional plans for land use or by strategic plans. The Master Plan is a subsidiary document of urban planning, between the regional plan and the General Adjustment Plan. The Master Plan includes territorial administrative boundaries to guarantee its efficiency.

The Master Plan in Albania is a medium-term plan. It is compiled for an unlimited period and remains valid until the coming into force of another master plan. The Master Plan is divided into general adjustment plans and partial urban studies.

## 3. General Adjustment Plans

An "Adjustment plan" represents a complex urban study for a limited area and includes the territory of a city together with its suburb zone or the area belonging to a village, any human settlement, a recreation area, an industrial site or other built-up area.

The General Adjustment Plan (GAP) is a complex trans-discipline document of urban planning, co-ordinating the whole development of a city or human settlement in its physical, social, economic and environmental aspects. GAPs are compiled on the basis of a draft duty (reference terms), prepared and approved by the relevant local bodies having jurisdiction over the territory of the city or human settlement. The GAP establishes and resolves the following:

    the boundaries of the city or human settlements;
    the urban and sub-urban boundaries;
    land use after evaluation of the seismological and hydro-geological conditions;

environmental protection from building works;

protection of areas with historical, cultural, monument, image or environmental value;

specific land use for civil construction, education, recreation, sports, business, infrastructure and so on;

the boundary lines of construction and of the suburbs.

GAPs are compiled to establish the development of a city or human settlement for a 10- to 15-year period.

It is worth mentioning that a component part of adjustment plans and strategic plans for urban development is the orientation, protection and enrichment of cultural, historical and monumental values of the ancient inheritance and of that which results in a process that is part of contemporary regional and European urbanism.

## 4. Operational Plans

The Operational Plan (OP) is a non-compulsory document covering a 5-year period. It is prepared in order to assist the co-ordination of a GAP and the operational actions for the necessary interventions made by the local government.

## 5. Partial Urban Planning Studies

The Partial Urban Study (PUS) is the main document of urbanisation in Albania in support of and in implementation of the technical criteria established by the master plans, general plans and operational plans.

A PUS is compiled on the basis of programmes approved by the relevant local unit according to the demands and interest of the relevant communities, while respecting the legal and technical criteria in force. A PUS for intervention in historical, cultural or natural areas is approved by the respective ministries. In historic zones and protected historic zones, intervention through town planning studies is categorically prohibited.

On the basis of the urban planning law, approval of studies and designs is decided at two levels:

1. Council of Territorial Adjustment of local units

2. Council of Territorial Adjustment of the Republic of Albania (CTARA)

In each local unit (municipality, commune and district) there is a Council of Territorial Adjustment, which approves all studies and projects in any phase where approval is needed, regardless of the size, type or other quality of the development. At national level, CTARA approves major studies and projects, as well as construction permits for important projects as established by Law No. 8405 dated 17.09.1998 on Urban Planning.

As a result of legal conditions applied during the compilation and preparation of projects, they must display all the conditions that guarantee the conservation of cultural values, the protection of cultural and historical monuments, and their integration and reflection in the process of sound development. This fact is conditioned by legal definitions in the Law on Urban Planning, in the Law on Cultural Heritage, and some laws on the environment, among others.

### 6. Land Use Plans

On the basis of Albanian legislation, land use plans are established in the legal structures of general and partial urban studies.

> Example: According to the law, building works are carried out within the legal boundaries (building lines) according to the definitions in the approved studies of the approved functional areas. Outside these boundaries, all building works are illegal. During the transition period in Albania there occurred the social phenomenon of population movement from poor districts to places that offered possibilities of a better life. This phenomenon created an chaotic urban situation and showed the need for integration of these areas in normal development. For this reason it was necessary to revise the studies then in force and the legal provision for this phenomenon.

In conclusion: Albania has inherited an ancient historical and spiritual culture along with, as a result, a purely material culture in the architectural and urban fields. In the context of this awareness and the present European activity, Albania is interested in promoting this cultural enrichment.

## 3. Authorisation, supervision and penalties

### 3.1. Authorisation

According to the Law on Environmental Protection (Law No. 8934), dated 5 September 2002, in order to develop an activity that affects or is likely to affect the environment, the physical and legal persons, native or foreign, are obliged to obtain approval of this activity from the competent authority defined by this law. The physical and legal persons should submit the request and relevant documents in order to get approval for their activity. According to the cases specified in this law, approval of the request is made by way of an environmental declaration, environmental permit, consent or authorisation. These are official documents that establish the conditions and circumstances that the approved activity must respect in order to prevent or mitigate its impact on the environment.

The Environmental Declaration is the official document issued by the Minister of the Environment, after review of the request and relevant documentation, for the approval of the project, plan or programme. The declaration may refuse or approve the forwarded request, accompanying it with obligatory conditions to be implemented by the proponent and competent authorities.

The Environmental Permit is the official document issued by the Ministry of the Environment, after review of the request and its relevant documentation, and consultation with all the concerned stakeholders. The permit approves the exercise of any activity having an impact on the environment, and determines the conditions and circumstances to be obligatorily implemented, in order that pollution and damage to the environment do not exceed the allowed norms.

Activities of a local character having an impact on the environment, but not included in the Council of Ministers' Decisions, are approved by Regional Environmental Agencies in co-operation with local government bodies. Approval for these activities is given in the form of consent or authorisation.

According to Albanian legislation, for each building permission that relates to a protected zone or a zone near an archaeological or historical site, despite normal procedures being followed by the owners or developers, approval must also be given by the specialised state institutions responsible for the preservation, protection and rehabilitation of architectural monuments, historical centres and archaeological sites through their decision-making boards. According to the Law on Cultural Heritage (Article 47), an investor who wishes to start construction work is obliged to consult the specialists of the Institute of Monuments of Culture and the Institute of Archaeology before and during the process of planning and implementing the project.

The Institute of Archaeology, after a survey has been carried out, gives its opinion if the place has or has not any archaeological value. If the place has no archaeological value, permission is given to the investor. Otherwise, the project proposal of the investor must be altered in line with the suggestions of the specialists of the state institution (Institute of Archaeology, Institute of Monuments of Culture) and the costs of this alteration are met by the investor.

The Institute of Monuments of Culture also verifies whether the change will affect any monument or its surrounding protection area. Permission for the proposal (i.e. construction permit) is given by the Ministry of Territorial Adjustment and Tourism.

Moreover, Article 48 specifies that if, during construction (immediately after construction works have begun), traces or objects of archaeological or ethnological value are found, work will immediately be suspended. Those who initiated the works must inform within three days the local authorities, the Institute of Archaeology and the Institute of Cultural Monuments, who make their assessments, report on the values found and make proposals on the continuation or not of the working procedures.

## 3.2. Supervision and penalties

In the field of cultural heritage, violation of these two articles is fined with a penalty ranging from 1 000 000 lekë (LEK) to LEK 5 000 000 (approximately €8 000 to €40 000).

Damage caused to unique objects of cultural heritage constitutes a penal act and is penalised according to the legislation.

In the field of environment, control is the duty of the Environmental Inspectorate and Regional Environmental Agencies; the Forest Police, the Construction Police, the Sanitary Inspectorate, the Plant Protection Inspectorate, the Fishery Inspectorate, the Hydrocarbons Inspectorate, the Zoo-Veterinary Inspectorate and the controlling bodies of local governments. The relevant local authorities exercise control on the basis of the normative acts that regulate their specific activities.

According to a decision of the Council of Ministers, No. 266 dated 24.04.2003 Concerning the administration of protected areas, the government is charged among other things with administration of protected zones, guarding protected zones (a police function) and oversight of the implementation of the zone's management plan.

According to Law No. 8934 dated 5 September 2002 on Environmental Protection, violations of this law constitute a penal act and the Environmental Inspectorate asks for penal proceedings. Violations that do not constitute a penal act are regarded as administrative contraventions in the field of environmental protection. For the administrative contraventions above, penalties are given according to three categories: from LEK 500 000 to LEK 1 000 000; from LEK 300 000 to LEK 500 000; from LEK 10 000 to LEK 300 000.

Besides any penalties, the sequestration of means and substances that pollute or damage the environment is decided. In addition, depending on the level of the pollution or damage already caused, the temporary or permanent interdiction of the permit is decided. For every case of opposition to the application of the above measures, the Environmental Inspectorate co-operates with the State Police. According to Law No. 8906, dated 06.06.2002 on Protected Areas, violations of this law that do not constitute a criminal offence shall constitute an administrative contravention.

According to Albanian legislation on construction, for each building it is obligatory to supervise each phase of construction and to ensure it is in conformity with the project approved by the responsible institutions. Each deviation from the project or non-fulfilment of approved schemes carries a penalty including the suspension of the works.

# Bosnia and Herzegovina

*Amra Hadžimuhamedović, Vesna Karacic and Azra Korac-Mehmedovic*

## 1. Documentation systems

### 1.1. Identification

The state level inventory has been established by the Commission to Preserve National Monuments and consists of a Register of designated national monuments (monuments, sites and ensembles), a Preliminary (tentative) List of properties and a List of Petitions containing properties that are in the process of designation. This register at state level is used as a basis for preparatory activities for the nomination of Bosnia-Herzegovina heritage to the World Heritage List.

There are also inventories of cultural and natural properties at regional level – Federation of Bosnia and Herzegovina, Republika Srpska and the Brčko District, mainly established before 1992. According to records from 1986 supplied by the Statistics Institute of the Republic of Bosnia and Herzegovina, 727 monuments and sites were then registered. The Spatial Plan of Bosnia and Herzegovina was drawn up in 1987; according to the Plan, 8 800 immovable cultural monuments were listed, of which 2 267 were registered. Based on chronological and stylistic features, the architectural heritage falls into eleven groups. Criteria are set in the Criteria for Valorisation of the Study on Cultural and Natural Heritage within the Spatial Plan of Bosnia and Herzegovina.

The process of drawing up inventories of cultural and natural properties at state level is under way, and a Law on the Cultural Heritage of Bosnia and Herzegovina (which is being drafted) will define the issue of administration of archives.

The Commission's register contains the following information about every designated national monument: location, land registry references, property data, construction and conservation order dates, historical, technical and artistic descriptions, photographs, technical documentation, maps and geodetic plans, valorisation. Registers of institutions at regional and local level contain the following information on the majority of the cultural heritage monuments: construction and conservation order dates, descriptions, photographs and plans (technical drawings).

Ministries and departments at national level: responsible for identification of cultural heritage include:

Commission to Preserve National Monuments
National Museum of Bosnia and Herzegovina

Ministries and departments at entity/regional level: responsible for identification of cultural heritage include:

   Federation of Bosnia and Herzegovina: Ministry of Physical Planning and Environment

   Institute for the Protection of Monuments operating within the Federation of Bosnia and Herzegovina: Ministry of Culture and Sports

   Ministry of Spatial Planning, Construction and Ecology of Republika Srpska

   Republic Institute for the Protection of Cultural-Historical and Natural Heritage, Republika Srpska

Ministries and departments at local level: responsible for identification of cultural heritage include:

   Institute for the Protection of Cultural-Historical and Natural Heritage of Canton Sarajevo

   City Institute for the Protection of Cultural-Historical and Natural Heritage, Mostar

   Institute for the Protection of Cultural-Historical and Natural Heritage, Tuzla

   Institute for the Protection of Cultural-Historical and Natural Heritage of Una-Sana Canton

   Regional Institute for the Protection of Monuments, Trebinje

Up until 1995 (the year when the General Framework Agreement for Peace in Bosnia and Herzegovina was signed), individual registers in the institutions were kept separately and it was possible to establish the exchange of information only upon written request. Given the fact that the list of units in the registers was not publicly known (not promulgated in the official gazettes or published on a website), it was often difficult to exchange information among institutions. Preparations are being made for setting up a single database that will provide for the automatic exchange of information. There are now established procedures for the exchange of information. A characteristic example of that kind is access to the documentation that forms an integral part of a decision of the Commission to Preserve National Monuments of Bosnia and Herzegovina.

The Government of the Federation of Bosnia and Herzegovina and the Government of the Republika Srpska, their relevant ministries, the heritage protection authorities, and the municipal authorities in charge of spatial planning and land registry affairs, are notified of the decision on the designation of a National Monument in order to carry out the measures stipulated in the decision, and the authorised municipal courts are notified for the purposes of registration in the Land Registry.

After the decision is signed, the enacting clause is promulgated in the official gazettes and the full decision is published on the Commission's website. All supporting documentation is accessible to everybody – institutions and individuals – on written request, in line with the Book of Rules for the use of monument-related records from the archives of the

Commission to Preserve National Monuments, published on the Commission's website (web: www.aneks8komisija.com.ba).

In the process of drafting decisions, the Commission submits a written request to municipalities, regional institutions and ministries to provide any relevant documentation that they have in their possession about the property referred to in the decision and the institutions have an obligation to submit the requested records pursuant to the provision of Article VIII of Annex 8 of the General Framework Agreement for Peace in Bosnia and Herzegovina.

## 1.2. Characterisation

A register of monuments is drawn up to include all national monuments, with all relevant data on the property (property rights, description of the site and its environment, architectural description, historical data, etc.).

Measures are being taken to permanently protect the monuments. The protection measures contain:

- – instructions for future works on the national monument, and its possible use, including
  - information on relevant administrative authorities in charge of issuing permits for conducting any kind of works on the national monument
  - information on the institutions protecting the property that are authorised to conduct and supervise any kind of works on the national monument
  - information on the works permitted to be conducted on the monument
  - information on urgent works on the monument, if needed
  - information on specific risks to which the monument is exposed
- – Measures to protect the immediate and wider surroundings of the national monument:
  - information on the works permitted to be conducted in the immediate vicinity of the monument
  - information on the permitted level of site development
  - properties disturbing the ambience to be identified and pulled down
  - define possible use of the properties in the immediate vicinity

The above protection measures are submitted to the relevant institutions at entity/regional level in order to be co-ordinated with the activities of conservation, and also to be used for drafting or amending spatial and urban development plans.

On the Commission's decisions, the relevant entity governmental authorities, the Government of the Federation of Bosnia and Herzegovina and the Government of Republika Srpska are responsible for ensuring and providing the legal, scientific, technical, administrative and financial measures necessary to protect, conserve, display and rehabilitate the national monument. The governments are responsible for providing the resources for drawing up and implementing the necessary technical documentation for the rehabilitation of the national monument.

All executive and development planning acts not in accordance with the provisions of the decision on national monuments are revoked.

*Church of St Nicholas in Trijebanj near Stolac (Council of Europe)*

## 1.3. Databases and computerised mapping

In the field of heritage, all data submitted to the Commission or collected in the process of drafting a decision to designate properties as national monuments are digitised and saved in a database. This comprehensive database – the digital archives of the Bosnia and Herzegovina heritage – includes three components: a database for the protocol (all data submitted to the Commission), a database of monument-related records (all data on a monument that is collected during the works, such as photographs, texts, drawings, copies of the plans, etc.), and a database on archived documents and plans. The comprehensive database is only partly in use at the moment (only a part of the base for the protocol can be used).

There are plans to link the above databases in a computerised mapping system – GIS, through MapInfo or another similar programme. As the databases themselves have not yet become operational, this segment either has not been fully worked out or is not yet in use.

The target group of direct users of the Digital Archive of Bosnia and Herzegovina Heritage project consists primarily of the Commission itself, together with various local, entity, national and international institutions and bodies directly or indirectly dealing with the cultural and historical heritage of Bosnia and Herzegovina: ministries responsible for civil affairs, education, science, culture, spatial planning and environment, foreign trade, economic relations and finance, institutes responsible for heritage issues in Bosnia and Herzegovina, museums, archives, galleries, and other institutions such as universities and non-governmental organisations.

Other target groups are institutions outside Bosnia and Herzegovina. Formation of a digital archive of the cultural and historical heritage in Bosnia and Herzegovina, backed up by the presentation and publication of part of the archived material via the Internet, will facilitate co-operation and communication between these and other interested parties.

A uniform spatial information system is assumed in spatial planning legislation, which means that all administrative units have the obligation to collect, process and classify all information relevant for spatial planning, and this also forms the database (UGIS) to be co-ordinated at entity level. Apart from data about spatial planning acts, land use, property, infrastructure and so on, the database will include relevant information about cultural and natural heritage.

The Commission has on several occasions submitted applications to various institutions for the project of establishing a digital archive of Bosnia and Herzegovina. After the entire system is set up, it would be necessary to organise additional educational courses for the Commission's staff and provide training so they can use the above database and connect it with the UGIS system, which has been established within the ministries of spatial planning.

## 2. Integrated management studies, plans and regulations

### 2.1. Environment

In Bosnia and Herzegovina, all activities related to environmental protection and improve-ment, including environmental impact assessments and related studies conducted prior to the adoption of large-scale plans and projects that have and/or could have negative impacts on the environment or elements of it, are to be in accordance with the Law on

Environmental Protection (published in Official Gazette No. 33/03)[1] and the Rulebook on Plants and Installations (see Official Gazette No. 19/04).[2]

The objectives of the Law on Environmental Protection are:

- preservation, protection, restoration and improvement of the environment's ecological quality and capacity, and of the quality of life,
- measures and conditions for managing, preserving and rational use of natural resources,
- creating the framework for legal measures and institutions for the preservation, protection and improvement of the environment,
- financing environmental activities and facilitating voluntary measures,
- allotting responsibilities, tasks and duties of public administration at different state levels.

The provisions of the Law cover:

- all environmental components (air, water, soil, flora and fauna, landscape, built environment),
- all forms of activities that utilise, load, pose a hazard to or pollute the environment, or have an impact on the environment (such as noise, vibration or radiation – with the exception of nuclear radiation, waste and other emissions).

The Rulebook on Plants and Installations for which an EIA is required, and which can be set up or operate only if they obtain an environmental permit, determines the following:

- the competent authority issuing environmental permits for plants and installations that must follow EIA procedures, which is the Federal Ministry of Physical Planning and Environment;
- the competent authority issuing environmental permits for plants and installations that do not come under EIA rules – that is, plants and installations that are under the limits determined by this Rulebook or that are not listed in this Rulebook – which is the authorised cantonal ministry;
- the content of the environmental impact study (EIS);
- the criteria for determining whether an EIA is necessary or not;
- planned activities that are not plants and installations, but have an impact on the environment.

---

1. The Law on Environmental Protection is based on the EU EIA directives.
2. The Rulebook on Plants and Installations which identifies the need to obtain an environmental permit before setting up and operating projects in cases where an environmental impact assessment is required is a by-law based on the Law on Environmental Protection.

The scope of the EIA is identification, description and assessment of the direct and indirect effects of a project on the following elements and factors:

- human beings, fauna and flora;
- soil, water, air, climate and the landscape;
- material assets and the cultural heritage;
- interaction between the factors mentioned in the previous three points.

Projects (plants and installations) subject to an EIA are specified and listed in the Rulebook on Plants and Installations for which an EIA is required. They must obtain an environmental permit before they can set up or operate, if they belong to the following spheres of activity:

- energy industry
- chemical industry
- metal industry
- waste management or mineral industry
- infrastructure systems
- water management
- extraction industry
- agriculture, water-power engineering or forestry
- food-processing industry
- textile, tanning, timber or paper industry
- tourism or entertainment

The Federal Ministry of Physical Planning and Environment, as the Competent Ministry for the EIA procedures in force, involves all relevant bodies at the cantonal and federal levels. The EIA may be carried out in two phases:

- prior environmental impact assessment (EIA),
- environmental impact study (EIS).

The competent ministry decides whether an EIS is needed on the basis of the prior EIA procedure. An EIS needs to have the following content:

- a description of the proposed project,
- a description of the environment that could be endangered by the project,

- a description of the possible significant project impacts to the environment,

- a description of the measures envisaged in order to reduce the negative effects,

- an outline of the main alternatives,

- a non-technical summary,

- an indication of likely difficulties.

The competent ministry publicises the application and organises a public hearing through newspapers with a public notification of the EIS draft.


## 2.2. Spatial and urban planning

According to the law, the spatial planning documents are spatial plans, as follows: the Spatial Plan of the Federation of Bosnia and Herzegovina, and the Spatial Plan of the Republika Srpska; the Spatial Plan of a canton; the Spatial Plan of an area with special features; the Spatial Plan of two or more cantons; the Spatial Plan of the cities of Mostar, Sarajevo and Banja Luka; the urban development plan, detailed environmental design plans: (regulatory plans, urban development projects) and other environmental design documents, defined by the Law on the Spatial Planning of Cantons.

In accordance with the Constitution of the Federation of Bosnia and Herzegovina and administrative division, spatial planning is the subject of divided jurisdiction of the Federation and ten cantons. The Spatial Planning Law defines the aims and scope of spatial planning activities, as follows.

The planned management, use and protection of land is ensured by the implementation of spatial planning documents, which are based on a coherent approach to the policy of spatial planning and principles of sustainable development.

Planned spatial development in the Federation of Bosnia and Herzegovina rests on the principles of:

- distributed legislative competence between federation and canton(s);

- equally balanced economic and social development of the federation area, including the cultivation and development of regional spatial features;

- protection of land in accordance with sustainable development principles;

- protection of integral values of land, and protection and improvement of the environment;

- harmonising the interests of land users and action priorities important for the federation;

- harmonising the spatial planning policy of the canton(s) with the spatial planning policy of the federation, and with other cantons;

- harmonising the spatial plans of the federation and the Republika Srpska;

- harmonising the spatial plans of Bosnia and Herzegovina and those of neighbouring states;

- publication of and free access to the records and documents important for spatial planning, according to these and other special regulations;

- establishing the system of information on the lands/areas important for the federation, for the purpose of planning, using and protecting the federation lands/areas.

According to the law, it is obligatory for the following spatial planning documents to be adopted:

- for the territory of Republika Srpska – Spatial Plan of Republika Srpska;

- for the territory of the Federation –Spatial Plan of the Federation;

- for the territory of the Canton – Spatial Plan of the Canton;

- for the cities of Mostar, Sarajevo and Banja Luka – Spatial Plan of the City;

- for significant areas – Spatial Plan of the Area with Special Features;

- for the urban area of the municipality in which is the Canton seat – Urban Development Plan;

- for a town-like settlement – Urban Development Plan of the town;

- for restricted urban areas, if included in the urban development plan – Regulatory Plan and Urban Development Project.

According to the law, the responsibility for the preparation and plan-making depends on the level of the authority. The ministry is the agent in charge of preparing a spatial planning document, and Parliament is in charge of adopting it. When two or more authorities are in charge of adopting a spatial planning document, they designate the agent in charge of preparing it through a mutual agreement. The agent in charge of preparing spatial planning documents that are to be adopted by a canton, city or municipality is determined by the cantonal law.

The technical work of drafting spatial planning documents is done by the executive authorities of the entity and canton, or city, through legal entities registered to conduct those affairs – or by other legal entities, on the basis of public competition, when the agent in charge of preparing the document is not the authority tasked with drafting the document by the foundation decision.

In the Book of Rules on requirements and criteria for the incorporation of companies and other legal entities to conduct technical works of spatial planning, the government, upon the proposal of the ministry, lays down the requirements that have to be met, along with general requirements, by companies and other legal entities in order to be part of the register of firms authorised to conduct spatial planning activities.

The procedure for any spatial planning document is given in a sub-law document, "A Decree on single methodology for drafting spatial planning documents – Official Gazette of the Federation of Bosnia and Herzegovina No. 63/04", which includes replies to most frequently asked questions.

The coherent approach to the policy of spatial planning and planned environmental designs includes particularly: exploration, examination and assessment of interventions within a given area; drafting spatial planning documents; and monitoring the implementation of spatial planning documents. The basic procedure is:

- decision of preparation and plan making (proposed by the entity or canton ministry (depending on the level) and adopted by Parliament or proposed by the City Government or Municipality and adopted by the Council);

- programme of public involvement (from local community tribune to public hearing) and programme of activities for plan preparation;

- plan Council formed by the ministry/city for process co-ordination and also for horizontal and vertical harmonisation, composed of members of different authority levels, different sectors, experts, NGOs etc.;

- preparation phase – collecting and processing all relevant information from different sectors and fields, which results in the Spatial Base. That process includes all relevant data on cultural and natural heritage and for protection and valorisation.

Pursuant to the law, the Spatial Base includes: recording of the current situation and problems within the area and its spatial planning; analysing and assessing the possibilities for its future development; general objectives of spatial development; special objectives of spatial development; drafting the basic scheme of spatial development and guidelines for the planned spatial development (which are to embody the principles, objectives of spatial development and plans resting on legal provisions, relevant documents by the United Nations, the Council of Europe, the European Union etc.) and drafting the environmental impact study. When the Spatial Base is finished, it is the subject of adoption by entity/canton Parliament or the city/municipality Council.

The plan-making process includes: pre-draft, draft and proposal. Each of them is subject to a public hearing. The contents of pre-draft, draft and proposal of the spatial planning document are part textual and part graphic.

The textual part of the Spatial Plan, its pre-draft, draft and proposal, is in four parts: general and special objectives of spatial development; projection of spatial development (working out the adopted basic scheme of development); projection of spatial system development; and decision on the implementation of spatial plan.

The general and special objectives of spatial development are taken over from the adopted Spatial Base. The projection of spatial development includes different thematic studies. These include specially protected areas (protected areas of nature, national parks, monuments of nature, nature parks, protected landscapes and the like, specially valuable sites of cultural and historical heritage, areas designated for tourism, recreation, climate resorts and so on, endangered areas and areas zoned for special use) and areas planned to be further developed.

According to the law, a projection of the development of a spatial system specifies its spatial development scheme and provides guidelines for the spatial development of a restricted area. Given the prevailing importance of the activity, the projection of the development also includes: the basis of spatial development of the environment (extra-urban), which provides guidelines for alteration, reconstruction and maintenance of the space between physical structures, while planning new activities and developing the existing ones (agriculture, use of water, mining, recreation, etc.) by way of ensuring the protection of nature, valorisation of natural and cultural heritage, permanent use of restorable natural resources, as well as the characteristics of the area easily recognisable by its natural and human created features (depending on the type of the Spatial Plan).

The decision on the implementation of a Spatial Plan contains, *inter alia*, measures to preserve the cultural-historical heritage, measures to preserve the protected areas of natural assets, and measures for spatial planning, preserving and improving the areas with special features of the federation and cantons.

The graphic part of the Spatial Planning Law is presented by means of an appropriate number of thematic maps and topographic maps. One of them is entitled "protected areas and properties of cultural-historical and natural heritage with the regimes and level of protection and other specially protected spaces, the spaces planned to be repaired, etc."

> Example: The old city of Pocitelj was a protected area in the former state. During the war of 1992-95 the old city was mostly destroyed. As it is an area of special interest for the federation, the federal government financed reconstruction of most of the buildings Most of the reconstructed buildings (which have no sacral character) are now at the disposal of artists and should become an art colony. In the Spatial Planning Act of the federation the area will be treated as a protected landscape, which provides for its protection and management since potentially it is a highly attractive tourist area.

Example: There are many similar cases, in particular the old part of several cities, Mostar Old Bridge, and various castles and fortresses.

According to the law, the funds necessary for preparing, drafting and implementing the Spatial Base and Spatial Plan of the Federation or of Republika Srpska, along with a two-yearly report and a programme of measures, are secured from the budgets of the entities.

Funds for preparing, drafting and monitoring implementation of the spatial plan of areas with special features are secured from the budgets of the entities, and for those important for the canton (or two or more cantons) from the cantonal budget. Funds for the preparation, drafting and monitoring of the implementation of urban development plans are secured from the budget of the canton/city/entity. Funds for the preparation, drafting and monitoring of the implementation of detailed plans are secured from the entity budget, for areas important for the entities, from the cantonal budget when the obligation to adopt them is laid down in a spatial planning document for a wider area adopted by the canton, or when the obligation is laid down in the law on spatial planning of the canton, or in the budget of the city or municipality and from other sources.

As mentioned above, the process of preparation, plan-making and plan adoption includes wide public consultation. Based on regulation, a "Programme for public involvement" should be made and adopted before preparation of the spatial or town planning documents begins. The programme describes how exactly the public is to be involved in the planning procedure. From the start, in the preparation phase, the tribunes, round tables and suchlike are organised in local communities. The public must be involved throughout the process of making the concept for the plan, along with local authority representatives, experts and NGOs, and also in the process of adoption of each phase of the plan – pre-draft, draft and proposal – each of which includes public hearings. All of these have an obligatory character for plan preparation, plan-maker and for the responsible authority.

## 3. Authorisation, supervision and penalties

### 3.1. Authorisation

According to the law, the ministry, without an urban permit having been previously issued, issues the construction permit for repairing properties of architectural heritage damaged or destroyed in war actions, where properties are designated as national monuments by the Commission to Preserve National Monuments, in accordance with Annex 8 of the General Framework Agreement for Peace in Bosnia and Herzegovina.

A permit for reconstruction, revitalisation, rehabilitation or other works is given in accordance with the legal regulation, which requires information on the main project (with necessary phases), control of the project, the reconstruction process, a use permit and technical examination. The permit reconstruction process includes, among other things, agreement on project documentation from the entity institutions in charge of protection of heritage and any conditions laid down.

"The decision from paragraph 3 of the Article may be subject to administrative litigation, by bringing suit with the Supreme Court of the Federation of Bosnia and Herzegovina/ Republika Srpska within 30 days from the receipt of the decision."

## 3.2. Supervision and penalties

According to the law, building inspectors from the ministry conduct inspections of buildings that fall under the competence of the ministry, namely those buildings for which the ministry issues urban and construction permits and permits for rehabilitation.

Supervision of implementation of the Law on Environmental Protection is carried out by the entity ministry. Entity and cantonal ministries shall, within the scope of their responsibilities, carry out the inspection tasks. The competent ministry has to draw up an annual/biennial inspection to set a systematic framework for inspections and monitoring, setting priorities for types of installations and areas according to pending environmental problems.

### Environmental damage

On compensation for environmental damage, the law says that, if the damage to the environment cannot be restored through reasonable measures, the person or company responsible is liable for the compensation of the value of the destroyed environmental assets. The compensation amount is based on the economic and ecological value of the environmental assets.

An administrative fine ranging from 1 000 marka (BAM) to BAM 10 000 (€500 to €5 000) shall be imposed on any legal entity for the following violations:

- building or operating installations or undertaking activities without the required permit or notification or contrary to such permit or regulation,
- not complying with requirements or conditions set out in the permit or in relevant regulations,
- not submitting to the competent authority the information, data or documents required by this act or respective regulations,
- not preparing a major accident prevention plan and not undertaking preventive measures when required,
- not adopting the approved internal intervention plan and not submitting it to the authority defined by the Law.

*Damage to cultural heritage*

In addition to issuing decisions designating National Monuments, the Commission to Preserve National Monuments monitors and considers the state of affairs and activities relating to National Monuments endangered by illegal construction, inexpert reconstruction, lack of maintenance or other forms of destruction. In specific cases, the Commission notifies the relevant entity or other authorities (governments, the appropriate ministries, institutes for the protection of monuments, municipal authorities, etc.) that a monument is endangered, and proposes measures for its protection in accordance with the law, including filing criminal charges with the relevant authorities pursuant to the provisions of the Criminal Proceedings Law.

Under the Criminal Laws of the Entities (Sluzbene novine Federacije Bosne i Hercegovine, No. 36/03 and Sluzbeni glasnik Republike Srpske, No. 49/03), a sentence of up to five years' imprisonment is stipulated for the person who:

- damages or destroys a monument of culture;

- exports or carries abroad a monument of culture or protected natural asset without a permit issued by the relevant authority;

- fails to bring back the monument of culture or protected asset upon the expiration of the deadline specified in the permit;

- carries out (without a permit from the relevant authority) conservation, restoration or exploration works on the monument of culture or, despite the prohibition or without a permit issued by the relevant authority, conducts archaeological excavations or explorations due to which the monument may be destroyed, severely damaged or lose the features of a monument;

- takes possession of or seizes items excavated or found during archaeological or other explorations, which are considered monuments of culture.

Pursuant to the above criminal laws and the Law on Criminal Procedure, the Commission to Preserve National Monuments presses charges with the relevant municipal prosecutors on the grounds of damaging and destroying the national monuments.

*Unlawful export of movable heritage*

The measures of protection against unlawful export in Bosnia and Herzegovina have been regulated in line with the international Convention on measures prohibiting and preventing the unlawful import, export and transfer of cultural assets, dating from 1970, ratified by Bosnia and Herzegovina in 1993. The principles from the Convention have been implemented through the following regulations:

- law on Protection and use of cultural-historical and natural heritage from 1985 ("Sluzbeni list SRBiH", Nos. 20/85, 12/87, 3/93 and 13/94), which applies in the

Bosnia and Herzegovina Federation, and in cantons that have not passed laws in that sphere (the law has been adopted in only three cantons: Sarajevo Canton, Zenica-Doboj and West Herzegovina Canton)

- law on Cultural Assets ("Sluzbeni glasnik Republike Srpske" No. 11/95)

- criminal Law of the Bosnia and Herzegovina Federation ("Sluzbene novine FBiH" No. 36/03)

- criminal Law of Republika Srpska from 2003 ("Sluzbeni glasnik Republike Srpske" No. 49/03)

- book of Rules on the activities of the Commission concerning international co-operation, adopted by the Bosnia and Herzegovina Presidency ("Sluzbeni glasnik BiH" No. 29/02)

- decision on classification of goods into import and export regimes, adopted by the Council of Ministers of Bosnia and Herzegovina ("Sluzbeni glasnik BiH" Nos. 22/98, 30/02 and 40/02)

- instruction of the Ministry of Foreign Trade and Economic Affairs on how to issue permits for export and import of works of art and antiquities ("Sluzbeni glasnik BiH" No. 41/02)

Basic reasons for not applying or finding difficulty in applying existing regulations on cultural heritage:

- permanent lack of funds to support institutions and measures to protect cultural heritage, with a large number of destroyed and damaged monuments in the recent war and postwar period;

- lack of political will at all levels of authority to protect heritage;

- lack of awareness of the importance and need to preserve cultural heritage;

- war-torn legal and institutional system, in which institutions have lost legal status, experts, budget, documentation and, to a large extent, the conditions to perform their activities;

- legislative hyper-inflation (Bosnia and Herzegovina now has twelve regulations covering heritage issues at all levels of authority; overlapping competencies are not a rare occurrence);

- the fact that there is no Ministry of Culture at state level is an additional, aggravating element that prevents the establishment of more effective mechanisms to protect the heritage.

The Commission to Preserve National Monuments – established pursuant to Annex 8 of the General Framework Agreement for Peace in Bosnia and Herzegovina, as the institution in charge of legal protection of the heritage, with the highest powers at state level – has through its work thus far tried to harmonise the legal chaos or vacuum in the field of the protection of cultural heritage. Many new questions, however, were opened by the postwar period of reconstruction, the period of transition and acceptance of European standards, and in 2004 these imposed on the Commission to Preserve National Monuments as a priority task the drafting of a legal framework to regulate heritage management issues at state level. Drafting of the legal framework is planned as part of the Regional Programme of Cultural and Natural Heritage for South-East Europe of the Council of Europe.

# Bulgaria

*Hristo Bojinov, Todor Krestev, Peter Miladinov and Lidya Stankova*

## 1. Documentation systems

### 1.1. Identification

#### Cultural heritage

Inventory systems exist in Bulgaria, covering all types and categories of monuments of culture. The systems are regulated by the State Archives Act and the Monuments of Culture and Museums Act (MCMA). The chief actor in this field is the Ministry of Culture and Tourism (MCT), which carries out inventory activities through its own bodies, local self-government bodies, specialised state institutions – the Archaeological Institute and Museum, and the Bulgarian Academy of Sciences [BAS] – and state, regional and municipal museums. The National Institute for Monuments of Culture (NIMC), as an MCT body, performs the main activities of inventory and documentation, and keeps the National Register and the National Scientific-Documentary Archives (NSDA) of monuments of culture. From this position it co-ordinates and harmonises the activities of documenting all the bodies mentioned.

According to the regulated procedure of declaring sites of immovable cultural heritage as monuments of culture, the first phase of the process is identification, whereby the sites are searched for, localised and described. The results are reflected in an identification map, along with a specialised study, photos and graphic documentation. In the succeeding phases (definition, final comprehensive assessment, endorsement, declaration and registration), a considerable volume of information is accumulated about the site and the terms for its preservation.

The National Archives Collection of the NSDA is composed of documentation of immovable monuments, created by the NIMC, other scientific institutes, non-governmental organisations, natural persons and legal entities. It contains the following documents:

- the National Register of Immovable Monuments of Culture (original); systematised information about the sites by registration county number, settlement, name, administrative and official survey data, type, category and registration data;

- lists of declared sites;

- original site dossiers;

- regulatory documents bearing on cultural heritage;

– documents relating to the sites and their preservation: scientific research, directive concept plans, support plans, land-development schemes, copies of development plans, archive plans and official surveys, photo-library, video-library and so on.

The NSDA stores about 800 000 archive units relating to some 40 000 immovable monuments of culture. The NIMC maintains in the NSDA, jointly with the Archaeological Institute and Museum and the BAS, an Automated Information System known as the Archaeological Map of Bulgaria, which collects, processes and stores information about the archaeological heritage of the country.

Specialised bodies in the municipalities, regions and mayoralties create and fill up local archives of immovable monuments of culture and organise their use according to regulations. Part of these archives consists of a mass of information about immovable monuments of culture, target-assured in connection with development plans at different levels.

Example: In connection with the general development plans of Sofia, Plovdiv, Assenovgrad, Gabrovo, Rousse and other cities, information databases have been compiled for the Cultural Heritage system, including data about monuments of culture, map information, and so on.

## Protection of nature

Pursuant to the Protected Territories Act (PTA), the state builds up and ensures the functioning of a system of protected areas, as part of the regional and world networks of such areas, in accordance with the international treaties on protection of the environment to which the Republic of Bulgaria is a party. Protected areas are intended to protect biological diversity in the ecosystems, and the natural processes taking place in them, as well as remarkable natural landscapes.

The Directorate of the National Service for the Protection of Nature (NSPN), with the Ministry of the Environment and Waters (MEW), keeps a register of protected territories declared under the procedure of the Protected Territories Act, namely: national parks, nature parks, reserves, protected areas and natural landmarks.

In this register, each protected area is filed under a certain number, while at the same time information is given about the order and year of declaration (the Official Gazette number where the order was published), settlement boundaries, the declaration area and protection category.

The respective regional MEW structures for protected territories also keep registers of the protected territories falling in their regional scope. An electronic register of protected territories is kept at the Executive Agency for the Environment with the MEW; immediately after finalising the procedure of declaration or change in a new or existing protected territory, the NSPN Directorate provides the necessary information for the entry.

Beside the registers of protected areas kept at the MEW, its regional structures and the IAOS, each protected area has its own dossier where all documents relating to the declaration and changes in the area, category or regime of use are stored. The archives of protected areas at national level are kept by the NSPN Directorate at the MEW, whereas at the respective regional MEW divisions similar archives are also kept of protected territories at the regional level.

## 1.2. Characterisation

### Cultural heritage

In principle, classifying the sites of immovable cultural heritage in Bulgaria is carried out according to target – in view of their registration as immovable monuments of culture. Information is collected according to the types and categories defined in the MCMA and Ordinance No. 5 of the MCT, which are already quite obsolete and to a certain extent do not correspond with modern notions of the content of cultural heritage. There are no documenting systems for the purpose of characterising the heritage in its broader context, as part of the comprehensive structure of the cultural environment.

Nevertheless, partial information of this type is documented within the framework of official inventory systems and outside them. This is carried out in the following ways:

- within the NSDA, especially in the process of identifying sites of immovable cultural heritage, the sites are sought, described and localised in connection with their broader territorial and historical context;

- within the specific territorial instruments worked out by the NIMC since the early 1980s (territorial schemes and directive concept plans for monuments of culture) for outstanding territories and settlements;

- in connection with general development plans for historical settlements. For example, as part of the general development plan of Plovdiv, a comprehensive study was made to include the broad context of monuments of culture and their evolution, historical stratification, etc;

- within the framework of research and local studies carried out by museums at different levels and directed at other dimensions of the cultural environment, such as non-material heritage, folklore and ethnographic valuables and traditional handcrafts;

- within the framework of programmes for the development of cultural tourism – for example, under the PHARE programme for cultural tourism (2003-5) nineteen projects have been selected, and in some of them the cultural heritage is explored in its broad natural and cultural context, as potential for cultural and ecotourism.

At present, there is no mechanism for disseminating this information among the general public.

*Protection of nature*

The Protected Territories Act determines the relationships between the institutions responsible for protected areas and it guarantees the more effective protection of nature and protection of local interests. The Act introduces a modern classification of protected territories in accordance with international standards. Under this classification, six protection categories are differentiated, namely: national parks, nature parks, reserves, maintained reserves, protected areas and natural landmarks.

These six categories differ in their conservation significance,and this determines their regime of protection and use. Thus, reserves and maintained reserves, which are managed mainly for the purposes of natural ecosystems and species habitat, have the strictest regime under the Protected Territories Act. In these two categories all activities are prohibited apart from measures for their security, the movement of people along marked paths and visits for scientific purposes. In maintained reserves, maintenance activities described in management plans are also allowed.

On the one hand, the Protected Territories Act stipulates a restrictive regime for each category of protected territory; on the other hand, each order declaring a protected area stipulates additional prohibitions, which are determined by the character of the individual site and its purpose, namely, the reason it is being protected. These prohibitions are strictly harmonised with the traditional way of using that particular protected area and the potential dangers it faces.

At present, digital models are worked out of the protected areas and, immediately after declaration, deletion or changing the boundaries of a given protected area, this information appears on the Map of Restored Property. The digital model of a protected area contains information about its area, ownership, manner of sustained use, regimes and category. The Map of Restored Property shows the protected area's boundaries, marked with a sign indicating its category. There is an agreement between the Ministry of the Environment and Waters and the Ministry of Agriculture and Forests (MAF) for reflecting the boundaries of newly declared protected areas and changes to existing areas on the Map of Restored Property.

Information from the Map of Restored Property is provided as an administrative service by the Ministry of Agriculture and Forests under a procedure established by an Ordinance on the Map of Restored Property Maintenance, against the payment of a set fee.

## 1.3. Databases and computerised mapping

*Cultural heritage*

In Bulgaria, there is no comprehensive, integrated policy of digitalising the cultural heritage. Existing practice in this field is still pragmatic and reactive, corresponding to specific problems and needs, and applied only within that framework. Creating an information system for immovable monuments of culture with the NSDA at the NIMC is at an early stage. There still is no comprehensive computerised database of cultural monuments connected to geographic information systems (GIS). There are no digitalised GIS maps even for World Heritage sites. But there are examples of active projects to create computerised databases.

> Example: The Archaeological Map of Bulgaria – created and maintained by the NIMC, Archaeological Institute and Museum, and BAS – is an Automated Information System for collecting, processing and storing data about archive sites, based on primary documents coming in from various sources.

> For some settlements and territories, digitalised surveys, regulation plans and maps showing monuments of culture have already been created, according to an ordinance of the Ministry of Regional Development and Public Works (MRDPW).

> General development plans for some historic cities (Sofia, Plovdiv, Asenovgrad) include comprehensive computer databases of their cultural heritage, sometimes including GIS.

> In 2005 a Multimedia Laboratory for Cultural Heritage was created in association with the University of Architecture, Civil Engineering and Geodesy (with the financial aid of the British Council in Bulgaria and the British Council Fund for Southeastern Europe), and this aims to assist digitalisation of the cultural heritage and popularisation of cultural treasures, with an orientation towards the general public as well.

The main problems related to such documentation systems are:

- there are no up-to-date systems of documentation or a national strategy for digitalisation of the cultural heritage in Bulgaria;

- a common shortcoming of the existing systems of documenting the national heritage is they are relatively closed and difficult of access, especially for the general public. The Register of Monuments of Culture and the NSDA are not accessible via the Internet. The prices charged for the use of archive documents by citizens are not always affordable. There is no public access to the database of the Archaeological Map of Bulgaria, and data from archaeological studies are published with great delays. There is no atlas of cultural heritage, and publications about cultural monuments – maps, guidebooks and other materials – are inadequate;

- there is no constantly updated information system for endangered sites of cultural heritage that require urgent conservation intervention.

### Protection of nature

A specialised map of protected areas is in preparation.

There is a mechanism for the exchange of information in the field of biological diversity – CHM, which is a part of the world mechanism of information exchange pursuant to the Convention on Biological Diversity. Its main goal is to ensure access to information about biological diversity, in particular about protected areas in Bulgaria, thus facilitating decision making on their preservation. The main object of activity of the mechanism is the management of data and information at national and international levels, with the aid of modern information technologies and the Internet especially.

Information in the Bulgarian CHM is collected, processed and structured through information nodes sited at key administrations and organisations supplying and using information on biological diversity. These are:

NSPN Directorate,

Department of Agro-ecology at the Ministry of Agriculture and Forests,

National Administration of Forests at the MAF,

BLUELINK Foundation,

Sofia University,

Park Node (Association of Nature Parks in Bulgaria),

Executive Agency of the Environment with the MEW, and others.

Creation of the Bulgarian CHM has been aided by a joint project of the MEW and UN Development, financed by the Global Environment Fund in 1993-95.


## 2. Integrated management studies, plans and regulations

Bulgaria has about 40 000 monuments of culture dispersed around the national territory, with certain concentrations in historic areas and settlements. The MCMA and Ordinance No. 5 of the MCT regulate preservation regimes – complexes of rules and norms, including data of the territorial scope of the site and its environment as well as provisions for its preservation. The special regime reserve is ensured for sites in the category "of national importance". The MCMA foresees joint action with the MCT and MRDPW in developments for preserving the cultural heritage.

In the 1980s the need to co-ordinate policies on preservation of the cultural heritage, archaeological exploration and development planning provoked the NIMC to create and implement specific plans of preservation, to be as instruments for a dialogue between these three fields. Regrettably, these very useful territorial instruments still remain unrecognised by the Territory Development Act (TDA) and the MCMA, which considerably reduces their effectiveness.

One positive measure is the TDA regulation of "territories with cultural-historical" heritage, for which specific rules and norms can be created in development plans, deviating from the general provisions.

The Protected Territories Act and the Ordinance on Working out Management Plans introduces a procedure for working out and endorsing management plans for protected territories. Management plans must be worked out for protected areas in the categories of national park, nature park, reserve and maintained reserve. The management plans are assigned by the Minister of the Environment and Waters to specialised teams of experts. The working out of management plans for other categories of protected area can be assigned by interested state bodies, municipalities, owners or non-government organisations after consent in writing from the Ministry of the Environment and Waters.

Management plans for protected areas of international importance or included on lists in international conventions are worked out in order of priority, for example, the Ramsar Convention, the Convention on World Heritage, UNESCO's Man and Biosphere and so on.

Management plans are worked out for ten-year periods. In the case of national parks, a public discussion is organised every four years on their implementation. The plans are worked out on the basis of detailed scientific and socio-economic information, data about the infrastructure in and around the protected area, data about use of the site by the local population, and other data. A major instrument in management plans is the zoning of the protected area and the determination of a specific regime of preservation and use of the biological diversity for each zone.

*Archaeological reserve "Nikopolis ad Istrum", Veliko Turnovo (Council of Europe)*

## 2.1. Environment

The Protection of the Environment Act (PEA) is the framework law in this field, determining state policy on protecting the environment. The Act specifies the place and role of central and local state bodies, leaving a broad field for enacting special legislation. The PEA regulates procedures for:

- environment Impact Assessments (EIAs) where required for proposed construction;

- strategic Environmental Assessments (SEAs), required for plans that may have a considerable impact on the environment.

The EIA and SEA aim to integrate provisions relating to the environment with the process of development as a whole and to introduce the principle of sustainable development.

EIAs are required for those investment proposals for construction or activities specified in Annexes No. 1 and No. 2 of the PEA. Proposals of the kinds listed in Annex No. 1 are subject to a mandatory EIA. As for the proposals for construction listed in Annex No. 2 to the said Act, the need for making an EIA for these is assessed by the director of the respective regional MEW structure or – in cases where a protected area is affected or a cross-border impact is possible – by the Minister of the Environment and Waters. If this assessment is negative – that is, an EIA is not needed, but a protected area is affected – the investment proposal is co-ordinated in writing with the MEW under the procedure of the Protected Territories Act. The terms for making an EIA are regulated in an Ordinance of the Council of Ministers.

SEAs are made for plans and programmes of the central and territorial bodies of the executive. SEAs are mandatory for plans and programmes (or changes thereto) in the fields of agriculture, forestry, fishery, transport, energy engineering, waste management, water-resources management, extraction of underground resources, and tourism and development planning, where the framework of future development proposals falls under Annexes No. 1 and No. 2 to the PEA.

The need for making a SEA is evaluated for each plan by the Minister of the Environment and Waters or the Director of the relevant Regional Inspectorate of the Environment and Waters (RIEW) under the procedure of an Ordinance of the Council of Ministers on Making Environmental Assessment. For plans and programmes under Annex No. 1 of the said Ordinance, an SEA is mandatory. For plans and programmes from Annex No. 2 of the said Ordinance, the need for an SEA is evaluated by the directors of the respective regional structures, or the Minister of the Environment and Waters in the cases when a protected area is affected. If the evaluation is that no SEA should be made but a protected area is affected, the plan or programme is co-ordinated with the MEW pursuant to the Protected Territories Act.

Actual production of an EIA for an investment proposal for construction, or for an environmental assessment of a plan or programme, is assigned by the investor or assignor of the programme or plan to registered experts, who declare that they are not personally interested in the realisation of the plan, programme or proposal. A public register of these experts is kept at the MEW. The expense of an EIA or environmental assessment is borne by the investor or assignor of the plan or programme.

EIA and SEA reports give a description and analysis of the components of the environment, with an evaluation of the presumed considerable impacts on the population and the environment resulting from realisation of the investment proposal, plan or programme. The experts give their conclusion, guided by the principles of reducing the risk to human health and the norms of quality of the environment enforced in this country.

The EIA of an investment proposal concludes with a resolution issued by the competent body (the Minister of the Environment and Waters or the Director of the relevant RIEW) and it is binding on the investor. The EIA resolution forms an integral part of the design visa, which is issued in accordance with the Territory Development Act (TDA).

The SEA concludes with the views of the competent body (the Director of the relevant regional structure or the Minister of the Environment and Waters) indicating the actions required and any control measures which are deemed necessary for implementing the plan or programme, which are co-ordinated with the Minister of the Environment and Waters or the Director of the respective RIEW and the assignor or authority responsible for the plan or programme.

The Protection of the Environment Act also envisages consultations with the general public in carrying out procedures of the EIA and SEA. Thus, for example, in the EIA procedure, the investor organises a public discussion on the EIA report, where all interested natural persons and legal entities, representatives of the competent body, municipalities, territorial authorities of the executive, public organisations and citizens can participate. Representatives of the public give their views in writing. The competent body adopts a decision on the EIA, taking into consideration the results of the public discussion.

In the process of working out an SEA, the assignor organises consultations with the interested public. The Environment Assessment Report reflects the results of these consultations, which are taken into consideration in the views of the competent authority. Public discussions are organised when this is stipulated in a special law or where there are more than two reasons for the negative views resulting from the consultations.

The Ministry of the Environment and Waters keeps a register of EIA procedures carried out, including public discussions, issued decisions and control of their execution. Access is ensured for the public, affected and interested parties to the views of the competent department in connection with the SEA.

## 2.2. Spatial and urban planning

Specific rules and norms are adopted by the authorities competent to endorse a particular development plan.

Issuing a regulatory base for the protection and development of the cultural and natural heritage is within the powers of the respective authorities of the central administration – the Ministry of Regional Development and Public Works (MRDPW), the Ministry of

Culture and Tourism (MCT) and the Ministry of Environment and Water (MEW). In the process of creating it, all interested central and territorial bodies of the executive, as well as other interested parties – specialised control bodies or exploitation companies, for example – take part.

The co-operation between the various ministries and units finds expression in a general co-ordination in creating the regulatory base, in implementing state policy in the relevant field, in the methodology and in operative guidance and control.

Public consultation in relation to land development, investment design and construction in the Republic of Bulgaria is undertaken according to procedures set out in the Territory Development Act (Article 1, Item 2).

Land development – meaning activities for using, protecting and building on land – is carried out in accordance with three types of plan: development schemes, general development plans and detailed development plans. Rules and norms for implementation are worked out as integral parts of the plan.

### Development schemes (DSs)

These are of two types, depending on their territorial scope:

- National Comprehensive Development Schemes, for the territory of the entire country, which are subject to approval by the Council of Ministers of the Republic of Bulgaria;

- Regional Development Schemes, for one or more counties or a group of municipalities, which are subject to approval by the county governor or the Minister of Regional Development and Public Works respectively.

Depending on their content, DSs are comprehensive when they solve general development problems in the territory and their mutual linkage, or specialised when they solve individual development problems in the territory.

The main goal of development schemes is to ensure that development of the territories matches socio-economic development with guaranteed protection of the environment (Article 99 of the TDA), by determining:

- the territorial structural zoning of the various types of territory with the regimes for their development,

- the development of sites, networks and installations of the technical infrastructure,

- the development of the settlement network and the centres of national and regional importance,

- the development of areas with specific characteristics and areas with environmental problems as well as the protected areas.

The provisions of endorsed development schemes and higher-level plans are binding on follow-up development plans. The implementation of DSs is assigned by the authorities competent to endorse them, with funds from the state budget and the municipalities.

## General development plans (GDPs)

GDPs are the basis for the overall development of the territories of municipalities, parts thereof or individual localities with their boundary areas. The provisions of general development plans – whereby the general structure and prevailing purpose of the territories, the type and purpose of the technical infrastructure, and the protection of the environment and sites of cultural-historical heritage are determined – are binding when working out detailed development plans (Article 104 of the TDA). General development plans are endorsed by municipal councils or, for settlements of national importance, by the Minister of Regional Development and Public Works.

## Detailed development plans (DDPs)

These specify permitted development and construction in the territory of a settlement and within its boundaries, as well as the settlement formations. Their provisions are binding on investment designs (Article 108 of the TDA). Detailed development plans (DDPs) are endorsed by the municipal councils or – where they cover only part of a settlement (up to three blocks) – by the municipality's mayor. If the DDP covers more than one municipality or county, it is endorsed by the county governor or the Minister of Regional Development and Public Works respectively, after co-ordination with the Municipal Council.

## Public consultation

Draft development schemes and general development plans are subject to public discussion prior to submitting them to expert boards of land development (Article 121; Article 127, paragraph 1, of the TDA). Public consultations are held mainly on the grounds of the provisions of the law related to creating and endorsing the development schemes and plans. Consultations are implemented through:

- co-ordination by the assignor of the DS, GDP or DDP with interested central and territorial administrations, specialist control bodies and exploitation companies (TDA Article 121, 127, 128);

- declaration by the assignor of the interested persons, such as owners/bearers of limited property rights to properties within the scope of the plan, who can object, propose or demand changes to a detailed draft DDP (Article 128 of the TDA); depending on the plan's scope, the declaration is made in the Official Gazette or, as stipulated in the Civil Procedure Code, by name;

- public discussions organised by the assignor, of drafts for DSs and GDPs.

Adopting a decision on the views, objections, proposals and demands is within the powers of the authority competent to endorse the respective plan, which assesses it in terms of its legality and expedience. Control of the administrative act whereby the respective plan is endorsed is exercised under court procedure (Article 215 of the TDA).

In comparison with the process of public consultation on development schemes and plans, public participation is insufficient in the process of cultural heritage management. There are no centres of consultation with the general public, and the contractual and traditional protection of the cultural heritage is poorly developed. Basically, the role of voluntary non-governmental organisations in the field of cultural heritage is quite limited.

### Preparation of plans

Working out GDPs is assigned by the municipality mayor on the basis of a resolution of the municipal council, when they are funded from the municipality budget, or by the Minister of Regional Development and Public Works when they are funded by the state budget. Working out DDPs is assigned to the municipality mayor, the county governor or the Minister of Regional Development and Public Works, depending on the manner of funding. DDPs can also be assigned by interested persons after consent of the municipality (Article 124 of the TDA).

Development schemes, and plans and investment projects, can be worked out only by designers – natural persons who, besides their technical capacity, also have full designer capacity (Article 230 of the TDA). Employees of municipal administrations can work out draft development plans for individual state and municipal land properties as part of their employment.

The technical basis for development schemes and plans is composed of survey plans and maps, levelling plans, specialised maps and others. Digitalised databases, surveys and specialised maps are used to ensure accurate records of the site or area (information record of the Survey Agency).

### Development plans and heritage

Sites of cultural-historical heritage (archaeological reserves, individual blocks or land properties in settlements of cultural-historical, ethnographic or architectural importance) are protected territories (TDA, Article 8, Item 4) or territories with special territory-development protection (TDA, Article 10, paras 2 and 3); they are reflected, regulated and reported as town-planning facts of special importance in development schemes and plans at all levels.

> Example: Positive results can be quoted for the development plans of a number of settlements with cultural-historical heritage, including Koprivshtitsa, Melnik and parts of Plovdiv, among others.

Territory-development plans are worked out under the procedure of the Territory Development Act, whereas their co-ordination with the Ministry of the Environment and Waters follows the procedure laid down in the Protected Territories Act, namely by making an environmental assessment. If it is considered that making a SEA is not necessary and the respective territory-development plan affects a protected territory, it is co-ordinated under the procedure established by the Protected Territories Act, namely, through co-ordination in writing.

The various types of development plan envisage the inclusion of cultural-heritage aspects. Development schemes determine the general territorial terms for the protection of natural and cultural heritage. It is possible to create a specialised development scheme for the cultural heritage of a given territory. In general development plans for territories of historical, ethnographic or architectural importance, special materials are required, characterising the cultural heritage and proposing measures for its protection.

Despite all this, as mentioned, the lack of specific development plans for protecting the heritage in historic areas has had a negative impact. The National Institute for Monuments of Culture has tried since the 1980s to compensate for this lack with a series of territorial protection plans – the National Development Scheme for Cultural Heritage, the Territorial Schemes for Cultural Heritage for parts of the Rhodopes Mountains, the Sboryanovo Reserve and others – but these lack regulatory legitimacy.

Since the 1990s some general development plans for large historic cities have realised attempts to overcome this lack. For example, the new Development Plan for Sofia offers a comprehensive concept of protecting and developing the Cultural Heritage system of development regimes and plans for integrated management of the cultural heritage, proposals for sustainable use of the cultural heritage for various functions, and so on.

The Territory Development Act envisages the issuing of both generally valid and specific rules and norms for land development (Article 13). For protected areas – which, besides sites of cultural-historical heritage, also cover sites of nature conservation such as nature reserves, national parks, natural landmarks, buffer zones, wetlands and protected littoral strips (TDA, Article 8, Item 4) – specific rules and norms can be created. They form an integral part of the respective development plans and they can regulate deviations from the general provisions (and here we have positive discrimination).

### Problems and solutions

Failures in heritage management – observed primarily in settlements where there is intensive investment interest (Antique Nessebar, Sozopol, etc.) – result mainly from insufficiently effective management mechanisms and systems, and delays in improving and bringing them into compliance with the requirements of socio-economic development.

In Bulgaria, there are no specific plans of integrated management of the cultural heritage in historical settlements like the French PSMV *(Plan de Sauvegarde et de Mise en Valeur)* and ZPPAUP *(Zone de Protection du Patrimoine Architectural Urbain et Paysager)*. As mentioned, initiatives have been implemented at the NIMC to overcome this lack, by launching directive concept plans for the cultural heritage for a number of historical settlements (Nessebar, Sozopol, Elena, Bansko, Blagoevgrad, Burgas, Varna and others). In some places, they have had an impact on conservation of the cultural heritage. In other instances, because of their illegitimacy, they have been ignored in development plans (for example, in Burgas, where the historical nucleus is crossed by a main street, contrary to the requirements of the Directive Concept Plan of the NIMC).

The "specific rules and norms" regulated today for settlements/zones with outstanding cultural heritage, while useful, are unable to fill the gap. In single cases, local authorities initiate the creation of specific conservation plans. For example, in Plovdiv a Strategy for Conservation and Sustainable Use of the "Antique Plovdiv" Reserve was worked out (2003), complementing the detailed development plan with a series of measures for integrated management and offering a General Conservation Plan, with a strategy and mechanism for managing the historical environment.

The main problems in managing the cultural heritage in historic areas and settlements are these:

- there are no effective development instruments – specific conservation plans, co-ordination of conservation policy with development planning, especially against the background of increasing commercial pressure on historic areas and zones;

- there are no effective mechanisms for co-ordinating the policy of archaeological exploration and conservation policy. Archaeological exploration is carried out without strictly complying with the possibilities for conservation, which places at risk any archaeological treasures found;

- there is no effective comprehensive settlement management. In a number of cases development policy has disintegrated into unco-ordinated partial town-planning suggestions for individual town fragments (squares, districts) while the public interest of conserving the cultural heritage in the town landscape is often ignored. This compromises the role of the development plan as an instrument of integrated management of the cultural environment. There are no rules for street advertising, lighting or town design in historic centres;

- there is no effective legislation and management that would protect the landscape as an integral treasure with cultural dimensions, in the sense of the European Landscape Convention – for example, the Black Sea coast is gradually degrading due to intensive urbanisation and improvident assimilation;

- the state does not have effective mechanisms and instruments to protect the public interest in integrated conservation of natural and cultural heritage, achieving and maintaining a balance between public and private interests;

– in accordance with the Protected Territories Act, settlements and settlement patterns do not fall within the boundaries of protected areas. For this reason, urban development plans have no direct relation to protected areas. Nevertheless, they are subject to co-ordination with the MEW under the procedure of the PEA.

## 3. Authorisation, supervision and penalties

The Protected Territories Act regulates a number of consultation procedures with the general public. For example, when a procedure for declaring or changing the area and regime of a given protected territory is under way, in the commission appointed by order of the minister, which takes a decision on the proposal, all owners must be invited to participate.

In declaring protected territories in the categories of nature park, national park, reserve and maintained reserve, prior to appointing a commission, public meetings are organised to which representatives of municipalities, county governors, local interested environmental and other public organisations, along with other interested representatives of ministries, administrations and research institutes, are invited. Minutes are kept of the views and suggestions from the public discussions, which form part of the documentation to be taken into consideration by the commission, when taking the decision for declaration of change.

In working out management plans for national parks, nature parks and maintained reserves, public discussions are also organised in which interested central and local authorities, owners, representatives of scientific institutes and non-governmental organisations can participate. The common views and recommendations from the public discussions are recorded in minutes, which are attached to the draft management plan, subject to endorsement under the procedure established by the Protected Territories Act.

Consultations with other state institutions are also regulated in the Protected Territories Act. For example, in the commissions appointed by order of the Minister of the Environment and Waters to examine suggestions for declaring and changing protected territories, representatives of the interested administrations, municipalities and county governors must be included.

In the public discussions organised as part of the procedure of declaring national and nature parks, or in the process of working out management plans for national parks, nature parks and maintained reserves, representatives of interested institutions also take part.

When endorsing management plans, representatives of the interested institutions are also included. Thus, for example, management plans for national and nature parks are submitted for adoption to the Council of Ministers after being examined at the

Supreme Environment Board in whose composition representatives of other institutions participate.

Management plans for the other categories of protected territories are endorsed by order of the Minister of the Environment and Waters, after they have been co-ordinated in advance with the interested administrations.

## 3.1. Authorisation

Pursuant to the Monument of Culture and Museum Act, all initiatives affecting monuments of culture and their environment are mandatorily subject to prior co-ordination with the National Institute for Monuments of Culture, before endorsement of the project documentation by the authorised state and municipal authorities and prior to issuing a construction permit. Such initiatives may include:

– programmes, plan assignments, tender papers, competition documents;

– development schemes and plans;

– concession terms;

– design visas;

– investment projects at all phases of intervention on sites of immovable monuments of culture (raising superstructures, raising extensions, restructuring, repair activities, change of purpose, partition, change of function);

– public works, setting-up movable installations, advertisements, lighting fixtures;

– demolition or elimination of immovable monuments of culture threatened by self-destruction, or life-threatening to residents and passers-by;

– projects for new buildings in an environment of monuments of culture;

– carrying out archaeological excavations, probing, underground exploration, geophysical and other investigations of monuments of culture.

Pursuant to the Monuments of Culture and Museums Act, the co-ordination procedure should start at the earliest stage of the investment initiative – as early as the level of plan assignment, competition or design visa so that restrictions on intervention are in place before work starts on the development or investment project.

The demolition of sites/monuments of culture is carried out on the basis of the procedure in Article 195, para. 2, and Article 197, para. 1, of the Territory Development Act. A representative of the National Institute for Monuments of Culture participates in the commission for establishing the condition of the immovable monument of culture and the Institute's consent is given before issuing the permit for eliminating a building or monument of culture.

Regrettably, there are quite a few cases where the owners of buildings or monuments of culture, or investors in new construction in an area of monuments of culture, prepare projects and even start the construction, with repairs and changes to the monuments of culture or their environment, without co-ordination with the NIMC and even without the relevant construction permit from the authorised authority – the municipality. The results of such actions are often fatal for the affected monument of culture – it is demolished or changed to such a degree that it loses its status. Commercial interests are the reason for considerable negative changes in group monuments and reserves – commercial sites and new residential construction deprive it of individuality and modify the architectural style, scale and structure of entire architectural ensembles and reserves.

Most threatened by destruction are the archaeological monuments of culture. A great part of these are unexplored, but known to society; such are the approximately 10 000 mounds, many of which – though they have not been declared monuments of culture – have lately been the object of treasure-hunting plunder accompanied by partial or complete destruction of the structures and the deletion of valuable archaeological data.

Frequent also are the cases when archaeological sites, unknown to explorers, are destroyed in excavation works. Some investors, apprehensive of a delay in construction or possible enforcement of a change to their plans, deliberately violate the law, which has expressly stipulated a text in defence of such random findings.

In this connection, the NIMC has declared as monuments of culture all archaeological sites in the territory of this country, including its water area, that have not yet been iden-tified and studied, and a preventive regime has been determined for them – a regime of conservation and the preliminary category "of national importance".

If in carrying out archaeological excavations and probes, a danger is created for the integrity and condition of the monument of culture, they can be discontinued by order of the Minister of Culture.

The permit procedures involve a certain degree of co-ordination between central bodies and the local authorities. The National Council for Conservation of the Monuments of Culture with the Ministry of Culture and Tourism includes representatives of various administrations. A number of co-ordination procedures envisage partnership between the MCT and the MRDPW.

According to the Territorial Development Act, construction can be carried out only if it is permitted by the competent body of the respective administration, usually the Chief Architect of the municipality. The law allows a small number of exceptions, among which is performing conservation-restoration works on a monument of culture that is not of world or national importance (Article 147, Item 11).

Allowing town planning intervention or a change in the provisions of development plans is also within the powers of municipalities and it is carried out by the mayor after a reasoned proposal from the chief architect. There is also the possibility of a combined permit – for town planning work and investment plan simultaneously (Article 150 of the TDA) from the relevant competent body.

Pursuant to the Protected Territories Act, the construction, reconstruction or extension of buildings and installations for which no EIA is required is co-ordinated in writing with the Ministry of the Environment and Waters. According to the said law, all other activities in protected areas are also co-ordinated in writing with the MEW.

As regards reserves and maintained reserves, which are exclusively state property and have the strictest conservation status of any category of protected territory, special permits are issued for visits for scientific purposes, and visitors can be allowed along marked paths determined by order of the Minister of the Environment and Waters. Maintenance and restoration works in maintained reserves are regulated by their management plans.

For the sustainable use of natural resources, the Ministry of the Environment and Waters issues permits. Under the TDA procedure, these include permits for pasture and extraction of wood to be used by the local population, which are issued by the respective National Parks Directorates with the MEW. The National Parks Directorates also issue permits for using wild and forest fruits and medicinal plants, pursuant to the Biological Diversity Act and the Medicinal Plants Act. According to the Biological Diversity Act (BDA), permits are also issued for the use of endangered species, which are under a special regime of conservation and use, control thereon being exercised by the respective MEW regional structures.

## 3.2. Supervision and penalties

The Ministry of Culture and Tourism exercises guidance and surveillance of monuments of culture through its own body (NIMC), local self-government authorities and the authorities of the executive in municipalities. Its dispositions as regards monuments of culture are mandatory for all institutions, organisations and citizens. In the event of violations of the law, the NIMC has the right to discontinue any activity – new construction, restructuring or repairs – affecting immovable monuments of culture and their environment, and what has so far been built is subject to demolition.

The MCMA and the Penal Code contain sanctions for natural persons and legal entities who by their actions (or inaction) cause (or contribute to) damaging or destroying monuments of culture. The Territory Development Act envisages the exercise of administrative control for observing its provisions and the regulatory acts covering its implementation in design and construction, as well as the respective administrative-penal responsibility in the event of established violations. Officials and participants in construction can be punished with fines of 100 to 150 000 leva if another law does not stipulate a heavier punishment.

Control is exercised by the authorities of the local administration and the Directorate of National Construction Control. The Directorate issues penal decrees and prescribes coercion measures, including removal of the illegal construction (TDA, Article 222 and subs). In executing its obligations, the bodies of the Directorate have the right to enforce access with the assistance of the authorities of the Ministry of the Interior. The main problem in implementing coercive measures is insufficient financial assurance and the difficulty in gaining reimbursement of funds expended for this purpose.

Control in protected areas is exercised by the Ministry of the Environment and Waters and its regional structures (National Parks Directorates and Regional Inspectorates of Protection of the Environment and Waters).

The Protected Territories Act foresees sanctions for all natural persons, legal entities or sole traders who carry out activities in protected areas that run counter to the Act itself, the relevant order of declaration, the management plan or other endorsed plans and programmes affecting the protected area.

The Protected Territories Act also envisages sanctions for officials who permit activities in protected areas in violation of the Act itself, the order of declaration or the area's management plan, or who have not imposed punishments for any activity or construction running counter to the Act, the orders or management plans for a protected area, or who have not co-ordinated with the competent bodies activities in protected areas for which there are no management plans.

The following problems can be outlined in the field under review:

– there are legislative contradictions in the field permit procedures, for instance: for conservation works on monuments of culture; for conservation works on façades of monuments of culture; for advertising, information and other elements in protected zones. These contradictions, as well as illegal construction, compromise to a considerable extent the Nessebar Reserve (a World Heritage site), for example.

– there is no effective control of cultural heritage and no adequate sanctions for violations in cultural-historical areas – this considerably increases the amount of illegal construction, treasure-hunting and non-maintenance of monuments of culture. There are cases of irreversible decay of buildings – monuments of culture of outstanding significance, left without elementary maintenance by their owners, without any sanctions on them. Such behaviour of the owners aims most often at the realisation of certain investment intentions of theirs to the detriment of the cultural heritage.

– some of the problems mentioned result from the strong centralisation and concentration of the management system, and the weak role of the local authorities in the process of conservation.

# Croatia

*Jasen Mesić, Nada Duic-Kowalsky, Tamara Ganoci Frisch and Marijana A. Mance*

## 1. Documentation systems

### 1.1. and 1.2. Identification and characterisation

#### Directorate for the Protection of Cultural Heritage

Within the Ministry of Culture of the Republic of Croatia, is the Directorate for the Protection of Cultural Heritage. It carries out administrative and professional tasks in researching, studying, monitoring, registering, documenting and promoting cultural heritage; establishing attributes of cultural monuments and their evaluation; keeping the register of cultural goods of the Republic of Croatia; prescribing standards for programmes of public needs regarding the protection of cultural goods; providing for, co-ordinating and supervising the financing of cultural goods protection programmes; evaluating conditions under which legal and physical persons carry out restoration, conservation and other cultural goods protection activities; providing conditions for the education and advanced professional training of personnel engaged in the protection of cultural goods; supervising the trade, import and export of protected cultural goods; establishing conditions for the utilisation and end-use of cultural goods, including the management of cultural goods in compliance with regulations; establishing special building conditions geared at protecting cultural goods; performing inspection activities in the field of cultural goods protection; administrative and administrative-expert tasks linked to the activity of archives and other tasks in compliance with the directions and instructions of the minister, who is the head of administration.

The directorate comprises eleven departments at present: Conservation Sectors of Zagreb, Rijeka, Split, Osijek, Dubrovnik, Zadar, Šibenik, Karlovac, Varaždin, Požega and Pula/Poreč. A further five departments are being set up at Gospić, Sisak, Bjelovar, Krapina and Pakrac.

#### Department for Immovable Cultural Heritage

The activities of this department are carried out in two sectors: the Sector for Individual Cultural Goods and the Sector for Cultural-Historic Ensembles.

#### Department for Movable and Intangible Cultural Heritage

The tasks of the department are carried out in two sectors: the Sector for Movable Cultural Goods and the Sector for Intangible Cultural Goods.

## Department for Archaeological Heritage

The Department for Archaeological Heritage carries out expert and administrative tasks pertaining to research and processing of archaeological cultural heritage, monitoring and establishing the status of archaeological heritage, preparation of proposed programmes and priorities for their protection, the implementation of measures for the protection of archaeological heritage and other tasks in compliance with the guidelines of instructions of the department, namely, the administration head.

## Croatian Restoration Institute

The primary activity of the Institute is the conservation and restoration of cultural heritage (architectural heritage, works of art, items of artistic handicraft, etc.). It comprises 18 specialised units, in 14 locations. The institute forms the framework for conservation and restoration in the state administration and public institutions, and it works under the authority of the Ministry of Culture.

## Documentation and observation of the state of cultural goods

The competent body prepares documentation concerning the protection and preservation of all cultural goods. The Minister of Culture prescribes the necessary level of documentation and the documentation standards for individual types of cultural goods, as well as the conditions, methods and procedures for safe-keeping and use.

The use of documentation concerning cultural goods may be granted for official purposes, scientific research, publication, teaching, exhibition and other approved purposes. In principle, only photographs of the documentation are supplied and they are made at the expense of the applicant. In exceptional circumstances, if required by scientific needs, the original documentation may be borrowed for a certain period along with its obligatory safe-keeping; this is in addition to the making of protective photographs at the expense of the applicant and in accordance with prescribed conditions. Approval for the use of documentation concerning cultural goods is given by the competent body, and by the Minister of Culture concerning borrowing original documentation.

The competent body constantly observes the state of cultural goods and establishes the state of cultural goods at least once every five years. The Minister of Culture stipulates the format of the report forms concerning the state of cultural goods and the process of establishing the state of cultural goods.

The central inventory of cultural heritage contains the following data:

- cultural heritage;
- architectural heritage;
- archaeological sites;

- legal status before the revision;

- historical sites;

- sites and environment.

## 1.3. Databases and computerised mapping

### Information System of Cultural Heritage of the Republic of Croatia TEUTA

The TEUTA information system of cultural heritage has been developed in the Ministry of Culture primarily to ensure efficient protection of cultural heritage, but also to serve the wider professional community and the general public, with open public access through the Internet. The system has three main purposes: the first and fundamental one is to ensure an insight into the complete stock of cultural monuments of the Republic of Croatia; the second one is the creation of a knowledge base necessary for fulfilling the tasks of cultural heritage protection by way of offering an insight into the existing documentation on a certain monument; and the third one is the preservation of cultural heritage in the most literary way – the digitising of documentation collections, which are already by themselves cultural heritage. This is the most efficient way to protect them.

The project of developing a universal information system for cultural heritage was defined in 2000/01, and the software development started in the autumn of 2002. Development is still in progress.

Through comprehensive information technology (IT) work, existing digital documents (databases developed in the dBASEIV programme package, and a few "home-made" MS Access applications) were successfully migrated to the SQL server and unified into a universal relational database, with Access user interface being developed. Nowadays multi-user information systems enable tracking of data changes as well as automatic network communication, bug reporting, automatic network system upgrading and permission assignment at the level of the individual user or group of users.

Although the skeleton of the system is the database of the central inventory of the cultural heritage of the Republic of Croatia, the system also includes documentation collections from the field of cultural heritage (photo library, photo CD library, plan library, microfilm collection, press clipping collection), the Register of cultural properties of the Republic of Croatia, conservation works programmes, address books of persons and organisations relevant to cultural heritage protection, and a whole range of auxiliary databases necessary for the efficient functioning of the conservation service.

The inter-operability of the system has been ensured by the application of international standards and guidelines (Council of Europe, ISO) in respect of data content and structure, and technical platform.

While defining the system concept, and later developing the system, special attention was given to the experiences of other countries in the field of documentation and inventory creation of cultural heritage, primarily to the Historic Buildings, Sites & Monuments Database developed by English Heritage and the French system *Mérimée*, developed by the Ministère de la Culture et de la Communication, Direction de l'Architecture et du Patrimoine. Contacts with neighbouring countries have been established as well, first of all with the Republic of Slovenia, whose information system is similar to the Croatian one and also complies with European standards, which provides the necessary preconditions for the systems' inter-operability.

### Databases within the TEUTA information system of cultural heritage

As stated in the introductory paragraph, the TEUTA information system will comprise a whole range of databases from the field of cultural heritage protection, which are divided into five basic groups in order to be as easy-to-consult as possible.

1. Central inventory of cultural heritage (historic buildings and monuments; historic ensembles; archaeological sites; movable objects; mosaics; organs)

2. Administrative databases (conservation works; register of cultural properties of the Republic of Croatia)

3. Documentation collections (photo library; photo CD library; plan library; microfilm collection; press clipping collection)

4. War damage (database of Croatian cultural heritage monuments and sites damaged in war, 1990-95)

5. Auxiliary databases (official list of places and towns in Croatia; address book of people and institutions relevant for the protection of cultural heritage; thesaurus of monument types)

### Central inventory of cultural heritage

This is a list or catalogue of the whole monument stock, immovable or movable, on the territory of the Republic of Croatia. It is divided into six databases – Historic buildings and monuments, Historic ensembles, Archaeological sites, Movable objects, Mosaics and Organs – because such different categories of cultural heritage cannot be documented and described in a uniform data structure, but some modification of the core data structure is demanded for each of them.

Data structures for each of the mentioned databases have been developed on the European standards for documentation and inventory creation of cultural heritage. Existing data, compiled during previous recorded activities, have been preserved and supplemented with new items, as recommended by the said European standards.

Regarding quantity, historic buildings and monuments are the most numerous category of immovable heritage in Croatia (circa 8 400 objects). For that reason, that database was the starting point for the development of the whole information system, to which all other databases have since been linked.

The data structure for historic buildings and monuments was carefully defined in accordance with the Recommendation of the Council of Europe on documenting historic buildings and their complexes (in other words, built heritage) and this model was then adapted to meet the needs of documenting historic ensembles and archaeological sites, after also consulting appropriate international guidelines.

## Administrative databases

These databases of conservation works are intended for use in administrative tasks related to collecting and processing proposals for conservation works on the cultural heritage, and updating the database of the Register of Cultural Properties, which serves as a tool for the on-going project of revising the protection status of all monument stock on the territory of the Republic of Croatia. It is a comprehensive task of harmonising the existing decisions on protection status with the current legislation, because the new Law on the Protection and Preservation of Cultural Property (OG, No. 69/99), which came into force in 1999, followed by Regulations on the Register of Cultural Properties (OG, No. 37/01) in 2001, brought drastic changes to the previous system of legal protection, based on a law of 1967. The old Register, also based on the law of 1967, was used to compile the Central inventory, so all data need to be revised and harmonised with the new legislation.

## Documentation collections

Databases of the Photo library, Photo-CD library, Plan library, Microfilm collection and Press-clipping collection form the next unit in the TEUTA information system. These computer-aided tools for inventory creation and cataloguing of documentation from the field of cultural heritage protection, are the property of the Ministry of Culture:

- the plan library, old maps and graphics collection comprises plans, projects, drafts and architectural drawings, dating from 1800 to 1970, in total 8 154 items.

- the microfilm collection contains microfilmed technical documentation (mainly architectural drawings and plans) of cultural heritage, whose originals are stored in the plan libraries of conservation offices and other institutions in the field. Technical documentation has been microfilmed since 1979. Up to 2006, about 94 000 items had been microfilmed. They can be divided into two thematic units: documentation from plan libraries of different institutions and microfilmed inheritances of certain renowned architects. Up to 2006, about 32 000 items had been entered on the microfilm database.

– the photo library comprises about 30 000 negatives and about 51 000 photo-graphs, from about 1860 until the present day, approximately 500 negatives on plate-glass and a collection of postcards (about two drawers full). Photographs have also been systematically digitised, so about 17 000 items are digitised and stored on the database.

– the photo CD library is the youngest collection, founded in 2002. It comprises photo material, shot exclusively by digital camera during campaigns of recording of cultural heritage. The photographs have been stored on about 100 CD-ROMs, which have been downloaded onto the database by a fast and simple procedure.

– the press-clipping collection comprises newspaper articles relevant to the cultural heritage protection. Articles are catalogued through the database and also digi-tised and attached to related records.

All the databases mentioned above are linked by cross-reference numbers with the data-bases of the Central Inventory and the simplified schema of the relational model, as follows: documentation, historic ensembles, administrative databases, auxiliary data-bases, archaeological sites.

### War damage database

The project of recording and evaluating war damage to the immovable cultural heritage resulted in the War damage database, which contains 2 423 records, cross-referenced to the database of historic buildings and monuments.

### Auxiliary databases

The rest of the databases in the TEUTA Information system of cultural heritage are auxiliary databases, including an address book of persons and organisations relevant to cultural heritage protection, an official list of places and towns in Croatia, and a thesaurus of monument types; they nevertheless form an extremely important part of the whole system.

The need to establish universal terminology and classification for cultural heritage has been long recognised in Croatia as a major precondition of creating consistent conservation and restoration documentation. Therefore, on the basis of ISO standards for the development of monolingual and multilingual thesauri and relevant foreign thesauri, as well as on the basis of Croatian experience so far, a complex application for thesaurus compilation has been developed in the frame of the TEUTA information system and the work of termi-nology compilation has been launched. So far, about 700 terms have been added to the thesauri, after being checked and processed from the lexical and conservationist aspects. Currently, indexing is under way of the records within the database of Historic buildings and monuments, using the terms from the thesaurus. This is expected to result in better consistency of data and the possibility of much more refined data retrieval.

Further development of the TEUTA information system of cultural heritage is conceived as an open-ended system that will be systematically upgraded with new thematic units. For example, the next phase is planned to include development of the intangible heritage database, along with the inclusion of geospatial data in the system and development of a geographical information system (GIS) for cultural heritage in Croatia, which will ensure a high-quality basis for physical planning and interpretation of cultural heritage in its natural surroundings as well as an inter-disciplinary approach to its preservation.

From the technological point of view, work is under way to upgrade the system from local area network application to a web-oriented platform based on XML standards, which has been recently developed. This will enable simultaneous work on the system in conservation offices scattered across the country, as well as inter-operability with the BREUH system. Finally, the whole system will be integrated into the BREUH information system, the database of registered works of art in process of restoration, developed by the Croatian Restoration Institute.

All these activities will facilitate access to data by professionals in the conservation and restoration field, but it is also expected that simultaneous work in conservation offices across the country will contribute to the quality and accuracy of data in the databases.

Simultaneously, the use of web technology will enable the Ministry of Culture, as a government body, to fulfil its obligation to inform the general public of its activities. In turn, this will help to raise awareness of cultural heritage, to affirm Croatians' common and personal identity, and encourage interest in heritage generally, which will bring about its protection and preservation. Therefore, we thrive on making our data accessible through the Internet to the widest public, but certainly bearing in mind the necessity of security measures. Situations such as careless publishing of data on the location of unprotected underwater sites in the Adriatic Sea, or unattended buildings with valuable inventories, should certainly be prevented. It is our task to avoid endangering the same heritage that we are trying to protect.

## 2. Integrated management studies, plans and regulations

*2.1. Environment*

*Types of document*

Environmental Impact Assessment (EIA) is carried out pursuant to the Environmental Protection Act (Official Gazette Nos. 82/94 and 128/99) and the Ordinance on Environmental Impact Assessment (OG Nos. 59/00 and 136/04). The List of Interventions, constituting an integral part of the Ordinance, defines those interventions for which an EIA procedure is required. According to the indicated List, EIA procedures shall be carried out for the following types of interventions: transport facilities, energy supply facilities, hydraulic structures, structures for waste management, sport structures, construction entities and extraction of mineral raw materials.

## Types of impact

EIAs examine potential adverse impacts that an intended intervention could have on soil, water, sea, air, forests, climate, human health, flora and fauna, landscape, cultural and historical heritage, and their inter-relationships, taking into consideration also other planned interventions and their potential interaction with existing or planned interventions in the area covered by the EIA.

The section of an EIA study dealing with cultural and historical heritage contains a part that refers to art conservation, and this establishes, on the basis of existing documentation of responsible institutions (art-conservation departments, museums, etc.), data from literature and visits to the sites of the planned intervention, the existence or non-existence of items of cultural and historical value, the potential threat to them, appropriate protection measures and a programme for monitoring the state of the environment.

## Competences

Implementation of EIA procedures falls under the competence of the Ministry of Environmental Protection, Physical Planning and Construction. The ministry appoints a commission, which on the basis of an EIA study assesses the environmental impact of the intervention, its evaluation and acceptability. Commission members are recruited from state administration bodies, representative bodies of local self-government in the intervention's impact area, scientists and professionals.

EIA studies are produced by legal persons registered for the performance of expert activities of environmental protection or for the production of EIA studies, respectively, and these legal persons are responsible for ensuring the EIA studies are well founded in professional terms.

The investor (executor) of the intervention shall obtain the relevant EIA study and provide the funds for its preparation. Within EIA procedure, carrying out public insight and public debate is mandatory.

## Impact on heritage

After completion of the EIA procedure, and upon proposal by the EIA Commission, the Ministry of Environmental Protection, Physical Planning and Construction issues a decision on the acceptability of the intervention, prescribing environmental protection measures and a programme for monitoring the state of the environment. Thereupon a location permit (or other permit for interventions for which no location permit is required) shall be issued, whereby the prescribed environmental protection measures and programme for monitoring the state of the environment shall be an integral part, thereof. Pursuant to regulations in force, the investor (executor) of the intervention shall provide to the environmental inspectorate details of the prescribed environmental protection measures and results of monitoring the state of the environment.

If the intervention is assessed by the commission as unacceptable, the ministry issues a decision whereby approval of the intended intervention is refused.

## 2.2. Spatial and urban planning

### Types of planning documents

The Spatial Planning Law (*Zakon o prostornom planiranju*, Nos. 30/94, 68/98, 61/100, 32/02, 100/04) quotes the following documents of spatial planning in the Republic of Croatia:

- Strategy and Programme of Spatial Regulation of the State
- other spatial plans, as follows:
  - Spatial Plan of a District (*županija*) or of the City of Zagreb (which has the status of a county);
  - Spatial Plan of Territories with Specific Attributes;
  - Spatial Regulatory Plan of the Municipality and/or Town/City;
  - Urban Regulatory Plan;
  - Detailed Regulatory Plan.

In addition to this Law, there is a Regulation on the Organisation and Protection of the Protected Coastal Area of the Sea (*Uredba o ure enju i zaštiti zaštićenog obalnog područja mora*, No. 128/04). Other conditions concerning the building itself and issuing of Construction (Building) Permits are defined in the Construction Law (*Zakon o gradnji*, Nos. 175/03, 100/04).

### Location permits

The Spatial Planning Law clearly states that a location permit is required for each spatial intervention, meaning that everything done on the terrain must be done according to the documents of spatial planning, special rules and location permit. A location permit is an administrative act issued in relation to documents of spatial planning, special laws and rules adopted in accord with those laws.

With a location permit, depending on the type of action undertaken on the site, the following elements are defined:

- shape and size of a building (construction) site, or spatial limit of the action undertaken,
- purpose of a building,
- size and area of a building,
- position of one or more buildings on a building (construction) site, or within a spatial limit,
- design of a building,
- regulation of a building (construction) site,
- ways and conditions of connecting a building (construction) site or the building itself to the public-traffic surface and utility infrastructure,
- ways of preventing unfavourable environmental effects,
- other elements that are important for some spatial activity, according to the specific rules.

A location permit comprises extracts from the documents of spatial planning according to which the location permit was issued.

In more general terms, the aims and scope of spatial planning are management and protection of the territories of the state, and an integral approach to spatial planning, for example:

- identification, verification and evaluation of the possibilities of spatial planning,
- drafting documents of spatial planning,
- follow-up activities related to implementation of the documents of spatial planning.

### Authorities responsible for the production of planning documents

The administrative divisions in the Republic of Croatia are:

- central administration (central government),
- offices of central administration in the units of local self-government (central government),
- local self-administration: municipalities and towns and/or cities (local self-government).

The efficiency of spatial planning of the state is assured through the institutions of the Croatian Parliament and the National Government, and through the representative and executive bodies of local self-government. These institutions are in charge of adaptation of the documents of spatial planning and other relating documents prescribed by the Spatial Planning Law.

The professional and expert elements of these documents are controlled by the administrative bodies of central government and local self-government. These bodies have permission to carry out stated expert tasks, together with legal authorities and registered architects that independently carry out tasks related to spatial planning.

Expert tasks for the state are done within the Institute for Physical (Spatial) Planning, which is part of the Ministry of Environmental Protection, Physical Planning and Construction. The Institute is in charge of making and maintaining the Strategy and Programme of Spatial Regulation of the State, and other documents that are adopted by the Croatian Parliament. On a medium-term basis for four years, the Institute drafts a Programme for the Advancement of Spatial Planning Conditions for the state, basic elements for usage of the territories of the state and Reports on Conditions of Territories.

To conclude, plans are adopted on all three levels – national, regional and local – depending on the importance and level of protection of the territory.

For areas of national interest, when plans are being executed – for instance, plans for some national parks – the entire work is undertaken in the Institute for Physical (Spatial) Planning at the Ministry of Environmental Protection, Physical Planning and Construction. National reports, programmes and strategies are produced in the same manner.

When local self-government produces a plan, there is a whole procedure that must be respected before the plan is actually adopted, and this procedure involves the relevant ministry, local self-government, the executors of the plan and the civil society.

### Public debate

Before a plan is complete, local self-government usually co-operates with the ministry, especially if planning for some strategic and/or protected area. Once the plan is finished, the first action must be to announce in an acceptable way that a public discussion is to take place. After the discussion, all remarks are collected. The plan and remarks, with responses, are then sent to the ministry, which gives final approval or sends the plan back to be further developed and modified in accord with some remarks. Once it is adopted, there is a public announcement of the plan in the local paper. After a period, the spatial plan becomes legally valid, with legal force and the status of a sub-statutory act.

### Collaborations

The Ministry of Environmental Protection, Physical Planning and Construction also collaborates with the Ministry of Culture on conservation provisions for historically valuable areas, and with the Ministry of the Sea and Infrastructure. Legal aspects are co-ordinated with the Ministry of Justice.

Zoning documents, dependent on the type and area of undertaking, are obliged to contain data from the conservation background material with a system of measures for the protection of immovable cultural goods that are found in the area encompassed by the plan.

The conservation background material is established by the competent body. It contains general and special conditions for the protection and preservation of cultural goods in the area encompassed by the plan. If the competent body has not established the conservation background material, it is required to establish, at the request of the body that passes zoning documents, a system of measures for the protection of immovable cultural goods found in the area encompassed by the plan.

The zoning document may only be brought forward with the previous approval of the competent body that confirms accordance with the conservation background material or the established system of measures for protection. The competent body is required to make a written statement concerning the requested approval within 15 days; if it does not do so, then it is assumed that approval is given.

Urban development plans are brought forward for the protection and preservation of cultural-historical sites in accordance with the provisions concerning zoning and the Law on Protection and Preservation of Cultural Goods.

## Financing of plans

Financing of plans is connected to their execution: the bodies in charge of making plans have a right to contract a private firm (this is usually the case with Detailed Regulatory Plans and Urban Regulatory Plans, that is, for the more detailed ones). In this case, they pay for the execution of the plans. Most of the spatial documentation of local self-government is financed from the local budget, but some less wealthy or underdeveloped areas with a lower budget have the right to apply for funds from the relevant ministry. Some funds for such administrative units are allocated to them, the amount depending on the ministry's budget. Such an approach is accepted because both wealthy and poor administrative units must respect the legal timetable for drafting a new generation of plans, in order to improve the state of spatial planning and spatial management in the Republic of Croatia.

The next step to be taken is to apply for the pre-accession funds that have been made available to Croatia lately. Previously, no such funds were available; only the CARDS programme was active.

## Documentation systems

A new generation of spatial plans ensures that all plans will be digitalised. Orthophotos and geophotos (black-and-white and full colour) are included in the process of digitalisation, and serve as a basis for and/or supplement to the plan documentation.

Some municipalities/cities have decided to skip the process of simple digitalisation and gone for GIS systems from the start. It took them more time to educate the staff, to get the right software and to ensure funds for all this, but such an approach has proved to be better because GIS is more adaptable, applicable and interoperable. In addition, many plans are published on the web, and GIS applications have proved to have a much better functionality than simple images of the plans.

At state level, the relevant ministry uses both: the GIS system ArcView and AutoCad Map for data extraction and manipulation. The ministry has not strictly prescribed which GIS software local communities should use once they get to it, but it has made some recommendations. As a consequence, most GIS users work with the ArcView application, though some use others, so that data exchange is not completely equalised and optimal. In addition, there are two computer-based systems in use for plans: the CAD-based one and GIS, which means that additional time has to be spent on attaining a single GIS plan system.

Data manipulated within the GIS systems include several plan levels, which means that the heritage level has to be taken into account.

### Consideration of the heritage in the planning system

Heritage can be understood in two ways: cultural heritage and landscape heritage. When it comes to cultural heritage, the Ministry of Culture is the one to give broad guidelines and the one that is authorised to make statements on culture in general. Conservation guidelines have to be respected, especially when it comes to planning on a more detailed level, and especially when architectural projects are included.

Landscape heritage involves both aspects: environment and spatial planning. That being so, within the Faculty of Architecture the subject of landscape/garden planning is part of the regular undergraduate and postgraduate syllabus. Landscape heritage includes natural, social and cultural aspects.

> Example: The vineyards of the town of Primošten have been listed as a Monument to Human Labour within the UNESCO World Heritage List. The Primošten vineyards include elements of astonishing natural beauty, human modification of the hills through the process of work and elements of construction with local materials; they serve as a three-dimensional document of humans' close relation with nature in the process of production.

It has happened, during work on big infrastructure projects like highways (for which the Ministry of Sea and Infrastructure is responsible), that valuable archaeological sites have been discovered. Such findings have resulted in the need for more detailed surveys before fixing the highway corridor.

Other ways of protecting specific areas (for example, national parks and/or nature parks) are described above (i.e. via spatial planning documentation).

# 3. Authorisation, supervision and penalties

## 3.1. Authorisation

### Special conditions for the protection of cultural goods when issuing location permits

When undertaking work on immovable cultural goods, or in the area within the physical boundaries of such cultural goods, where a location permit is obligatory according to special provisions, the location permit must ensure special conditions for the protection of the cultural goods. The special conditions for the protection of cultural goods are issued by the competent body at the request of the administrative body competent to issue location permits.

In undertaking work on protected cultural-historical sites, the special conditions of protection for cultural goods are established by the administrative body competent to issue location permits, in accordance with the system of measures for protection established in the urban development plan in Article 57 of the Law on Protection and Preservation of Cultural Goods.

### Previous approval for works on cultural goods

Works that may cause changes to the cultural goods or their immediate vicinity – in other words, that may disturb the integrity of the cultural goods – may be undertaken with the prior approval of the competent body. The prior approval of the competent body is necessary for any construction in an area protected as a cultural-historical site.

The Minister of Culture prescribes the documentation to be attached by the person filing the request for previous approval. The competent body comes to a decision on the request for previous approval. A building permit may be issued only if there is a final decision. In cases where, according to the Law on Construction, it is not necessary to have a building permit, construction may not begin without the final decision.

In particular circumstances, the competent body may issue consent for the removal of immovable cultural goods, or a portion thereof, if it is established that the removal is related to deterioration or larger damage that directly threatens the stability of the building or a portion thereof, that it represents a danger for neighbouring buildings and individuals' lives, and that the danger cannot be removed in any other way. The competent body may only give consent with the previous opinion of the Croatian Council for Cultural Goods.

### Prior approval for activity within immovable cultural goods

Legal entities and individuals may not begin the performance of economic activities in an area within immovable cultural goods or a protected cultural-historical site without the prior approval of the competent body. Approval is also necessary for every change in purpose of the business premises, in other words any change in the activity.

## Preventative protection of cultural goods in extraordinary circumstances

Institutions that undertake the duties of protecting and preserving cultural goods and the owner of the cultural goods are required to secure the following during times of peace, in co-operation with the competent bodies:

– conditions for work on the protection and preservation of cultural goods in cases of extraordinary circumstances (armed conflict, earthquake, flood, fire, ecological incidents and catastrophes or other extraordinary circumstances);

– measures for the prevention of theft, looting, illegal appropriation of cultural goods in any way, and all activities intended to destroy or damage cultural goods.

The Minister of Culture may order the undertaking of special measures for the protection of cultural goods in cases of disappearance of the cultural goods or if extraordinary circumstances are declared. The local government of the county, the City of Zagreb, the municipality or city on whose territory the cultural goods are found must secure the resources necessary for the implementation of measures.

*Jusuf Maskovic Han, Vrana
(Council of Europe)*

## 3.2. Supervision and penalties

### Supervision

The Ministry of Culture performs the administrative and expert duties connected with the protection and preservation of cultural goods envisaged in the Croatian Law on Protection and Preservation of Cultural Goods, as well as inspection for the protection and preservation of cultural goods.

Cultural goods are considered to be endangered if they are immovable cultural goods entered in the List of World Heritage or the List of World Heritage in Danger, or they are cultural goods entered in the Register whose status as endangered cultural goods is established by a decision of the Minister of Culture, and at the recommendation of the Croatian Council for Cultural Goods.

The Minister of Culture may appoint a committee whose task is the monitoring and planning of measures to be implemented for the protection and preservation of endangered cultural goods. The tasks and method of work of that committee are established in the act on its appointment.

Inspection is performed by civil servants of the Ministry of Culture with the rank of Inspector or Senior Inspector of the protection of cultural goods (hereinafter: Inspector). A Senior Inspector may be a person who has a university degree; at least ten years' experience in duties connected with the protection of cultural goods, and has passed the national examination. An Inspector may be an individual who has a university degree, at least five years' experience in duties connected with the protection of cultural goods, and has passed the national examination.

Inspections connected with the protection of cultural goods may be performed by other employees of the Ministry of Culture on the basis of special authorisation of the Minister of Culture. Inspectors have special identity cards and badges with which they prove their official capacity, identity and authority. The form of official identity cards and badges and the method of issuance thereof, as well as the form of the record and the method of keeping thereof, are prescribed by the Minister of Culture.

An inspector keeps a record of the performance of supervision. The inspector has the right and obligation during the performance of supervision to inspect cultural goods, the area in which the cultural goods are located, documentation and equipment, and if necessary to listen to individual persons in the administrative procedure.

The person who is being supervised is required to provide for the Inspector proper conditions for the implementation of supervision, to enable them to review the cultural goods, to provide access to the documentation requested and to give them necessary data and notifications.

With direct insight into general and individual acts, conditions and methods of work of the persons who are being inspected, the inspector establishes whether they are in compliance with the laws and other provisions concerning arrangements for protecting and preserving cultural goods, and if the persons being inspected have the approval, permission or other prescribed act that allows them to perform duties in connection with cultural goods, especially in the case of restoration institutes, museums, galleries, archives and libraries, as far as relates to the protection of cultural goods, other institutions that perform duties connected with protecting and preserving cultural goods, and specialised legal entities and individuals who perform duties connected with protection, preservation, renovation and transactions of cultural goods.

The inspector checks the state of the cultural goods and the implementation of measures for the protection and preservation, use and transactions of cultural goods, execution and implementation of the provisions of Croatian Law on Protection and Preservation of Cultural Goods, and especially:

– performance of conservation, restoration or other similar work on the cultural goods and their immediate vicinity, as well as adherence to the issued conditions and approvals;

– archaeological excavation and research, including those under water, as well as underwater activities and removal of submerged cultural goods with adherence to the prescribed conditions and approvals;

– transactions of cultural goods, application of the right to first purchase, and the export, import and movement of cultural goods;

– application of other provisions and measures established in this Law.

### Penalties

In the execution of his or her tasks, the Inspector has the right and obligation to order:

– removal of established insufficiencies and irregularities,

– removal of the consequences of illegal actions or omissions,

– interruption in performance of unapproved work, actions or activities on the cultural goods,

– removal of damage,

– temporary seizure of movable cultural goods for their protection,

– other measures for the protection and preservation of cultural goods in accordance with the law and other provisions.

In the execution of his or her tasks, the Inspector has the right and obligation to forbid:

– implementation of illegal actions,

– works, actions or activities on the cultural goods carried out without permission, without issued special conditions for protection or not in compliance with them,

– archaeological excavation or research undertaken by unauthorised or non-expert legal entities or individuals,

– unauthorised transactions of cultural goods and transactions without application of the right to first purchase,

– export, import and movement of cultural goods contrary to provisions of law,

– unauthorised performance of restoration and conservation, performance of restoration or conservation work on cultural goods contrary to the law and provisions
based on the law, and other illegal work according to the law and provisions based
on the law.

If the inspector establishes that the person being inspected has gained possession of
cultural goods through an illegal act, they may temporarily seize the cultural goods
or any item used to commit the illegal act, until a decision is taken on the violation
or a judgment given on a criminal offence. A written confirmation of the temporary
seizure is issued, in addition to the simultaneous initiation of misdemeanour or criminal
proceedings.

### Emergency measures for the protection and preservation of cultural goods

If a contractor undertakes work on cultural goods without the necessary previous
approval, or they undertake work contrary to the approval, the competent body temporarily interrupts such work by way of a decision. In the decision the competent body may
order the contractor to return the cultural goods to their previous state and may also
threaten implementation at the contractor's expense.

An appeal against the decision does not suspend the execution. If the contractor does not
cease the work begun on the cultural goods, the competent body notifies the competent
police administration and the competent building inspector, to prevent further damage
to the cultural goods.

If the owner of cultural goods, or any other individual, acts contrary to the provisions
of the Law on Protection and Preservation of Cultural Goods, resulting in damage to
cultural goods, or brings about a direct threat of damage, the competent body without
delay requests from the competent administrative bodies the undertaking of measures
within their competence. The competent body of national administration is required to
act immediately in response to the request and undertake measures within its competence to prevent damage or destruction of the cultural goods.

### Proposal for the substance of conservation principles behind physical planning

The problem of the protection of cultural and historical treasures in a given territory
is present at all levels of planning. For this reason, the conservator must incontestably
be one of the essential participants in the planning process. The problems that appear
when drafting conservation principles for physical planning, and the need for regulation
of the necessary level of collaboration with those who draw up the plans, indicate
the urgency of them being settled. In the proposal put forward, which is based on
general principles, knowledge of conservation tasks and activities, and many years of
experience in the practical application of them, particularly in protecting the integral
values of a territory, an attempt is made to provide a basis for a permanent solution of
this problem.

# Montenegro

*Lidija Ljesar and Vasilije Buskovic*

## 1. Documentation Systems

### 1.1. Identification

#### Cultural heritage

The cultural heritage of Montenegro is defined by the Law on Protection of Cultural Monuments of 1991.

In the territory of Montenegro, 357 immovable cultural monuments have so far been placed under protection. The cultural monuments consist of: immovable and movable objects; groups of objects and buildings; historical, archaeological, artistical, aesthetical, ethnological, architectural, urban, sociological and technical ensembles; and other scientifical and cultural treasures important for the history and culture of Montenegro. Cultural monuments named on the World Cultural Heritage List enjoy special protection defined by this and other laws.

Cultural monuments are classified in three categories according to their value:

- first category      – monuments of exceptional value

- second category – monuments of great importance

- third category     – significant monuments

The 1992 rule book on the contents of a register of cultural monuments, and how to present them, sets down the way to keep the Register of cultural monuments in the territory of Montenegro, according to which there are three types of inventory:

- Central Register of cultural monuments,

- register of cultural monuments,

- indexes of cultural monuments with preventive protection.

There is a place in the register for each cultural monument containing the basic dates for it, entered under the following headings:

- registration number,

- number and date of the official Decision to designate the cultural monument,

- name and type of the cultural monument,
- its relative values and legal status,
- exact location of the cultural monument,
- period when the monument was erected, including all important values and legal changes made to the cultural monument or in any way related to it, and all necessary documentation related to it (cadastre facts/real estate registry/ sales contract etc.),
- list of the most important professional literature dealing with the cultural monument,
- professional documentation of the cultural monument enabling its identification during restoration,
- information on financial investment in the cultural monument,
- documentation of conservation and other work executed on the cultural monument,
- grade of the cultural monument,
- special remarks,
- privy seal and the signature.

The Republic Institute for Protection of Cultural Monuments, in Cetinje, has been managing the Central Register of the cultural monuments on the national level, and the Regional Institute for Protection of Cultural Monuments, in Kotor, has been managing the Register of cultural monuments in the area of the municipalities of Kotor, Herceg Novi and Tivat. There is a uniform system of documentation.

*Former French Embassy, Cetinje (Council of Europe)*

*Natural heritage*

The natural heritage of Montenegro is regulated by the Law on the Protection of Nature of 1977, including modifications and annexes from 1989.

So far 106 655 ha. of natural property in Montenegro have been placed under protection, which is 7.72% of the overall territory of the state. On the other hand, 237 899 ha. have been placed under international protection (UNESCO, Ramsar), in other words 17.2% of the state territory.

For each protected natural object, the Central Register of protected natural property and protected objects of nature keeps the following information:

- registered number,
- name,
- type,
- republic (national) category,
- international category,
- location,
- short description,
- description of the boundaries,
- information about the owner and holder,
- physical and legal changes,
- number and the date of the designation document,
- information about conservation work and scientific research,
- details of maintenance and conservation costs for private property financed by the state, and
- remarks.

The dossier on a protected natural object holds the following information:

- general information: name; type; the republic (national) category; the international category; location, with geographical co-ordinates and description of boundaries; information about the owner and the holder; information about the main types of habitat; information on inhabitants and settlements; the official limitations/allowed action;

- information about the environment: geophysical (climate, precipitation, insolation, evaporation, bio-climate, winds) and hydrological (rivers, lakes, sea), soil, fauna and flora (including the abundance and status of protected species);

- iInformation about activities and influences;
- maps and graphics (aerial-photo shots, topographic maps, thematic maps, town and urban spatial plans, satellite photo shots);
- photo-documentation;
- bibliography, including research projects and a list of programmes of work implemented on the protected natural property.

The Republic Institute for Protection of Nature, based in Podgorica, is responsible for keeping the Central Register, as well as the dossier of individual protected natural objects. The Republic Institute of the Protection of Nature has been working at the national (republic) level.

## 1.2. Characterisation

### Cultural heritage

The Law on the Protection of Cultural Monuments of 1991 defines the type of documentation needed if an immovable object is to be eligible for the procedure for its designation as a cultural monument. This documentation should consist of the following:

- a description of the immovable object followed by the basic documentation,
- the boundary of the immovable object and its immediate surroundings,
- the programme for protection, arrangement, use and maintenance of the immovable object,
- an indication of the owner and the holder of the immovable object.

In accordance with the Law on Protection of Cultural Monuments, the Republic Institute for Protection of Cultural Monuments is responsible for creating professional documentation of the protected cultural property.

The main information sources needed for making planning documentation are the documentation centres of the Republic and Regional Institute for Protection of Cultural Monuments (Project Analyses and Studies), the Central Register and the Register of protected cultural monuments.

### Natural heritage

Information about the character of the protected natural property is given in its dossier (see section 1.1. above). The decision to put a natural property under protection is based on expert findings (project analyses or studies of the protection process) and development plans (the projection of the protected natural property in the Republic Spatial Plan and municipal spatial plans). The regulation putting the natural property under protection is passed by the municipality, following the opinion obtained from the Regional Institute for the Protection of Nature, except for the national parks whose protection is regulated by the Law on National Parks of 1991.

The national categories of protected natural property and protected area do not completely correspond to the World Conservation Union (IUCN) categories for managing protected natural areas.

There is no specific regulation that more thoroughly defines the information in the documentation systems mentioned above. The law defines only the categories of necessary information within these documentation systems. More detail of these categories of necessary information is incorporated in the design of individual documents by the engaged expert(s) – who are, in each case, the people with the best knowledge.

In accordance with the Law on the Protection of Nature, the Republic Institute for the Protection of Nature produces the expert findings (project analyses or studies of the protection process) needed before putting an area of natural property under protection.

In accordance with the Law on Spatial Planning, the Ministry for Protection of the Environment and Spatial Planning carries out the administrative actions in making spatial plans for areas with a particular purpose (typically, National Parks).

Specialised institutions used to be responsible for creating development and protection programmes for the national parks, whereas the latest one has been created by a specialised agency, the public body called National Parks of Montenegro. This agency is responsible for making annual/operational plans along with protection and development programmes for the national parks.

The main sources needed for planning documentation, in the creation of basic studies for spatial plans, are the documentation centre in the Republic Institute for the Protection of Nature (project analyses and studies of the protection process), the Central Register of protected natural property and dossiers of individual protected natural properties.


## 1.3. Databases and computerised mapping

### Cultural heritage

Electronic databases for this purpose do not exist in the Republic of Montenegro. Neither is there any computerised mapping system or GIS (Geographical Informative System).

### Natural heritage

For the time being, there is neither any sign of the authorities creating an electronic database for the documentation systems previously mentioned, nor is there an official digital thematic map of protected natural property. Only recently have scanned topographical maps, or some parts of them, been included in a single dossier of protected natural property. A Geographical Information System (GIS) has not been established so far, so there is no suitable electronic documentation (of protected natural areas) that could be incorporated in a GIS.

## 2. Integrated management studies, plans and regulations

### 2.1. Environment

On the basis of the Law on the Environment 12/96 and the Regulation on Evaluation of the Influence of Various Activities on the Environment 14/97, environmental assessment studies represent an indispensable part of technical project documentation. Environmental assessment is performed for a wide spectrum of works or activities that could cause permanent or temporary environmental degeneration, including those related to land use, construction or reconstruction of buildings, new or modified technology, exploitation of natural resources and other types of works. All activities in a protected natural property are, without exception, subject to environmental impact assessment.

Therefore, the preparation of an Environmental Impact Assessment (EIA) is requested for different projects in the field of industry, mining, energy, agriculture, forestry and fishing, infrastructural activities, civil engineering and tourism. However, the regulations do not make any distinction in the size or capacity of the projects; in other words, they do not propose any threshold for the need for this kind of study. This attitude has had a negative influence on practice and on the quality of studies themselves, since their preparation is obligatory even for activities that have no impact at all on the environment. New regulations are being drafted, and this field will be regulated in accordance with European legislation; also, the obligation of making a strategic environmental assessment will be introduced. It is expected that the new regulations will improve EIAs in practice, making them more efficient.

Instructions on the contents of EIAs suggest that, in the preparation period, all direct and indirect influences the project might have on all elements of the environment should be considered, including the level of noise and vibration, and the effects on inhabitants, objects, cultural-historical monuments, archaeological sites, landscape, flora and fauna, geological features, soil, water, air and climate. The obligatory elements of the Environmental Impact Assessment are description and analysis of the quality of the environment at the location planned for the project; for that purpose, existing documentation is used to the extent that is necessary according to those who evaluate the study.

The Ministry of Protection of Environment and Spatial Planning (MZŽSUP) is authorised to evaluate the study, that is, to issue an ecology consent so the project can go ahead if the study and the project are judged acceptable. If the projects are complex, the ministry can engage an external expert to evaluate the study. The ministry may also organise (this is not obligatory) a public discussion on a specific project, especially if the projects might cause huge negative consequences. Other forms of consultation, particularly in the preparatory phase of the study, are not formally envisaged, and informal consultations are very rare.

Financing the EIA is the obligation only of the investor or the project applicant. As far as preparation of the study is concerned, the project applicant, for that purpose, may engage independent consultation companies or legal persons registered for preparing that kind of documentation (they may be from the private sector, or public scientific or research institutions).

## 2.2. Spatial and urban planning

Spatial and town planning in Montenegro is regulated by the Law on Spatial Planning (Official Gazette of the Republic of Montenegro, Nos. 16/95, 22/95, 10/00), which provides for the following:

> Spatial Plan of the Republic, enacted by Parliament
>
> Spatial plans for areas of special treatment (national parks and coastline), enacted by Parliament
>
> Spatial Plan for a municipality, enacted by the Municipal Assembly for the territory of a town.
>
> General Town Plan, enacted by the Municipal Assembly for a part of the town
>
> Detailed Town Plan, enacted by the Municipal Assembly for parts of the General Town Plan
>
> Town Plan, enacted by the Municipal Assembly for specific entities, such as the historic city core.

It is obligatory to enact a Town Plan for a residential part or parts of a settlement that is listed in the Registry of cultural monuments. The Law allows for enacting: spatial plans of regions, spatial plans of areas with the function of a monumental zone, recreation/tourist regions, exploitation fields and so on, but none of these types of plan has been passed so far, nor is there at present any initiative to do so.

The Ministry responsible for the Environment and officials of the authorised municipal agency take care of the administration and preparation of spatial and town plans. The process includes: decision to create a plan, setting up co-operation with relevant institutions, preparing a draft plan, evaluation by the authorised bodies (who give their opinion) and revision of the plan, after which the draft plan is adopted (by government or local authority) and public discussion is organised (for up to 30 days); suggestions and improvements are incorporated in the plan proposal, it is submitted for consideration and detailed modification, and finally it is adopted (by government and local authorities). Spatial and town plans can be designed by companies or institutions registered for those activities.

Spatial and town plans are enforced by provisions in the Law on Spatial Planning and the Law on Construction of Buildings: for activities set out in the law, it is first necessary to obtain a Decision on Location (issued by the relevant ministry or authorised municipal agency), then carry out preparatory examinations, and produce a feasibility study and technical documentation (which must be revised after technical review). After the technical documentation revision, urban consent must be obtained, as well as consents from relevant ministries (ecology, waterpower engineering, sanitary, transport, fire-fighting, cultural monuments), and after that a building and occupancy licence may be issued.

Protection of the environment and cultural and natural heritage is enforced through regulations and procedures referring to the environmental sector, although both fields have their own legal provisions and procedures for specific issues in their domain.

### *Consultation procedures*

Public consultations or discussions are an integral part of implementation of the planning regulations. Spatial and town plans, when in draft form, are subject to public discussion organised by the relevant ministry. In practice, these public discussions are organised by the Ministry responsible for the Environment for plans enacted by the Republic Parliament, whereas for plans enacted by the local authority (Municipal Assembly) public discussions are organised by the authorised agency/secretariat for spatial planning/town planning. Public discussions last for 30 days. When the public discussion is finished, the relevant ministry or secretariat makes a report and submits it to the plan-maker for consideration, so that it can be incorporated into a plan proposal.

In case of spatial plans for areas with special purpose, such as national parks, there used to be thematic meetings within the public discussions, based on the interests of professionals not the general public. There have been no public discussions in the process of enacting development and protection programmes for the national parks, since the law did not provide for them. This weak point was noticed, and it was the right time to start such a practice, not only in the phase of drafting the programme, but also during its consideration in public consultations. The public should be involved not only in the public discussions of planning management of the cultural and natural heritage, but also in the management itself, and that is not the case here.

The Ministry of Culture and Media and the Ministry of Protection of the Environment and Spatial Planning give their opinions on spatial and urban draft plans. The Ministry of Protection of the Environment and Spatial Planning may initiate and organise public discussions and consultation on the finalised Environmental Impact Assessment, although consultative tools, which could be applied in early phases of the project (e.g. simultaneously with the creation of a study) do not exist. The experience with public discussions in this field is quite limited.

In the preparation of Environmental Impact Assessments, there is no formal require-ment to request either horizontal or vertical co-operation with other bodies involved in the decision-making process. The Ministry of Protection of the Environment and Spatial Planning may request additional opinions from, for example, institutions in charge of public health or the protection of nature, but these cases are rather a rarity than a general practice.

## 3. Authorisation, supervision and penalties

### 3.1. Authorisation

According to the Law on Construction of Buildings, new development and other works on protected cultural and natural properties can be carried out only if these actions comply with the spatial plan, and its development and protection programme, and if a building licence has been obtained before work starts. In the process, the manager of the works must give his opinion about the work, as do the Ministry of Culture and Media, and the Ministry of Protection of Environment and Spatial Planning.

Urban licences, and then building and use licences, are issued by a body authorised for spatial planning (ministry or local agency/secretariat) after any other necessary licences and consents of authorised bodies have been obtained. The investor in the development (or their agent) is responsible for gaining the necessary licences and consents, and the bodies and agencies named above perform their part in the process for provision of licences, opinions and consents. If one of the requested licences/opinions/consents is not given, for whatever reason, the process is suspended.

### 3.2. Supervision and penalties

Supervision of environmental matters and management of protected natural properties is carried out by the authorised inspection agencies (ecology, waterpower engineering, building, urban etc.), primarily at the republic level, although some of these services operate at local level as well (municipal inspection). Special services of the bodies respon-sible for managing protected natural properties (such as the forest guard service of the national parks) control activities in those areas. The police supervise certain potentially illicit activities. However, because of inconsistent legal solutions and overlapping compe-tencies, it is sometimes unclear how to act in practice. Who has the primary authority?

Inspection services for cultural monuments supervision do not exist. The Ministry of Culture and Media and the Ministry of Protection of the Environment and Spatial Planning are responsible for administrative supervision of works carried out by institutions and services dealing with the protection of cultural and natural heritage.

The inspection services are obligated to co-operate in the supervision process, according to the Law on Inspection Control (Official Gazette of the Republic of Montenegro No.

50/1992). For most inspections in the field of environment, they are additionally obliged to make joint inspections for specific procedures according to the Regulation on Joint Market, Sanitary, Veterinary and Agriculture Inspection in Foreign Trade (Official Gazette No. 12/2001).

The Law on Protection of Cultural Monuments, the Law on Protection of Nature, the Law on Protection of the Environment and the Law on Protection of National Parks, as well as the Criminal Statute of the Republic of Montenegro, set out fines and/or sentences of imprisonment as sanctions for illicit activities that are a threat to the cultural and natural heritage, and the environment. However, the level of application of penalties for offences related to the cultural and natural heritage is very unsatisfactory.

The main reasons for poor enforcement of the laws protecting the cultural and natural heritage are:

- the social and economic transition is unfinished, so we have a combination of laws inherited from the former socialist system and new laws to some extent adapted to EU legislation;

- the services/bodies enforcing the law have insufficient capacity (technical and human);

- in some cases, it is very difficult to enforce legal obligations (especially prohibitions, limitations, imposition and collection of fines) because of the poor economic situation of the industries affected (the economy generally, users of natural resources especially);

- there is little awareness of the law, as well as a generally low level of respect for the law;

- penalties are seldom applied, and courts are slow to act.

The process of solving the problems mentioned, and others, has started within the context of the current social and economic reforms. In the near future it will be necessary to pay much more attention to: transforming and reinforcing services in the field of cultural and natural heritage; harmonising national legislation with EU legislation in the same fields; improving the efficiency of services responsible for law enforcement; and starting activities to raise general public awareness about cultural and natural heritage, and better respect for the law.

# Romania

*Mircea Angelescu and Adriana Baz*

## 1. Documentation systems

Romania's legal frame for its cultural patrimony falls into three domains: laws on historical monuments, laws on archaeology and other legislation. In the domain of historical monuments are:

Law No. 157/1997 on Ratification of the European Convention on Architectural Patrimony – Granada 1985

Law No. 5/2000 on Approval for National Planning of the National Territory: Section III – protected areas

Law No. 422/2001 – see Appendix 1 of the Law on the Protection of Historical Monuments

Law No. 564/2001 on the Special Protection Measures for Romanian Sites inscribed on the World Heritage List

Law No. 451/2002 on Ratification of the European Convention on Landscape adopted at Florence in 2000

In the domain of archaeology are:

Law No. 150/1997 on Ratification of the Archaeology Patrimony Convention adopted at La Valetta in 1992

Law No. 378/2001 – see Appendix 2 of the Law on the Approval of Government Ordinance No. 43/2000 referring to archaeological patrimony protection

Law No. 462/2003 on the Improvements of Government Ordinance No. 43/2000 referring to archaeological patrimony protection

Among other relevant laws are:

Law No. 149/1997 on the Ratification of the UNIDROIT Convention – adopted at Rome in 1996 – referring to stolen goods and their illegal export

Law No. 182/2000 on Protection of Movable Cultural Patrimony

Law No. 105/2004 and Law No. 314/2004 – Improvements of the Law No. 182/2000

In the sense used in Romanian law, by 'protection' is understood inventory-making, classification and record-keeping, among other things. In the context of Law No. 422/2001 the meaning of 'historical monument' is: monument, ensemble and site.

## 1.1. Identification

The National Inventory contains the List of Historical Monuments (hereafter: the List). It was published as an official document in the Official Monitor of Romania No. 646 bis/16.07.2004. In this the objects are arranged by counties and the list contains:

- the current number,
- the code,
- the name,
- the location (town, village) and address (inside the town, or village),
- the main historical data.

The List is structured by the following categories:

- archaeology,
- architecture,
- monuments for public forum (public statues),
- memorial or funeral monuments.

The List, containing about 29 000 sites, can be seen on the Ministry of Culture webpage at: http://www.ministerulculturii.ro. Urban documentation is detailed in section 2.2.

### The bodies responsible for documentation systems

The Ministry of Culture and Religious Affairs is in charge of managing the List, which is in fact continually changing due to the addition or removal of sites. These changes are regulated by a procedure described in the second title of Law No. 422/2001, and the Service for Historical Monuments (within the ministry) does the necessary work. Every five years the revised List of historical monuments is edited. All changes to the List are kept at the National Institute for Historical Monuments (NIHM) in the general database.

The ministries, departments and services involved in documentation are:

- at national level: the Ministry of Culture and Religious Affairs (MCRA), the Ministry of Environment and Water Management (MMGA), the Romanian Academy, and the Ministry of Transport, Construction and Tourism (the MTCT, whose General Division for Spatial Planning, Urbanism and Housing Policy is in charge of the management of protected areas as part of urban and spatial planning);
- at regional level: the departments for culture, cults and cultural patrimony, and the regional development agencies;
- at departmental or local level: county or local councils.

The documentation of historical monuments is mainly kept in the archives at the NIHM. These public archives contain the technical and historical documentation from the beginning of conservation activity in 1911. There is some co-ordination between departments and other bodies.

MTCT has ordinary meetings with principals, associations of architects (at departmental/municipal level) and recently established a Settlements and Historical Areas Association, similar to the French one. MTCT has also organised many national and international meetings between 2001 and 2004 in the field of protected areas, in some cases with private sector support and participation. The website of the MTCT on urban and spatial planning (www.mt.ro) is still under construction. It will have a specific section for protected built areas.

Communication between the three ministries is superficial. There existed in 2004 an interministerial commission (MTCT/MCRA) for protected built areas, but unfortunately it did not work. Now there exists a common participation within the advising commissions of each ministry and also joint meetings have been organised.

## 1.2. Characterisation

Classification is based on the methodology approved by the ministry in Order No. 2682/2003. This methodology describes the criteria that should be fulfilled for entry on the list, the form of the evidence and also the short form. These criteria are a qualitative standard for evaluating non-movable patrimony with a view to being entered on the list in one of the following groups:

    A. Historical monuments of national or universal value,

    B. Historical monuments representative of the local cultural patrimony.

For urban areas, the documentation directly related to the built patrimony is the urban plan for the protected built area, along with the corresponding local urban planning regulations (see section 2.3.). The detailed methodology is included in the regulations ordered and funded by MTCT. The last version of "The elaboration methodology and the frame-contents of urban documents for protected built areas – UPPBA" was published on 12.02.2004 in the Official Gazette of Romania (as an appendix to the Order of the Ministry of Transport, Construction and Tourism No. 562/20.10.2003) and was drafted by the URBANPROJECT Institute (subordinate to MTCT). In 2001 the same institute produced the "Methodology of the frame-content of historical studies representing the fundamental urban documents", which was not published officially, the obligation to produce these studies being imposed only in urban documents, such as General Urban Plans (GUP) and Detailed Urban Plans (DUP), and the commissions that approve documents related to the built patrimony.

The Ministry of Culture and Religious Affairs is in charge of classification, additions, erasures and correction of the list. At national level, NIHM deposits all the information. At county level, information on historical monuments can be found at the Department for Culture, Cults and Cultural Patrimony (DCCCP) and public institutions of the Ministry of Culture and Religious Affairs around the country.

Documentation of protected urban areas is created through initiatives of the government (MTCT), county/local councils or private investors (for smaller regions), based on their importance. Generally, those who produce the documentation are chosen by public tender (in smaller regions, investors choose qualified companies). The responsible bodies for documentation are:

- MCRA – The National Commission of Historical Monuments or DCCCP,

- Regional Commissions,

- MTCT – the Commission on Spatial Planning, Urbanism and Architecture,

- specific structures of county/ local councils.

The extent to which this information is passed on and taken into account varies. At the preparation stage of an urban plan, this information is taken into consideration, especially to establish the protected area and its buffer zone.

Otherwise, information communication is scanty. For important regions, these documents require approval from both ministries (MCRA and MTCT) and – for protected natural areas – from the Ministry of Environment and Water Management (MMGA). Zonal Urban Plans (ZUP) are taken from higher urban and territory arrangement documents such as General Urban Plans (GUPs). Generally, these documents are managed by county councils (or, for municipalities and larger cities, by local councils), which should have the entire database to detail strategies at county level.

Example: UPPBA – Oradea Fortress (Oradea City, Bihor County) was the subject of, among other things, feasibility studies, historical studies and management studies. When the GUP update was carried out, information from UPPBA and the management study was incorporated (the study can be accessed in English at http://arhitectsef.oradea.ro/cetstu_e.html).

## 1.3. Databases and computerised mapping

### Computer databases

As a result of a co-operation agreement between MTCT and the French Ministry of Infrastructure, Spatial Planning, Tourism and the Sea, in 2004 an urban data bank was established (national documentation-information register of constructions, architecture, spatial planning and habitat) at the CDCAS (Centre for Documentation on Construction, Architecture, Urban and Spatial Planning, an institute subordinate to MTCT). This data bank will include all settlements, with research and studies financed by the ministry.

Information on historical monuments is not computerised in GIS, nor linked up to the Romanian Survey (Cadastre) Map. At the moment work is being carried out on a national computerised map.

The main documents made in GIS are some general urban plans. Currently General Urban Plans (GUPs) are being prepared using GIS for 10 to 15 municipalities, but only three are finished, those for Timisoara, Oradea and Satu Mare. The County of Valcea has GIS-based GUPs for all settlements (municipalities, cities, communes). Currently the problem is the lack of cadastral plans: there are official surveys for only 141 cities and a few communes, due to the lack of funds (they are co-funded from the state budget).

### *Benefits of these integrated documentation systems*

The advantages are considerable:

- ease in managing and administering monuments (official survey, historical, viewing of façades, possibility of making films outside and inside, impact of interventions on the area),
- on-line (real-time) administration of the protected area/monument (authorisations issued, list of interventions, development proposals),
- elimination of the arbitrary from political and administrative decisions,
- maps of natural hazard areas (earthquakes, landslides, floods, etc.).

Example: Valcea County Council, National Institute for Historical Monuments, Bucharest Technical Construction University (Department of GIS) and county directorates for culture, religious affairs and national patrimony have a partnership to manage all protected areas in Valcea using GIS.

Systems should be accessible to other interested public authorities and also, with some restrictions, to the public (especially target groups):

- the details of historical analysis, level of conservation, potential risks and ownership type are useful for general use; in fact, they are indispensable for a conservation or rehabilitation project. It is not recommended that the owner's name, technical documentation and official correspondence be freely accessible.
- DCCCPs have full access to the future database system.
- for urban plans, the system is not fully available at central level; it is partly accessible, depending on the administrator.

### *Difficulties in setting up such systems*

The main difficulties encountered are either financial – in setting up an intranet connecting DCCCPs and the ministry, in obtaining a GIS application, and in training people who will improve the database – or in developing software, especially for the management of forms.

At NIHM there is a plan to achieve a database. The first step has been taken and each county DCCCP has been equipped with a PC and connected to the Internet. Some of them now provide a home page for the public.

The property regime in Romania is far from clear. Many fields and buildings are under litigation, and their judicial situation will not be cleared up very quickly. There are financial problems (for equipment and software), a lack of specialists and no co-ordinating structure at national level. Each ministry and institution tends to work independently, and information is not centralised or communicated.

The solution requires a political decision to create a governmental structure at county level, that includes specialists from all fields.

*Histria Fortress - Archaeological Site, Istria commune, Constanţa County (Council of Europe)*

## 2. Integrated management studies, plans and regulations

*2.1. Environment*

*Environmental impact studies*

The URBANPROJECT Institute drafted the regulation "Methodological guide of the elaboration of impact assessment analysis, as an integral part of territorial arrangement and urban plans", which was approved by common order of the ministries (MTCT and MMGA) and published in August 2000. Fundamental environmental impact studies are included in territorial zoning and urban plans; they are a part of analytical fundamental studies, with the aim of obtaining environmental accord.

In Romania, environmental impact assessments (EIAs) must follow specific regulations in line with EU directives on environmental impact assessment (EIA) and strategic environmental assessment (SEA). Ministerial Order No. 860/2002, on approval of EIAs and the issuing of environmental agreement procedures, regulates the conditions for application and issuing of environmental agreements for projects with a significant environmental impact.

Appendix I.1 of this procedure contains the List of activities and/or installations of significant environmental impact that are subject to environmental impact assessment; Appendix I.2 of this procedure contains the List of activities and/or installations with potential significant impact on the environment that must be made subject to environmental impact assessment procedure.

## Types of environmental impact

For spatial planning documents, impact analyses are treated generally, in the nature of guidance; in urban planning documents, impact analyses are more detailed, to be acted on as part of the implementation of plans.

Government Decision No. 918/2002 set up the framework for EIAs and for approving public or private projects listed as subject to this procedure, along with the framework for issuing environmental agreements where projects are likely to have significant effects on the environment by their nature, size or location.

An EIA must identify, describe and assess in an appropriate manner in each individual case the direct and indirect effects of a project on the following factors:

- human beings, fauna and flora;

- soil, water, air, climate and the landscape;

- material assets and the cultural heritage;

- the interaction between the above factors.

The EIA should state the measures required to reduce or avoid the negative impact of the project on the factors listed above and it gives a decision whether the project can go ahead on the chosen site.

The EIA is achieved in three stages:

- EIA screening;

- the EIA's scope;

- review of the environmental impact statement.

Ministerial Order No. 863/2002 approved guidelines on the stages of the EIA framework procedure for certain public or private projects. The methodological guidelines specify what the EIA must contain, making reference to all environmental factors, including archaeological sites, as well as schemas and maps. There are two types of methodological guidelines for EIA:

– methodological guidelines on the scope of the EIA assessment and preparation of the report;

– methodological guidelines on reviewing the report on the environmental impact study.

In the framework of the screening stage, the EIA process must consider the vulnerability of the environment in the areas affected by the project, taking into account especially:

– the actual use of land;

– the richness, quality and regeneration capacity of natural resources in the area;

– mountain areas and forests;

– nature reserve and parks (in accordance with Law No. 5/2000 on Territorial Planning and Law No. 462/2001 for the approval of Governmental Decision No. 236/2000 concerning the Regime of natural protected areas and the conservation of wild flora and fauna);

– lands classified and protected by national legislation, especially laws on the conservation of natural habitats, wild flora and fauna;

– areas of particularly high environmental quality;

– densely populated areas;

– landscape with special historical, cultural or archaeological importance.

### Responsibility for environmental impact studies

The Ministry of Environment and Waters Management is not responsible for preparing EIA studies and does not finance them. EIA studies are produced by the physical or juridical persons certified by the Ministry of Environment and Waters Management. The initiator of the project sustains the costs of the environmental impact assessment study.

The public authority for environmental protection shall encourage the project developer to identify the public concerned and to engage in a direct dialogue with them, before and throughout the procedure, including presentation of the project objectives. Public debates are organised for proposed projects; where the resulting suggestions are justified, these will be taken into account in the final decision.

The project developer must inform the public, by announcements in the mass media, and support public participation in the EIA process in the environmental agreement procedure. The project developer shall inform the public on the following steps:

- submission of the environmental agreement application for the project;

- the decision at the project screening stage;

- the public debate of the report on the EIA study;

- the decision at the project review stage.

Article 37 (1) of the law on EIA states that, in presenting the decision at the project screening stage, the developer shall inform the public, at public meetings (in the municipal council), in the national or local press, and on radio or TV if possible, of:

- name of the developer;

- the project and site presentation;

- where and when information on the project may be obtained;

- who any well-grounded public views on the environmental impact assessment of the project should be addressed to.

Para. (2) says that public information on the data referred to in para (1) shall be available within 10 days of receiving the decision at the screening stage, for any project included in this stage. Para. (3) adds that the public shall have the right to present to the competent authority for environmental protection a proposal to reconsider the decision on the screening stage, within 10 days of its publication.

The public may forward justified proposals on the EIA up to the date set for the public debate, and no later. The public debate meeting must take place in the presence of representatives of the competent authority for environmental protection, in a manner convenient to the public, in the area where the project is to be implemented, and after working hours.

In some cases, MTCT fund impact studies for land zoning and urban plan documents, especially in areas of natural hazard. The studies are prepared by specialised institutions and private companies, chosen by public tender. Although laws require the population to be consulted, this is done formally.

*The effect of impact studies on heritage*

In the urban context, impact studies are prepared when a new building is to be inserted in a historic context in the protected area. This frequently happens. In the city of Bucharest, an impact study was produced for the oldest areas, defining where new buildings could be inserted and where new higher buildings, including skyscrapers, could be sited.

Unfortunately, some impact analyses are superficial, and landscape arrangement is a rarity. For documentations on protected areas, their approval requires the environmental accord (MTCT and MCRA cannot analyse impact on nature studies).

## 2.2. Spatial and urban planning

### Spatial planning

| | Spatial Planning of the National Territory | Spatial Planning of Zonal Territory* | Spatial Planning of County Territory |
|---|---|---|---|
| Character | Guidance | Guidance | Guidance |
| Objective | Synthesis of sectoral strategic programmes | Solving specific problems of the territory | Spatial dimension of socio-economic programme |
| Content | Communication routes, water, protected areas, areas of natural risk, tourism, rural development | No legal regulations | Sustainable Development Strategy |
| Legal initiator | MTCT | MTCT/County/Local Council | County Council |
| Legal financing | MTCT | MTCT/County/Local Council | MTCT/County Council |
| Legal adviser | Government | MTCT/County /Local Council | MTCT/County Council |
| Legal approval | Parliament | MTCT/County/Local Council | County Council |

*intercommunal/ interdepartmental/ regional/ boundary/ metropolitan/ peri-urban

All these documents include a section on protected natural heritage and built cultural heritage areas, at a general level, and their approval requires documents from all departments or institutes of specialised ministries (in this case, MTCT, MCRA, MMGA). Information is taken from more detailed, lower-level (urban) plans. The heritage documentation is used as a historical study and is the basis of the resulting proposals.

The third section of the Spatial Planning of the National Territory is "Protected Areas" (Law No. 5/2000), and in these Annexes are stipulated all types of protected areas of national interest.

Spatial Planning of Zonal Territory and Spatial Planning of County Territory define all existing protected areas within the zone/county and require the preparation of urban plans for protected areas with further detailed regulations in case of objectives included in the World Heritage List.

## Urban planning

There are six types of urban plans:

### General urban regulation plan

These plans have a compulsory legal regulation (HG 525/1996). They establish the rules for land usage and building land limits according to functions. They include a system of technical and economic norms as a basis for elaboration of urban plans and regulations. These plans are legally initiated and financed by the MTCT with assistance and final approval by the Government.

### General urban plan + local urban planning regulations

These cover specific regulations for urban and rural localities. They establish the rules for localities, especially for land usage and building land limits. They include a Development Strategy and Regulations for localities in correlation with the approved spatial planning documents. These plans are approved by the relevant Local Councils.

### Zonal urban plan + local urban planning regulations

These provide specific detailed regulations for parts of localities and are designed to solve problems relating to a specific part of a locality as well ensuring correlation with the General Urban Plan regulations. They include a Development Strategy and specific regulations for part of a locality. These plans are approved by the relevant Local Councils.

### Zonal urban plan for core area + local urban planning regulations

These provide specific detailed regulations for core areas within localities and are directed at solving specific problems within such core areas and ensuring correlation with General Urban Plan regulations. They include a Development Strategy and specific regulations for core areas. These plans are approved by the relevant Local Councils.

### Urban plan for protected built area + local urban planning regulations

These provide specific detailed regulations for protected built areas and are aimed at solving specific problems within protected built areas and ensuring correlation with General Urban Plan regulations. They include a Development Strategy and detailed regulations for protected built areas. These plans are approved by the relevant Local Councils.

### Detailed urban plan

These have specific detailed regulations for establishing the rules for one or two adjacent parcels and are also approved by Local Councils.

We do not have a national inventory or maps identifying special ethnological/arts and crafts areas, historic itineraries and landscapes. There are financial and technical problems with land registry (cadastral) maps, topographical surveys, geological maps and so on. At the moment, the only urban plan for a protected built area created in GIS is that made by the Local Council of Timisoara.

There are special regulations for historic urban protected areas.

> Example 1: There are 98 defined protected areas in Bucharest, with regulations on how empty sites can be built on, the permitted use of land, conservation of vegetation and erection of advertisements.

> Example 2: Urban plans for protected built areas contain rules for the conditions of occupation and use of land, traffic and parking, town equipment, services and general limitations on the exterior of buildings and landscaping. Following a co-operation agreement with the French Ministry of Culture and Communications (signed in 2002) important steps were taken in this direction. The urban plan for the protected area of the Alba Iulia Fortress will be the first approved plan to regulate each site in detail, documenting for each building its physical state, proposals for demolition, conservation, restoration, function and allowed interventions (materials, colours, services, interior arrangements, landscaping), as well as urban spaces and signage. Requested and funded by MTCT, this pilot study is to be provided to all important county and local councils as an exemplar.

The DCCCP are in charge of surveying and giving permission for such areas.

In the field of landscape, Romania has ratified the European Landscape Convention, but for implementation we are starting from zero. Because it is responsible for spatial planning and actively takes part in CEMAT meetings and activities, MTCT has set up a department for landscape and protected areas (with Council of Europe support). Since 2002, a good collaboration has been established between the Council of Europe and MTCT: two regulations concerning the European Landscape Convention have been drafted, translated and published; the European Rural Heritage Observation Guide (CEMAT) has been adapted, translated and disseminated; the international seminar on Landscape and Spatial Development (Tulcea, Romania, 6-8 May 2004) was organised under the aegis of the Council of Europe, concluding with the Tulcea Declaration; and, at the Third meeting of the Workshops for the implementation of the European Landscape Convention (Cork, Ireland, 15-19 June 2005), MTCT received high appreciation for its efforts and the quality of its presentations, and it was commonly agreed that the next meeting (the fourth) should be hosted by the municipality of Sibiu, Romania. (Sibiu was designated the European Capital of Culture in 2007).

## Consultation procedures

Public debates on rehabilitation are usually organised by the local administration for the area of the proposed project, and justified suggestions will be taken into account before final decisions are made. This kind of debate often concerns the historic downtown areas of cities, as in Bucharest, Sibiu and Piatra Neamt.

The public authority for environmental protection requires the project developer to identify the public concerned and to engage in a direct dialogue with them, including a presentation of the project's objectives, at every stage of the procedure and even before its initiation.

From a legal standpoint, the prepration of urban and territorial arrangement plans requires the population to be consulted, but the procedure is not established. Most of the time this is done only in a formal way due to the lack of funds, personnel and time. There are some cases where public opinion can influence these projects (for example, the General Urban Plan of Vama Veche).

## 3. Authorisation, supervision and penalties

### 3.1. Authorisation

Before any official land-use change or work on property, the authorisation procedures require two documents, both released by the local council administration:

- urban development certificate (for information only), specifying the legal conditions (judicial regime, economic regime, restrictions, projects to be detailed, obligatory approvals, fees) necessary to obtain a construction/demolition permit for buildings/ structures in protected areas
- construction/demolition permit for the execution of works

#### Prior permission required on protected property

According to Law No. 422/2001, all kind of interventions on a protected site should be submitted for approval, in the form of a heritage permit. Only maintenance work is not subject to a permit.

Town-planning documentation referring to historic monuments is also submitted to the Ministry of Culture and Religious Affairs (or its decentralised institutions, i.e. DCCCP) for a permit.

#### Forms of authorisation

Law No. 50/1991 with its successive revisions regulates the procedure for building permits and it has a unique form. It is given by the local administration, based on several permits or approvals. The procedure consists of two main steps:

1. The owner demands permission for building and receives a document called an urban certificate from the town hall. This indicates the permitted land use under the urban regulations for the site and the permits to be obtained for the project. The owner sends details of the project to the institutions or authorities to obtain the approvals or permits demanded by the urban certificate. Depending on the type of building, these approvals can be as many as thirty. Among them, based on Law No. 422/2001, is the heritage permit for historic monuments inscribed on the protected List (inventory) or sites inside a buffer zone or protected area.

2. The project, adapted to the conditions demanded by all approvals or permits, is submitted to the town hall and it is analysed. In some cases, it may be subject to public consultation. Following this, the building permit is given to the owner. After this, work on the site can begin.

The final decision belongs to the local administration. If the owner feels he has not received justice, he can appeal against maladministration, at a tribunal.

The approval of the responsible authority is decisive, but mediation is possible in some cases.

## 3.2. Supervision and penalties

### Main legal framework

– Law No. 50/1991 (with later modifications and completion) on *Building Autho-risation and Some Measures for Housing Construction;*

– Law No. 350/2001 (with later modifications and completion) on *Urban and Spatial Planning;*

– Law No. 422/2001 (with later modifications and completion) on *Historical Monuments Protection.*

### Supervision of heritage, spatial planning, town planning and environment

Qualified persons (according to Law No. 422/2001) ensure the supervision of all kinds of interventions upon historic monuments and buffer zones. The public servants of the DCCCP inspect conservation work and check whether it respects the conditions of the heritage permit.

The State Buildings Inspectorate verify the work sites and also check that the approvals, permits or norms are truly respected. The local police can verify whether the works on site have building authorisation. Each work site must display a panel specifying the developer, the originator of the project, its duration and details of the building authorisation.

The Ministry of Culture and Religious Affairs finances the National Conservation Programme, which includes works on important sites. These display special announcement panels.

There are cases where laws are broken by unauthorised construction or intervention, illegal deforestation, violation of authorisation, irregularities among public employees and controlling bodies, among other causes. Exaggerated bureaucracy contributes substantially to the violation of laws.

There is informal mutual help between the State Buildings Inspectorate and the DCCCPs in assessing works on protected sites.

Generally, ministries and county/local councils should place such responsibilities with judicial bodies or the State Buildings Inspectorate.

An example of good practice: UNDP (United Nations Development Programme) Beautiful Romania is a programme that aims to consolidate, restore and display important objects (not benefiting from other financial support) in Romania. This programme is based on co-funding (UNDP, MCRA, MTCT and local councils). Its structure permits more rigorous control and correct supervision of execution of works, since UNDP is impartial and directly interested in the success of the programme.

### Penalties in respect of heritage, spatial planning, town planning and environment

The sanctions for violation of Law No. 422/2001 are mentioned in Title VI: Sanctions, which contains four articles (Article Nos. 54-57) covering administrative and criminal penalties.

For archaeology, Ordinance No. 43/2000 indicates at Chapter VI: Infractions and Contraventions (Article Nos. 23-27) the administrative and criminal penalties.

Violations of the laws result in civil penalties, fines (€275-2 750), disciplinary, administrative or penal responsibilities (for each case individually), but the control system does not work properly. For land or building owners, illegal constructions can even be demolished (though this happens in very few cases, compared to the number of illegal constructions/interventions).

### Main problems and obstacles encountered in trying to implement these laws

The State Buildings Inspectorate is a relatively independent body (within the General Secretarial Office of the government). It worked until recently under the authority of MTCT, being controlled by that ministry in some degree. Major problems are: lack of personnel, pressures from politicians and investors, mild penalties and complex bureaucracy.

The solutions are at the level of political decision – creating solid controlling structures, with more serious penalties applied whenever necessary. A conformity certificate ought to be introduced, attesting that the building permit has been respected in the completed works, for which the signatory should assume full legal responsibility.

# Serbia

*Tijana Zivanovic, Milica Risojevic, Bozidar Kovacevic and Borislav Šurdić*

## 1. Documentation systems

### 1.1. Identification

#### Archaeological and architectural heritage

Regulations on identifying and maintaining the inventory of cultural heritage are adopted at national level. Their enforcement is the responsibility of the Ministry of Culture of the Republic of Serbia.

Archaeological and architectural heritage is a set of cultural assets determined under the Law on Cultural Property of 1994. Note, however, that the term 'archaeological and architectural heritage' is not found in this law, which mentions only 'immovable cultural properties'. However, since the country is a signatory to the Granada (1985) and London (1969) conventions, we employ both terms.

Archaeological and architectural heritage comprises the following types of cultural properties:

- monuments,
- spatial cultural-historical ensembles,
- archaeological and historical sites,
- significant sites (memorials).

This classification is not fully in line with the principles of the 1985 Granada Convention. Spatial cultural-historical ensembles most often consist of groups of buildings, but they may also include sites.

There are three types of inventories:

- register of immovable cultural property;
- Central Register of immovable cultural property;
- records on previously protected cultural property.

Registers of immovable cultural property are maintained by provincial institutes (Vojvodina or Kosovo and Metohija) and regional (intermunicipal) institutes for the protection of cultural property. The 1994 Law equated the competences of provincial institutes with the competences of regional institutions.

The term 'region' should be regarded tentatively. In Serbia, there are no administrative regions in the sense they are organised in the countries of the European Union. By special regulation, certain bodies (regional institutes for the protection of cultural monuments in Subotica, Novi Sad, Pancevo, Sremska Mitrovica, Belgrade, Smederevo, Valjevo, Nis, Kragujevac and Kraljevo) have been authorised to identify the immovable heritage within the municipalities surrounding these centres. In this way, the regionalisation pertaining only to the protection of cultural heritage has been carried out.

## Registers of cultural heritage

These registers comprise:

– general identification data: ordinal number, number, date of entry into the register, name of cultural property;

– location data: municipality, address, cadastral lot, zone borders;

– legal grounds: formal decision, data of official publication;

– ownership data: form of ownership, entry into land-ownership records;

– data on the appearance and significance of the property: description, specific observations.

The documentation accompanying the registers consists of:

general documentation:

- decision on designation of cultural property,
- land certificate,
- decision on categorisation.

technical documentation:

- layout,
- ground plan,
- sections,
- other important details.

photographic record:

- photograph of the general appearance (18 × 24 cm),
- photographs of characteristic details.

The Central Register is maintained by the Republic Institute for the Protection of Cultural Monuments. The Central Register is actually a national inventory of architectural and archaeological heritage. Types of data kept in this register are basically not different from those kept in the registers of regional institutes. The form of the register is different.

Co-operation in the field of the protection of cultural property includes:

- co-operation with institutions for the protection of nature – determining and protecting the environment of a cultural property, giving opinions on management programmes of certain landscapes and other natural property;

- co-operation with planning institutions – in most cases this co-operation is inadequate and unco-ordinated. There are even differences in terminology, which sometimes create great difficulties to citizens and institutions. Nevertheless, it is worth stressing that there is a better co-operation during the preparation of planning documents.

### Protection of nature

The State Union of Serbia and Montenegro has not signed or ratified the European Landscape Convention (2000), which means that the national legislative framework on environmental protection does not define the term "landscape" in line with the international treaty. Likewise, the national legislative framework on environmental protection does not define the term "natural heritage".

The Law on Environmental Protection from 1991 defines a "landscape of exceptional characteristics" as a type of protected natural property in the Republic of Serbia, thus: "a landscape of exceptional characteristics is a relatively small area, with vivid landscape features, undisturbed principal values of landscape appearance with presence of forms of traditional way of life and cultural properties, including the protected environment of immovable cultural properties". Apart from this protected natural property, the 1991 Law on Environmental Protection also defines other types of protected natural properties: national park, nature park, landscape of exceptional characteristics, nature reserve (general and special), natural monument and natural rarities.

### Register of protected natural heritage

The same law provides that all protected natural properties are entered into the register of protected natural properties maintained by the Institute for the Protection of Nature of Serbia. This register comprises the following information:

- ordinal number
- type of the protected natural property – according to the old law
- type of the protected natural property – according to the new law
- municipality where it is located
- cadastral municipality [registration district] where the property is located

- the year of enacting the first document on protection
- the year of enacting the second document on protection
- the state of the natural property
- guardian
- area of the protected natural property

A great shortcoming of the register is an inadequate updating of data and lack of photographic record, which makes examination more difficult and does not present the real picture and state of the protected area.

At the moment, there is a lack of successful co-operation and co-ordination of information exchange between the competent ministry and the Institute for the Protection of Nature of Serbia, as a professional institution and manager of the protected area.

## 1.2. Characterisation

### Archaeological and architectural heritage

"Characterisation" in policy and cultural heritage management strategies (both architectural and archaeological) is undeveloped, in fact almost non-existent. It has not been defined as a mandatory, not even desirable methodological approach and is therefore carried out rarely and unsystematically.

Records of previously protected cultural property may be of relevance for "characterisation". This database, envisaged by the law of 1994, comprises the inventory, description and summary of the historical significance of individual objects, groups of buildings and ensembles that have not been declared as cultural property by the law, but whose value is evident (though not yet professionally and technically valorised).

### Protection of nature

Data on landscapes of exceptional characteristics are maintained in the register of protected natural property. A detailed description of a natural property with all its characteristics and natural values is specified in the Study of the Protection of a Natural Property, a document which precedes enactment of the decision on the protection of that property, and an integral part of the documentation kept with every protected natural property.

## 1.3. Databases and computerised mapping

### Archaeological and architectural heritage

There are no systematised digital databases of cultural (architectural and archaeological) heritage. They have neither been provided by the Law of 1994 nor by sub-acts.

The creation of a digital map and database of the Danube region is under way (prepared within the Programme INTERREG III C Argedonau).

### Protection of nature

Depending on the type and kind of data, there are different databases and they are maintained in different institutions: Institute for the Protection of Nature of Serbia, Museum of Nature, Faculties, Botanical Gardens, etc.

There is no integral database (documentation system) where all existing and valid information would be stored and this presents a problem in the integrated planning of the protection and development of protected natural property. These databases are not connected with a computerised mapping system or GIS.

## 2. Integrated Management Studies, Plans and Regulations

### 2.1. Environment

The Law on Strategic Environmental Impact Assessment (Official Gazette of the RS, No. 135/2004) regulates the conditions, manner and procedure of strategic environmental assessment (SEA) of the impact of certain plans and programmes, with a view to ensuring environmental protection and promoting sustainable development by integrating the basic principles of environmental protection in the procedure of preparation and adoption of plans and programmes.

A strategic assessment is carried out for plans, programmes and fundamentals in the field of spatial and urban planning of land use, agriculture, forestry, fishery, hunting, energy, industry, traffic, waste management, water management, telecommunications, tourism, preservation of natural habitats and wild flora and fauna, which establishes a framework for the approval of future development projects determined by regulations on environmental impact assessment (EIA).

### Phases in the strategic assessment process

The preliminary phase includes:

- making a decision on the preparation of a strategic assessment,
- selection of the drafter of the strategic assessment report,
- participation of interested bodies and organisations.

Then a strategic assessment report is prepared.

The decision-making process involves:

- participation of interested bodies and organisations,
- public participation,

- report on the results of participation of interested bodies/organisations and the public,
- evaluation of the strategic assessment report,
- approval of the strategic assessment report.

The authority responsible for environmental protection is the ministry if the case in question is at republic level, or the provincial secretariat if the case is at *vojvodina* (regional) level, but the city assembly or municipal assembly if the case is dealt with at local level. The authority has a role in:

- giving an opinion in the preliminary phase whether a strategic assessment is needed, and

- the decision-making process, where the authority gives approval to the strategic environmental impact assessment.

The authority will give its opinion that the preparation of a strategic assessment is not required only when the area in question consists of smaller areas for which a strategic assessment or other similar document containing adequate and comprehensive measures of environmental protection has already been done. In that case, the ministry responsible for the protection of environment gives opinion that the strategic assessment is not required.

Since the strategic assessment report is an integral part of a planning document, the strategic assessment is carried out and the strategic assessment report is compiled by the institutions preparing the plans (legal entities registered in the appropriate registry for carrying out activities of spatial and urban planning). Authorities responsible for adopting the plans (see 2.2.1. and 2.2.2., below) also adopt the strategic assessment report, provided that they have obtained the opinion of the authority responsible for environmental protection. The entire procedure of preparation, control and proposing of plans is carried out by the Republic Agency for Spatial Planning and the competent ministry at the republic level, using the services of a local authority at local level.

During the preparation of plans adopted at the republic level, there is co-operation with the ministries responsible for traffic, economy, agriculture, energy, protection of cultural and natural heritage, and science. These ministries monitor the entire development of plans and give opinions before the plans are adopted. As regards urban plans, the co-operation is with relevant institutions, which stipulate the conditions of plan development (protection of cultural monuments, protection of nature, different infrastructure systems).

The preparation of the strategic assessment for spatial and urban plans is funded as part of plan development funding. Public consultations are carried out during the period of 30 days (see section 2.2.2.).

The main problem in preparing spatial and urban plans is inadequate recognition of the environmental impact of their realisation, which is precisely the point of an EIA (where planning solutions are primarily based on the existing state of environmental quality, instead of on the perceived planned impact of planning solutions).

## 2.2. Spatial and Urban Planning

### 2.2.1. Spatial planning

The Law on Planning and Construction specifies different types of planning documents at national, regional and local levels.

#### At national level

There are three types of document: strategy, scheme and plan.

#### Strategy of the Spatial Development of the Republic of Serbia

This is prepared by the Republic Agency for Spatial Planning, proposed by the Government of the Republic of Serbia and adopted by the National Parliament of the Republic of Serbia (as the supreme legislative body in Serbia). It:

- defines the long-term objectives of spatial planning and development in accordance with overall economic, social, ecological, cultural and historical development;

- contains the basis for creating policies and regimes for the protection of natural and cultural values, objects and landscapes.

#### Scheme of Spatial Development

This is a planning document for the entire territory of the republic; it is adopted by the Government of the Republic of Serbia, based on a proposal of the competent ministry. It more closely defines the spatial development of certain areas as defined in the Strategy, *inter alia* for areas of culture and natural and rural areas.

#### Spatial Plan for a Special Purpose Area

This is adopted by the government upon the proposal of the Republic Agency for Spatial Planning, that is, by the assembly of an autonomous province for an area within its territory that, due to its characteristics, has a special purpose that requires its own regime of organisation, development, use and spatial protection. It is adopted for larger areas of immovable cultural properties and their protected surroundings, with a view to defining the spatial conditions for their protection, including rules for development and land use. Most often, three protection zones are defined, namely: an immediate protection zone (only the cultural property; all activities in this zone are prohibited except a strictly controlled presentation of the cultural property), a narrow protection zone (the first belt around the cultural property, where only facilities for protecting and presenting the cultural property may be built) and a broad protection zone (a broad belt around the narrow protection zone, where activities are prescribed and allowed only if they do not have any adverse impact on the cultural property.

*At regional level*

A Regional Spatial Plan covers:

– the territory of an autonomous province,

– the territory of the city of Belgrade,

– areas corresponding in size to a region (from 100 000 to 4 000 000 inhabitants).

It is adopted by the government upon the proposal of the assembly (that of the autonomous province or the city of Belgrade) or, in the third case, a proposal of the Republic Agency for Spatial Planning.

Apart from the objectives of spatial planning, rules for the use, development and protection of the planning area and guidelines for the implementation of the spatial plan, it also comprises measures for the organisation of inter-municipal co-ordination in the region, measures and instruments for an immediate application of rules pertaining to spatial development and use of space in spatial and urban plans of smaller territorial units and settlements, as well as guidelines for the elaboration of local programmes and plans.

*At local level*

A Municipal Spatial Plan is adopted by a municipal assembly either just for its own territory or for that of one or more other municipalities (up to 100 000 inhabitants) as well. The procedure for preparing and adopting a spatial plan for two or more municipalities is regulated by an agreement between them. A Municipal Spatial Plan spells out the principles on which it is based and determines the objectives of spatial development, organisation, protection, use and purpose of spaces.

If the task of preparing the planning document is allocated to a company (either public or private), which must be found in the appropriate registry for carrying out spatial and urban planning activities, this is usually done by public tender, conducted by the body competent to adopt the planning document. The preparation of plans is funded from the republic budget or municipal budgets.

Before its adoption, the planning document is subject to professional expert review and is then presented to the public.

All relevant available data are used in preparing plans. However, the data are usually not in digital form, nor connected to an integrated system. There is a legal obligation to prepare spatial plans in both analogue and digital form.

Several laws require spatial plans to accept and respect the conditions in regulations issued for this purpose by bodies responsible for the protection of cultural monuments, natural property and the environment, as well as the Ministry of Defence. For example, the Government of the Republic of Serbia adopts spatial plans within its competence only after having obtained a positive opinion from the ministry responsible for the protection of cultural monuments and the ministry responsible for the protection of nature and the environment. There is positive discrimination in favour of cultural and natural heritage in all spatial plans. Past planning practice dealt exclusively with the strict protection of heritage, but plans prepared more recently pay special attention to the planning of development and sustainable use of heritage.

### 2.2.2. Urban planning

The Law on Planning and Construction defines the following types of urban plan:

- general urban plans – the general plan and the general development plan;
- regulation plans – the general regulatory plan and the detailed regulatory plan.

Urban plans define long-term projection of the development and spatial growth of different types of settlement. Development rules and construction rules are constituent parts of urban plans, which also include graphics. Urban plans dealing exclusively with heritage have not been defined by law, but the conditions for protection, maintenance and use of cultural property (as defined by a competent institution) must be incorporated in all urban plans.

The adoption of urban plans is within the competence of local self-government (municipality or city). Urban plans are prepared following a decision of the body competent for the adoption of plans. Before any decision to develop an urban plan, a programme for the development of such a plan has to be devised (and forms an integral part of the decision); for this it is necessary to obtain, from the authority responsible for the protection of cultural and natural monuments, data on the existing state and conditions for the use of registered or protected structures, cultural monuments or ambient ensembles, as well as natural monuments.

Protection conditions have significantly gained in importance with the entry into force of new regulations under which the protection conditions are secured by the drafter of the urban plan, during the preparation of the plan development programme. In that way, the conditions are contained in the plan itself and are submitted in the form of an excerpt from the plan to the investor, who has to observe these conditions during development of the project. When giving approval for construction, the competent authority checks whether the project is in conformity with the excerpt from the plan and the conditions for protection specified therein.

Some of the aforementioned urban plans may be drafted for an area where there is a priority to protect a piece of heritage.

*Consultation procedures*

During the development of spatial plans, there are certain times when consultation and co-ordination with planning entities are carried out, namely:

- in the preliminary phase, when adopting the decision and the programme for preparing a spatial plan, there are consultations among administrative bodies when objectives and priorities are defined; then the programme is sent for consideration and, after the harmonisation of opinions, a decision on preparation of the plan is made;

- in the phase of expert review of the development strategy, professional experts check the first synthesising planning material and the consultations with different actors;

- in the phase of professional review and public presentation of the spatial plan proposal – the most important phase – the general public is involved in the planning process. The spatial plan is presented to the public for 30 days in the centres of all local self-government units whose territory is covered by the plan; during the period at least one plan presentation and expert discussion is organised, in which all interested legal and natural persons may take part. Upon completion of the presentation to the public, the body in charge of preparing the plan drafts a report containing answers to all remarks submitted during the public presentation. After that, the plan is revised in line with the report, that is, in line with the accepted remarks;

- in the phase of signing a spatial plan implementation agreement, there are consultations with administrative bodies and other relevant participants for the purpose of drafting and signing the plan implementation agreement, which defines the participants, their obligations and the funds to be used for the implementation of planning solutions, for a period of four years.

In developing spatial plans in Serbia, the public presentation phase has had a dominant place. It was only after new legislation in 2003 that other phases gained prominence, too. The basic aim was to ensure consultations between planning bodies and involve the public in the planning process in parallel with the development of the plan, not only as a formality at the end of the plan development.

The phase of public presentation has been carried out without any problems so far. Participants who take an active part in debates and make comments on the plan are: local government bodies (about 40% of the remarks), other legal entities such as enterprises (about 20%) and local inhabitants (about 40%). The basic principle applied by the decision-maker (the body in charge of spatial plan development) during public consultations is to accept as many of the presented remarks as possible (provided they do not affect the basic concept and aims of the plan, that is, they do not impair the public interest). On average, 75% of the remarks submitted during public consultation are accepted.

# 3. Authorisation, supervision and penalties

## 3.1. Authorisation

### Archaeological and architectural heritage and the protection of nature

Archaeological excavation, irrespective of its proportion, may only be carried out with the permission of the Ministry of Culture of the Republic of Serbia. The procedures for issuing conditions for the work that changes the form or purpose of either archaeological and architectural heritage or natural property are similar or even identical in many parts.

When changing the purpose of an area within a protected natural property, the administrator or investor is obliged to obtain the "Conditions for the protection of natural property" from the Institute for the Protection of Nature of Serbia, but there is no issuing of permits, only the stipulation of conditions. Likewise, a nature protection organisation may issue a decision temporarily prohibiting the performance of works if it is assumed that the natural property has the characteristics of a natural monument. The decision on the temporary prohibition of the performance of works is forwarded to the investor, the contractor, the authority that issues construction approvals and the authority competent for the protection of natural property.

It should be underlined that the document "Conditions for the protection of natural property" stipulates measures and conditions that, for the purpose of preservation, protection or promotion of a natural property, prohibit certain activities and actions, such as tree cutting or exploitation of minerals.

Construction work that may change the form, appearance or characteristics of a protected natural property or protected zone may be approved under certain conditions. These are conditions that the authority competent to issue the document obtains from the organisation for the protection of natural monuments and also the conditions for spatial development.

A similar procedure applies to the issue of permits for the performance of work on architectural or archaeological heritage. The institution in charge of activities protecting immovable heritage prescribes technical measures for any change of appearance or restoration process, stipulates conditions for the performance of works and gives consent to projects.

### Construction work

Construction of a structure is done on the basis of a construction approval, in line with technical documentation for such works. A construction approval is the only form of approval, but a "combined permit" can be issued: this incorporates conditions imposed by the service responsible for the protection of cultural monuments.

The construction approval for a structure of importance for the republic is issued by the ministry or province, whereas construction approvals for other structures are issued by units of local government. Structures of importance for the republic include cultural property of national and international value, and structures in their protected environment, but it should be mentioned that the Law on Planning and Construction and the Law on Cultural Property do not have a harmonised terminology concerning the categorisation of these properties, and consequently the issue of competencies is not harmonised either, which often presents problems to citizens and legal entities.

No construction approval is issued for the construction of auxiliary structures, maintenance work, works to remove obstacles for the handicapped, or works to adapt and improve an object. For specified works on objects of cultural and historical significance, consent to the conceptual project should be obtained from the institution in charge of protection of cultural monuments.

*Sirmium – Roman Market, Sremska Mitrovica (Council of Europe)*

## 3.2. Supervision and penalties

### Archaeological and architectural heritage and protection of nature

Expert supervision of conservation works is the responsibility of the Institute for the Protection of Cultural Monuments. Inspection bodies of the Ministry of Culture supervise implementation of the Law on Cultural Property (1994).

The Institute for the Protection of Nature of Serbia conducts expert supervision of work implementing programmes and projects of protection and development. Implementation of measures for the protection of natural property is inspected by the republic inspector for environmental protection. If the inspector finds violations where other inspection bodies also have competence, the inspector is obliged to perform the supervision jointly with another body so that adequate action may be taken.

Legislation in the field of environmental protection (Law on Environmental Protection, Law on Environmental Impact Assessment, Law on Strategic Environmental Impact Assessment, Law on Fishery, and Law on Forests) provides for fines and imprisonment for offences against these laws. These laws also provide for confiscation of objects or prohibition of an activity.

There are two levels of penalty for disregard of the Law on Cultural Property, that is, by destroying or damaging the cultural property. The first level is covered by the 1994 law and refers to offences caused by inadequate protection, irregular procedure, damage to previously protected property and similar cases. The law envisages fines for these offences. For major, deliberate damage caused by abuse of the protected heritage, the penalties provided by the Criminal Code include imprisonment. Fines are relatively low, and criminal proceedings are very rarely instituted.

### Spatial and urban planning

Supervision of spatial and urban planning activities, construction of structures and related matters is carried out by the competent ministry. Inspection is conducted by the competent ministry through its inspectors. Autonomous provinces, municipalities and cities are assigned to inspect and supervise the construction of structures for which they issue construction approval.

Urban inspectors (at the level of the Republic), control whether spatial and urban plans are developed in conformity with the law, whether the excerpt from the plan is issued in accordance with the plan, whether the conceptual project is prepared on the basis of the excerpt from the plan, etc. An urban inspector is authorised to prohibit further development of the plan, as well as to order by a decree the competent administration to annul the excerpt from the plan.

Construction inspectors (at the level of the republic and provinces) check the process of constructing the structure, specifically checking whether construction approval has been issued for the structure, whether it is in conformity with the project, whether the construction works are being carried out in an adequate manner, whether they are in conformity with the project and construction approval, whether the contractor fulfils the conditions prescribed by law, and so on. A construction inspector is authorised to order demolition of the structure or the suspension of works as they see fit.

# "The former Yugoslav Republic of Macedonia"

*Biljana Prentoska, Danica Pavlovska, Robertina Brajanoska, Biljana Tanovska, Juilja Trickovska, Snezana Gerasimova, Mirko Andovski, Rada Filipovska, Pene Penev, Valentina Cavdarova and Daniela Stefkova*

## 1. Documentation systems

### 1.1. Identification

Inventory and registration of cultural heritage in the Republic of Macedonia (RM) has been a permanent activity for more than fifty years. Until the adoption of the new Law on Protection of the Cultural Heritage (Official Bulletin No. 20/04, enforced 1 January 2005), several specialised institutions of the Ministry of Culture were implementing the process of inventory and documentation of a large part of the movable and immovable heritage: the Institute for the Protection of Cultural Monuments of the Republic of Macedonia, the Institute for Protection of the Cultural Monuments of the City of Skopje and the institutes in Bitola, Prilep, Stip and Strumica, which are responsible for the cultural heritage of their near vicinity and which function also as museums. With the new Law on Protection of the Cultural Heritage and reforms in heritage protection, these institutes became special protection institutions (conservation centres) or museums; the inventory remained an obligation in both new types of institution.

Documentation of the identification and registration of the cultural heritage differs from one institution to another since there was no unified methodology in its creation. In past practice, documentation was sent to the Information-Documentation Centre (INDOC) within the Institute for Protection of the Cultural Monuments of RM (Central Register). Information and documentation from the Centre was then used in conservation projects on specific monuments as well as meeting the needs of spatial and urban planning.

According to regulations and obligations resulting from the new Law on Protection of the Cultural Heritage, the Ministry of Culture – or, rather, the new Cultural Heritage Protection Office within the ministry – is drafting a number of by-laws setting down the methodology for all aspects of protection of the cultural heritage as well as the type and scope of documentation for defined needs. Thus, documentation is being unified: it will now be created upon standards defining the type, content, norms and ways of documenting cultural heritage as well as conditions for preservation and use of documentation for certain needs (according to Article 36 of the Law on Protection of the Cultural Heritage). All data from the inventories owned by the institutions mentioned, obtained according to the methodology set down in the Book of Rules, are submitted to the Cultural Heritage Protection Office to be entered in an established information-documentation system.

No single inventory of immovable cultural heritage has been created so far. However, a basic document based on the new Law (Articles 12 to 127) – a National Classification of the Cultural Heritage – has been drafted recently, with the aim of designating all different types of cultural heritage that the Republic of Macedonia possesses. The Government of the Republic of Macedonia is expected to adopt it in the following months. In parallel, a process of re-evaluating the whole cultural heritage is supposed to develop (in the next two years for immovable heritage and within one year for movable heritage), aimed at categorisation of the cultural heritage. This will establish the level of significance of the cultural heritage for the public interest of the Republic of Macedonia, identifying cultural heritage of special significance (in two subcategories: of exceptional and of great significance) and a separate category of significant cultural heritage (Articles 28 and 29).

The first stage is identification of the cultural heritage, by means of an inventory. It can reasonably be assumed that cultural goods already listed possess valuable features, which is why they previously obtained the status of protected heritage by law. In order to create the so-called protection inventory, special rules have been laid down for cataloguing cultural heritage (Article 34), establishing the type of information needed to confirm the value of cultural goods, their degree of preservation and the type and scope of documentation required to be prepared for that purpose.

The goods are evidenced in basic, native and central records. According to the new law (Article 34), the national institutions, conservation centres (formerly institutes for the protection of cultural monuments) keep the basic and native records of documentation on immovable cultural heritage, while the Cultural Heritage Protection Office maintains the central records of documentation. For each item of immovable heritage in the inventory, there is a record card, registration number and file, according to type of goods.

There are three types of immovable heritage: individual monument, (cultural) site and cultural landscape (articles 12, 13 and 14 of the law). In the former legislation on cultural and natural heritage, and in past practice, cultural landscapes were not treated as a separate type of immovable cultural heritage. Hence, we still do not have a single monument listed under the term "cultural landscape", which is defined as a type of immovable heritage in Article 14 of the new law. Industrial heritage was listed in the framework of cultural sites (economic structures and ensembles), but only three buildings have been identified so far – all in the Municipality of Demir Kapija (wine cellar, hydro-power pepper plant and hydro-power station).

The new law on Nature Protection (Official Gazette of RM, No. 67/2004) regulates the categorisation of protected areas – in accordance with the World Conservation Union (IUCN) definition – including the category of "protected landscape". According to Article 84, a protected landscape shall be an area where the interaction of people with nature has created, over time, a landscape with particular characteristics and aesthetic, environmental, cultural, and historical or ethnographical importance, specific to that area only and which at the same time has a significantly high biological diversity.

Based on the inventory, experts from the national conservation centres prepare a justification for the evaluation of any given immovable cultural heritage, meaning a thorough assessment of historical art features and the degree of preservation. On this basis, a specific category of heritage importance is proposed along with a general protection regime defining the type and scope of interventions permitted or not permitted. The rules (the adoption of which is pending) for evaluation, categorisation and re-evaluation of the cultural heritage provide the methodology and necessary documents for this purpose. After acceptance of the justification by an expert commission, the immovable cultural heritage item is given the status of cultural heritage (in a specific category) protected by law.

According to the previous regulations, registers of cultural heritage were kept at two levels – municipal and central registers. Municipal institutes kept the municipal registers, each covering its own area, while the Institute for the Protection of the Cultural Monuments of the Republic of Macedonia kept the central register as well as the municipal registers for municipalities where institutes of protection for the monuments were not established. Even though municipal institutes had an obligation to submit documents to the state institute to be processed in the central register, this was not done consistently and it was not checked.

According to the new Law on Protection of the Cultural Heritage (Article 45), the Cultural Heritage Protection Office keeps the National Register of Cultural Heritage for immovable, movable and intangible cultural heritage. Besides the main register, additional registers are kept as well:

- register of goods under temporary protection;

- register of cultural heritage in danger;

- register of reserved archaeological zones.

According to the Rules on Maintaining the National Register of Cultural Heritage, every entry record of immovable cultural heritage on the registration form contains the following data: Name/type of the register and its composite part; registry number; name of the protected goods; Individual Native Identification Number (IIN); Act of Protection (designation, with number and date when the act was promulgated in the Republic of Macedonia Official Gazette); decision on registration (number and date); level of protection; date of object's creation; description of cultural goods; reasons for being protected; regime of protection; responsible protection institution; additional entries; removal from the register; date of compiling the information; name of expert compiling the information; notes; classification; category; location (municipality, inhabited area, region, address); type of ownership; owner, (name, address and legal grounds of acquiring the goods); user (name, address, legal grounds and period of using the goods); author(s)/creator(s) of the goods; relation to other protected goods; relation to an individual or event; relation to previous protection status; relation to previous registration; specific photograph and its author; description of the goods' boundaries; description of the goods' contact zones; cadastral (land tax register) municipality; cadastral plots within the goods; cadastral plots within the contact zones; protected area (of the protected goods, of the contact zones and the protected area as a whole); topographic data; use/function of the goods (original, additional changes, present); condition of the goods and immovable heritage at various levels of function.

The necessary data for the national register are to be provided from all processes of protection of the cultural heritage, from drawing up an inventory to the implementation of specific protection-conservation projects, such as revitalisation and special treatment in the framework of certain types of spatial planning (spatial and urban plans); the Cultural Heritage Protection Office takes care of their appropriate preparation and inclusion in the information system.

## 1.2. Characterisation

Before intervening to directly (physically) protect the cultural heritage or its treatment in spatial and urban planning, the competent institutions that protect immovable cultural heritage – that is, the new conservation centres – and legal bodies licensed to conduct certain protection-conservation activity should put forward a protection regime, based on their insight into the condition and the importance of certain cultural goods. They should propose certain investigations aimed at establishing the type and scope of conservation necessary for specific immovable cultural heritage and also how it should be treated in spatial planning. The way to conduct these investigations and the type and scope of necessary documents are set down in two rulebooks (in accordance with the Law on Protection of the Cultural Heritage):

- the rulebook on necessary conservation investigations, the adoption of which is pending (Article 82), on the need to undertake specific conservation measures on the monument itself or to produce scientific-expert studies on certain conservation procedures needed in protection;

- the rulebook on the Content and Methodology for the Preparation Protection-Conservation Criteria of the Cultural Heritage (Article 71), referring to investigation and treatment of cultural heritage for the needs of spatial and urban planning.

A conservation investigation for the needs of spatial planning is in fact a study analysing the historical development of the protected goods, with an inventory of artistic and architectural styles, analysis of features and value of the protected goods and their immediate environment, and investigations of socio-economic and other aspects aimed at defining the programmes that decide suitable measures for direct (physical) protection and a protection regime within the plan.

For cultural sites/ensembles included in planning, a comprehensive documentation base is prepared, based on analysis of all aspects of the place of the immovable cultural heritage in its wider vicinity.

In previous practice, conservation investigations mainly examined the monument itself or a cultural site or ensemble, but without detailed analysis and treatment of their immediate or wider vicinity. Also, there was no requirement to use a standardised methodology that would more precisely detail a protection regime, not only for the zone containing the cultural heritage but also for the contact zone. This was because the protection institutions, which generally prepared these studies, had different approaches in setting the general frames of protection regimes and defining specific conditions for their implementation. This practice is expected to end with the new law, i.e. the Rules on Protection-Conservation Bases.

There have been several analytical studies of the historical nuclei of cities in relation to the needs of urban planning (for Skopje, Bitola, Gevgelija, Struga, Veles, Tetovo, Gostivar, etc.), and these contain results from historical, architectural and urban research. However, no large-scale multidisciplinary studies, which would incorporate other types of analysis in the framework of strategies for sustainable development (from a socio-economic aspect or from the aspect of human environment) created at an inter-departmental level, have been created so far.

Public institutions for the protection of cultural heritage, working as national institutions for the specialism in which they are competent, conduct conservation investigations for the needs of spatial and urban planning. These specialist bodies are now – pursuant to the new Law on the Protection of Cultural Heritage – the conservation centres.

The competent institutions for spatial and urban planning generally use data from investigations and the documentation that institutions for the protection of cultural heritage already possess. The new Law on Spatial and Urban Planning, adopted by the Assembly on 30 June 2005 (Official Gazette No. 51/05) requires them also to take action.

The Law on Protection of the Cultural Heritage requires documentation setting out the basis for protection-conservation to be prepared, and this must be incorporated in the adopted plan (Integrated Conservation – Chapter 3 of the Law).

In the past, there were several cases (especially with secular architecture or historic city centres) where the planners themselves or their external collaborators drafted, evaluated and decided the protection regime without the involvement of institutions or protection experts, and therefore without incorporating the results of any investigation.

There were also cases where, in contributing to the planning process, the institutions responsible for this work very often simply noted the buildings or ensembles of cultural heritage, without indicating anything about their status as protected goods (Appendix to this national report: Examples 1 and 2).

## 1.3. Databases and computerised mapping

A compatible information-documentation system of cultural heritage, connected to specialised and/or general systems at national level, has not yet been created.

Digitalised processing of documents of immovable cultural heritage does not exist at the moment. Until recently, only photo-documentation was prepared electronically. Architectural documentation in electronic form began in 2002, but much of it is still being manually copied on tracing paper, and the format varies.

Descriptive documentation is prepared on paper in A4 format. Most of it has not been put onto electronic media (CD), except for recent documentation, which mainly refers to specific reports on conservation interventions on the cultural heritage.

The Ministry of Culture is working to create a digitalised information system for cultural heritage, in the framework of the project Development of Municipalities through Culture, funded by the World Bank. In that context, a "Data Model for the Information System on Cultural Heritage of RM" is being prepared.

There is also continuous implementation of HEREIN – the Council of Europe's digital network for cultural heritage, which unites all government services dealing with protection of cultural heritage. The Ministry of Culture submitted an Assessment Report on the Cultural Heritage in RM, looking at policy. A pilot project on digitalisation of museum (movable) cultural heritage will now follow.

These preparatory activities are in the context of regulations deriving from the Law on Protection of the Cultural Heritage, which provides for the Cultural Heritage Information System of RM to be set up and run by the Cultural Heritage Protection Office (Article 115). For that purpose, Article 36 provides for special regulations on the type, scope and method of creating documents on cultural heritage. All stakeholders involved in the protection of cultural heritage must apply the new rules on the type, content, standards, norms and manner of cultural heritage documentation and the conditions for its maintenance and use. In preparing these rules, information is now being collected on the type and scope of standard documentation from previous practice, comparable rules for other protection processes and generally accepted international standards.

## 2. Plans for integrated management and regulations

### 2.1. Environment

In the past, the procedure for environmental impact assessment of certain projects was not unified at a national level and was conducted on the basis of several laws and regulations: Law on Environment and Nature Protection and Promotion (Official Gazette of RM Nos. 69/96, 13/99, 96/00, 41/00 and 45/02), Law on Construction of Investment Facilities (Official Gazette of RM Nos. 15/90, 11/91, 11/94, 18/99 and 25/99), Law on Mineral

Resources (Official Gazette of RM Nos. 18/99, 48/99 and 29/02), Energy Law (Official Gazette of RM Nos. 7/97, 40/99 and 98/00), Law on Concessions (Official Gazette of RM No. 25/02), Law on Waters (Official Gazette of RM Nos. 4/98 and 19/00), Law on Spatial and Urban Planning (Official Gazette of RM Nos. 4/96, 8/96, 70/96, 5/97, 28/97, 18/99, 53/01 and 45/02), Rulebook on Standards and Norms for Spatial Development (Official Gazette of RM No. 2/02), Rulebook on Standards and Norms for Design of Buildings (Official Gazette of RM Nos. 69/99, 102/00 and 2/02).

In past practice, the process of environmental impact assessment (EIA) was compulsory for investment projects indicated in Annex I of the Convention on Environmental Impact Assessment in the Transboundary Context – the Espoo Convention, ratified by the Republic of Macedonia in 1999 (Official Gazette of RM No. 44/99).

The national EIA procedure has previously consisted of three phases:

– investment facility planning (in accordance with the Law on Construction of Investment Facilities). In this phase the investor is obliged to obtain an opinion from the Ministry of Environment and Physical Planning (MoEPP), which must be taken into account when the body running the construction permit procedure (Ministry of Transport and Communications) defines the conditions for construction;

– issue of a construction permit (in accordance with the Law on Environment and Nature Protection and Promotion and the Law on Construction of Investment Facilities). In this phase, the investor is obliged to prepare an EIA for projects that might cause damage to, or be a risk for, the environment or human health.

– the EIA is treated as a phase of the main project and is submitted for inspection and analysis by MoEPP. Assessment and analysis are carried out by the Environment Service within MoEPP, which approves or rejects the submitted EIA.

EIAs prepared in the past contained a description of the proposed site, with a map at a scale of 1:25 000 and a site plan showing spatial planning documentation, along with details of the quality of the environment (including a special review of existing sources of pollution), climate characteristics, water resources, geo-morphology, population and density of inhabitants, existing infrastructure, flora and fauna, protected natural goods, landscape characteristics and immovable cultural goods, description of the object and land-use regulations, together with possible changes and impacts on the environment during construction, in operation and in the case of a major accident, as well as a review of measures for environmental protection.

Past practice was fully replaced when the new Law on the Environment came into force on 1 September 2005, having been adopted by the Parliament of the Republic of Macedonia on 22 June 2005. The law implements in full the EU Directive amending and supplementing the Council Directive 337/85 on the Assessment of the Effects of Certain Public and Private Projects on the Environment, the Council Directive 42/2001 on Strategic Environmental Assessment, and the Espoo and Aarhus Convention regulations.

The law sets out basic principles for environmental protection, establishing procedures for environment impact assessment and public participation in the decision-making process, and deals with issues of access to environmental information, integrated environmental permits and so on.

The new law contains a separate chapter on environmental impact assessment, which describes EIA procedures. A draft decree (to be adopted by the Government of the Republic of Macedonia) defines the projects for which an EIA is compulsory, and those projects where the need for an EIA is to be assessed on a case-by-case basis. An EIA with justification must be prepared for all other projects not covered by the decree.

An investor planning a project is obliged to notify the MoEPP of the intention to implement a project and submit an opinion on the need for an EIA. Having received the notification, the MoEPP shall, by means of a decision, notify the investor whether an EIA is needed. The scope of the EIA depends on the type of project. The opinion must include alternatives, along with the main reviews and surveys that need to be carried out, the methods and criteria applied to estimate the effects, the improvement measures that should be taken into account, legal entities that need to be consulted in the course of preparing the EIA and the structure, contents and scale of environmental information. In case of projects requiring an EIA, the investor is obliged to produce an EIA, which is then submitted to the MoEPP. Once the EIA is submitted, a report on its acceptability is prepared.

On the basis of the EIA, along with the report, public debate and opinions received from the public, the MoEPP issues a decision by which consent is awarded or the request for consent is rejected. The decision remains in effect for a period of two years after its issue, and its validity may be extended if no significant changes result from modifications to the project, changed conditions in the affected area, new knowledge related to the main contents of the EIA or development of new technology that could be used in the project.

The body responsible for the project implementation may not issue a decision/permit for the project before the investor submits a decision by the MoEPP approving implementation of the project. There is no obligation on the state body issuing the permit to notify the MoEPP that a request for project implementation has been submitted without completing an EIA in advance.

During this procedure, the MoEPP consults the local government units within whose boundaries the project is to be implemented, NGOs in the field of environment protection and improvement, and the general public, by forwarding and disseminating the relevant documentation, organising public debates and placing the presentation on the MoEPP website. The MoEPP decision must include the public opinions that have been taken into account, and explain why any opinions have not been taken into account.

The MoEPP is not responsible for preparing EIAs. In the past, they were prepared by authorised companies, at the request of and financed by the project investor. Authorisation of such companies was approved by the Minister of Environment and Physical Planning, if they fulfilled the criteria specified by law. According to the new Law on Environment, only experts who fulfil the criteria and pass an exam to acquire EIA expert status can be responsible for the preparation of EIAs.

In past practice, departments dealing with cultural heritage protection were involved in the EIA process in the phase of investment facility planning and in cases of natural resource exploitation (Appendix to this national report: Example 3). The previous Institute for Cultural Monuments Protection of the Republic of Macedonia – now the Cultural Heritage Protection Office – gives its opinion of the project documentation, and approves geological investigation and natural resources exploitation (Article 79 of the Law on Protection of the Cultural Heritage). Project documentation must be *ex officio* obtained from the Ministry of Economy and the Ministry of Transport and Communications.

The new Law on Protection of the Cultural Heritage provides for an obligation to obtain an opinion on EIAs from the Cultural Heritage Protection Office. The office is also authorised to carry out monitoring of pollution impact on the conservation of immovable cultural heritage and its immediate vicinity. (Article 111). These regulations have not yet been put into practice.

*The Husamedin-Pasha mosque, Leninova, Shtip (Council of Europe)*

## 2.2. Spatial and urban planning

Spatial and urban planning is a continuous process of preparing, adopting and implementing spatial and urban plans. The preparation and adoption of spatial and urban plans are issues of public interest.

The basic aim of spatial and urban planning is to provide balanced spatial development, rational arrangement and use of space, suitable conditions for human life and work, protection and improvement of the environment and nature, and protection of cultural-historical treasures, with protection from destruction by war or natural and technological disasters.

The procedure for preparation and adoption of plans – until the new Law on Spatial and Urban Planning (Official Gazette of RM No. 51/2005) was adopted by the Assembly of RM on 30 June 2005 – was regulated by the Law on Spatial and Urban Planning (Official Gazette of RM No. 4/96, 28/97, 18/99, 53/01, 45/02), the so-called Old Law. The old law, with some innovations from the new law, has been used to get a more realistic picture in this report.

The process of planning and land use on the territory of RM has a national as well as a local level. In accordance with existing regulations on the arrangement and use of land, a Spatial Plan of the Republic presents the strategy for spatial development of the state. To implement the Spatial Plan of RM, a Law on Implementation of the Spatial Plan of the Republic on Macedonia was adopted (Official Gazette of RM No. 39/04). The National Spatial Plan, Regional Spatial Plan and Spatial Plan of National Parks are adopted at national level, by the Assembly of RM.

Municipal Spatial Plans are adopted locally by municipal councils. Urban planning documentation (General Urban Plan or GUP, Detailed Urban Plan or DUP, and urban planning documentation for a populated area) is adopted at local level by the municipal council, in the old and new laws.

The co-operation between institutions dealing in planning and land use and those responsible for the protection of cultural heritage in preparing spatial and urban plans is based on regulations set out in the Law on Protection of the Cultural Heritage (Official Gazette of RM, No. 20/04), the Law on Spatial and Urban Planning (Official Gazette of RM, No. 51/2005), the Law on Protection of Nature (Official Gazette of RM, No. 67/04) and the Law on Local Self-Government (Official Gazette of RM, No. 5/02).

According to the Law on Protection of the Cultural Heritage, integrated conservation of the cultural heritage is established through co-operation between institutions responsible for protection of cultural heritage and institutions responsible for planning and land use, at all stages of preparation, adoption or change of plans.

The Ministry of Environment and Physical Planning, as the competent institution in the field of spatial planning, is responsible for spatial planning documentation. The Ministry of Transport and Communications is the responsible institution for issues of land use and is charged with preparing urban planning documentation.

The Government of RM adopts an annual programme for the preparation of spatial and urban plans proposed by the Ministry of Environment and Physical Planning. Annual programmes of preparation of spatial and urban plans are funded from the national budget. Annual programmes for the preparation of urban plans may be financed by interested legal or private bodies.

According to the Law on Construction Land (Official Gazette of RM, No. 53/01) the arrangement of any construction land that lies outside the urban area, or is not listed in the Annual Programme, is financed by the investor.

Spatial and urban plans are prepared as Draft and Proposal Plans by the State Enterprise for Spatial and Urban Planning (PESUP), established by the Government of RM. Urban planning is a business category. Not only PESUP, but also domestic or foreign legal entities may prepare urban plans after fulfilling conditions set out in the Law on Spatial and Urban Planning and gaining a licence for urban plan preparation acquired in the home country. There are no licensed legal or private entities for the preparation of spatial plans, other than PESUP. The new Law on Spatial and Urban Planning provides for transformation of the state enterprise into an Agency for Spatial Planning.

The procedure for adopting spatial and urban plans, besides involving government institutions, provides for active public involvement through participation in organised expert debate and public opinion surveys. Expert discussion is organised on the Draft Spatial Plan and General Urban Plan, with participation of representatives from institutions and organisations in the area covered by the plan. A public opinion survey is organised on the draft Detailed Urban Plan and Urban Planning Documentation of populated areas. The public opinion survey is conducted through presentation of the plan in a public place for at least ten days, during which interested citizens and legal entities in the area covered in the plan submit written comments on questionnaires to the organiser of the survey. An announcement of the time and place of presentation of the plan is made in the public media, thus providing transparency in the process of plan adoption. The new Law on Spatial and Urban Planning provides for longer duration of the public opinion survey, from 10 to 15 working days.

To be able to justify the rejection of certain comments and proposals in the process of adopting urban plans, the new law provides for the preparation of a report on the public opinion survey. This report is prepared by an expert commission with the responsibility of writing to every individual who submitted a comment on the questionnaire and informing them why their comments or proposals have been accepted or rejected.

To provide a professional approach and transparency in the process of planning, the new law provides that the Municipal Council should establish a Participative Body composed of representatives of the council, officials from the local administration, prominent experts in the field of urban planning, representatives of civic organisations and citizens. The aim of this body is to convey the position, opinions and needs of the citizens.

According to the Constitution of RM (Official Gazette of RM, No. 91/2001), citizens at the local administration level participate directly or via representatives in the decision-making on issues of local importance, especially in the field of urban planning, rural planning, culture and other fields determined by the law.

The authorities responsible for protection of the cultural heritage provide opinions on draft urban plans as a basis for the expert discussion of the plan. In this case, the opinions of these authorities are not binding, and most often they are only partly accepted in the final version of the plan. These authorities never receive feedback on whether their comments were accepted or rejected, as a result of which the implementation of policies in plans for the areas where cultural heritage exists has been impeded. The authorities protecting cultural heritage are not included in the adoption stage of the draft plan.

The Office of the Spatial Information System (SPI), within the MoEPP, has available digital spatial data for the whole territory of RM at a scale of 1:50 000. These data provide the basis for presenting graphically the structures and sites of immovable cultural heritage (Appendix to this national report: Example 4).

Planning the protection of immovable cultural heritage is an inseparable part of the planning of spatial development in this country. The Law on Spatial and Urban Planning and the Law on Protection of the Cultural Heritage provide an obligation that all types of spatial and urban plans contain planning measures for protection of immovable cultural heritage. These measures are regulated in accordance with the basic documentation (protection-conservation criteria) of the plan, which is prepared by authorised departments staffed by experts on protection of cultural heritage.

According to the Law on Protection of the Cultural Heritage, an appropriate regime of protection of immovable cultural heritage in spatial and urban plans is implemented in accordance with approved and certified protection-conservation criteria. The Protection-Conservation Criteria form the basis for the treatment of cultural heritage in spatial and urban plans created on the basis of existing data (in the database): textual, graphic and documentary presentation of the heritage and contact zones relevant for planning and land use.

Without impairing the protection of cultural heritage in the process of planning (except where special measures are laid down for areas with particular cultural value), it is possible to adopt plans at a lower level if necessary, in the case of DUPs, Urban Planning Projects and detail development of rehabilitation and reconstruction projects (Appendix to this national report: Example 5).

The Basic Law applied in this field is the Law on Spatial and Urban Planning (Official Gazette of RM, Nos. 44/96, 28/97, 18/99, 53/01, 45/02). Under the old law, cultural heritage was dealt with by regulations based on the law: the Rules on Land Use, the Rules on Content, Preparation and Adoption of Urban Plans and the Rules on Building Design (Appendix to this national report: Example 6).

It should be mentioned that, in the preparation of a General Urban Plan, under the new law the part relating to cultural heritage is omitted (Article 10). Institutions relevant for the protection of cultural heritage remain involved in the expert discussion.

In the past, when urban plans were being prepared, the authorities responsible for protection of the cultural heritage were required by law to submit (to the planning authorities) data on the protection regime for all types of cultural heritage in the zone concerned; the data had to be related to a specific type of plan and incorporated in the planning solutions. One protection regime was prepared for the area with cultural heritage and another for the adjacent zones.

However, urban plans usually only noted the existence of cultural heritage. The planning authorities were required to obtain the opinion of the competent authorities on a protection regime for the cultural heritage, but only at the stage when the plan was being implemented, and cultural sites or ensembles of any type were left as zones under special regime. Urban plans did not provide any guidelines for development of the zone or inclusion of the heritage in future planning solutions. Problems occurred, especially with monitoring implementation of DUPs (Appendix to this national report: Example 7).

Both general and special urban planning conditions have been specified for the contact zone of one cultural ensemble – the Bazaar – being quite liberal in allowing the construction of structures of greater height and different shape. This could destroy the silhouette of the historic centre of Skopje. In such cases, when urban planning conditions are already specified, without considering the entire protection treatment of the buildings, it is almost impossible for the protection authorities (primarily the Cultural Heritage Protection Office which, by the Law on Protection of the Cultural Heritage, specifies the conservation criteria and conditions) to act to preserve the authenticity and integrity of the ensemble as such.

In the past, cultural heritage had no appropriate treatment in urban plans, except that it was present in the documentation prepared for the plan; but there were no planning guidelines for its development or its inclusion in the general development flows of the cultural heritage area covered by the plan.

The new Law on Spatial and Urban Planning, which was adopted by the RM Government and came into force on 30 June 2005 (Official Gazette of RM, No. 51, 06/05) significantly resolves past incompatibility among the regulations on cultural heritage. In the basic principles of spatial planning, particular attention is paid to immovable cultural heritage (Article 4) and the National Spatial Plan contains obligatory measures for protection of the immovable cultural heritage (Article 8).

The new law contains other significant innovations in spatial planning. It lists more specifically the required types of investigation, in the context of protection/conservation criteria, for cultural sites/ensembles and buildings having cultural and historical significance (Article 11). Special treatment (in documentation) is provided for cultural ensembles of rural character, where it concerns Rural Urban Planning (Article 12), and for ensembles/sites and buildings of cultural heritage and cultural landscapes outside populated areas (Article 13). The expert discussion on draft general urban plans must include the institutions responsible for protection of cultural heritage (Article 23). Also, there is an obligation when preparing an urban planning project (for complex buildings on one building plot) that such a project must be prepared also for those buildings and areas protected by the law because they represent the cultural heritage (Article 50).

## 3. Authorisation, supervision and penalties

### 3.1. Authorisation

For immovable cultural heritage of particular significance, urban planning projects are prepared (besides spatial and urban plans) and approved by the ministry responsible for issues of land use. Approval is given only after an opinion has been obtained from the Cultural Heritage Protection Office authorised to conduct expert works within the field of protection of cultural heritage.

The Law on Investment Construction in force until 1 July 2005 treated the protection of immovable cultural heritage only in Article 19. In order to obtain a building permit from the planning authorities, the investor must now provide an opinion on the technical documentation submitted by relevant state institutions for protection of cultural heritage (the new conservation centres), but only for those buildings on the list of protected assets (Article 4 of the Amended Law on Investment Construction). For other elements in the cultural site/ensemble and other buildings in the contact zones, the law does not lay down such an obligation, though it can be specified in the DUP for a given area.

The new Law on Investment Construction (Official Gazette of RM No. 51, 06/05), in spite of some terminological inconsistency with the Law on Protection of the Cultural Heritage when it deals with buildings of cultural heritage (in defining reconstruction, maintenance, removal, etc., in defining types/stages of design, and in the chapter on project documentation), contains significant differences where it refers to cultural heritage listed on the National Register, especially provisions for requesting approval from the institution authorised for the protection of cultural heritage in the case of reconstruction (Article 10), in cases of destruction of the building as a result of natural or human factors (Article 65) and where there is need of removal of a structure (Article 85). In the procedure for issuing construction approval for buildings of the fifth category (with "memorial monument and commemorative marking", as per Article 50), an opinion on presented documentation is required within a specified period (Article 52). Only practice will show how much the new regulations are respected.

Furthermore, all types of immediate protection (conservation, rehabilitation, restoration, adaptation, reconstruction and construction on a protected area, or any archaeological excavation) require an appropriate opinion, agreement or approval from the authority responsible for the protection of cultural heritage, namely the new conservation centres and Cultural Heritage Protection Office.

The new legislation on cultural heritage provides for a conservation opinion (Article 75 of the Law on Protection of Cultural Heritage) or agreement (Article 75) to be obtained on taking measures for immediate (physical) protection of all goods within the protected area. In the case of protected goods listed in the National Register of cultural heritage, it is necessary to obtain conservation approval before undertaking any intervention of immediate protection,. The conservation opinion, agreement and approval are issued by the Cultural Heritage Protection Office (Articles 75 and 87). To change the use or function of protected goods, approval from the same office is required (Article 121).

If there is no DUP or if there are separate provisions in the existing DUP on specific urban planning conditions, the authorities responsible for land use issue architectural/urban planning conditions, after having obtained an opinion on the protection/conservation conditions from the office, defining special architectural/urban planning conditions as the basis for preparation of the project documentation (Article 74). These conditions must not contradict the plan provisions.

Before any intervention on a protected asset, it is necessary to obtain a building permit from the authorities responsible for planning. The building permit may be issued only after obtaining a prior opinion, agreement or conservation approval from the Cultural Heritage Protection Office (Article 87). A problem occurs when, at the stage of preparing the DUP, the protection regime of the cultural goods was not respected. In such a case, the dispute ends before the court or, as usually happened in the past, the work is carried out according to the regime of the protected cultural goods (Appendix to this national report: Example 8).

## 3.2. Supervision and penalties

The legislation protecting cultural heritage provides for inspection and supervision of the cultural heritage and penal provisions in cases prescribed by the Law on Protection of the Cultural Heritage (Chapter IX, Articles 165-171 and Chapter X, Articles 172-174). The inspectors monitor the protection of cultural heritage in the field and, where they find operations contrary to provisions of the Law; they act by taking decisions on removing the irregularities (Article 171). At the same time, the responsible Construction Inspection and spatial planning authorities are informed (Article 169) and, if necessary, a request is submitted for a misdemeanour procedure or criminal case (Article 169).

By law, the holders of protected goods are obliged to keep and maintain them (Article 130). If the holder does not undertake in due time the prescribed technical protection measures, the Cultural Heritage Protection Office is entitled to order the holder to undertake such measures or to impose them being carried out by the relevant institution for protection at the expense of the holder (Article 130). If there is a danger that the protected goods may be damaged or destroyed by the holder due to negligence or unprofessional handling, the Office may, upon proposal of the responsible state institution for protection, appoint a guardian for the protected goods who will undertake the necessary measures of protection and maintenance (Article 136).

At the time of writing, the inspection service (a Section within the Cultural Heritage Protection Office, under Article 167) has functioned for only a few months and is short-staffed (with only four experts in different fields), but visible effects of the work of this service and its further development are expected in the future. There is little awareness yet of the seriousness of the inspection authority interventions, so the cases of infractions in the treatment of cultural heritage remain numerous.

On site, there is a continual problem of illegal construction of buildings and unprofessionally carried out interventions on protected goods. Examples can be found in many urban areas in Macedonia. In most cases, the institutions for protection merely alert the competent inspection authorities, without significant results.

For the purpose of undisturbed inspection or supervision, co-operation is needed with the responsible planning and inspection authorities. The current situation is unsatisfactory because the co-operation between the inspection authorities in the municipal units for urban planning and the inspection authority for cultural heritage is only incidental. So far, no formal or informal co-operation agreements have been made among the authorities responsible for cultural heritage and spatial and urban planning with the purpose of controlling illegal works in the field.

However, since the Cultural Heritage Protection Office started work (employing staff from 1 January 2005), many efforts have been made to establish co-operation with municipal units of urban planning (within the Ministry of Transport and Communications) and with the relevant authorities in the Ministry of Environment and Physical Planning. Besides established contacts, working meetings are planned in order to agree on and prepare a mutual strategy for resolving common problems in protecting cultural heritage.

According to the provisions of the new Law on Protection of the Cultural Heritage, the fines for misdemeanour by legal or physical entities range from 5 000 Macedonia Denars (MKD) to MKD 300 000. In certain cases the penalty can include a ban on carrying on the business, lasting from 6 months to 2 years (Articles 172-174). Considering the short period that this law has been in force and the inspection authority has existed within the Office, results in this respect are expected in the future.

According to the new Law on Environment, the penalties for disrespect of the procedure for EIA are as follows: the fine for legal entities ranges from MKD 100 000 to MKD 300 000; for private entities it is from MKD 10 000 to MKD 30 000. In certain cases, besides the fine, it is possible to impose a protective ban on carrying on the business, for a period from six months to five years.

# Appendix

*Example 1*

A study of the protection of the building heritage of Gevgelija was made at the request of the local administration, who needed it for the development of urban planning documentation. Although the making and adoption of this study was transparent and many stakeholders had an interest (the municipality was the investor, the city architect was actively involved, the study was promoted in public debate in which all parties were involved, including urban planners, conservators, city authorities and owners and/or users of cultural heritage), no feedback on the use of data from the study has been received yet.

*Example 2*

The document "Protection regime for the building heritage of Neighbourhood No. 3 – Tetovo" was prepared by the heritage protection services to meet the needs of the Detailed Urban Plan (DUP). The area included in the plan was investigated, the architectural heritage evaluated and a protection regime prescribed for particular cultural goods and ensembles. Feedback on the treatment of cultural heritage was not received until the plan was being implemented, when it was established that, among other things, the building plot containing the protected cultural goods "Begov Konak" had been divided into seven parts for planned residence blocks. The plan is being implemented without the removal of these anomalies.

*Example 3*

A special chapter on the archaeological and cultural-historic sites was prepared in the EIA Study for the construction of the oil pipeline from Miladinovci to Thessalonica (on the border with Greece, 160 km long). A detailed archaeological investigation was made along the railway from Beljanovce to Kriva Palanka. For the highway section from Demir Kapija to Udovo, a special chapter describing the archaeological sites was prepared as part of the EIA Study. For the high-tension line from Negotino to Chervena Mogila (Bulgaria), the EIA Study contained a list of sites with cultural-historical significance, based on the data from the Institute for Protection of Cultural Monuments of the Republic of Macedonia.

*Example 4*

In the National Spatial Plan there is a map of the cultural historical heritage, drawn on the basis of satellite photographs at a scale of 1:200 000.

*Example 5*

The National Spatial Plan covers the cultural heritage, which means there is "positive discrimination" in planning land use. The effect of this positive discrimination may be seen only if the urban plans, as plans of lower level, are in accord with the spatial plans, especially the National Spatial Plan.

RM provides, according to existing regulations, protection of immovable cultural heritage. Even though there are instruments for integrated protection and implementation of the policy of arrangement, use and protection of space in RM, in practice there is a clash with inappropriate management of spatial planning documentation and disrespect for regulations directly threatening the immovable cultural heritage.

*Example 6*

The rules on standards and norms of land use treat cultural heritage only in the chapter entitled "Standards and norms on arrangements of cultural monuments and archaeological sites" (Articles 58 to 60).

*Example 7*

The Detailed Spatial Plan of the Skopje Old Bazaar (in respect of the cultural ensemble within) provides only general urban planning conditions applicable to all buildings. It gives conservation treatment only for individual protected goods listed in the Central Register. Urban Planning blocks define the character and values of the cultural ensemble. The plan determines the maximum allowed height, which is not equal to the existing one, in practice introducing the possibility of destruction of the bazaar silhouette and changes to the integral facing walls, which form an important part of the value of the protected ambience. To determine particular urban planning conditions, the preparation of urban planning projects for each block has been prescribed.

*Example 8*

Planned destruction of protected goods is frequent in practice. In cases where the urban plan defines additions, upgrading or construction of a new structure on the site, it usually happens that the protected goods are destroyed. An obvious example of this approach is the DUP for the site "Debar Maalo 2" covering the protected ensemble/site "Central city area 1" in Skopje, where in line with the adopted plans new buildings are being rapidly constructed in place of old buildings protected by law, indicating large-scale destruction of the cultural site/ensemble by clearing away the inherited buildings that defined the values and character of the protected goods.

# PART 2

## CHARACTERISATION AND DOCUMENTATION SYSTEMS

# Comparative summary of documentation systems – RPSEE countries

*Myriam Goblet*

## 1. Heritage documentation systems

In order to manage the heritage effectively, it is first necessary to be fully familiar with it. The establishment of an appropriate documentation system provides the first integrated heritage management and study tool.

The next stage is to carry out environmental impact assessments and draw up spatial and urban planning schemes and regulations. Planning permission is then granted and inspections are carried out and, where necessary, penalties applied.

## 2. Competent authorities

In all the countries analysed, the Ministry of Culture is the principal public authority in charge of cultural heritage documentation. It is responsible for research, conservation and regularly updating information; it is assisted in its efforts by regional or supra-local bodies that possess more information about the situation on the ground. It collates and makes available the information collected in the documentation centres or national archives.

The ministries of culture are, however, not the only authorities responsible for the heritage.

Some of them work with separate authorities responsible for archaeology, such as the Archaeological Institute of the Academy of Science in Albania or the Archaeological Institute within the Academy of Science in Bulgaria.

In Romania, protected urban complexes are the responsibility of the Spatial and Urban Planning and Housing Department.

Responsibility for protection of the environmental value (species, countryside) of the natural heritage may lie with the Ministry of the Environment (Albania and Bulgaria) or be shared with the Institute for Nature Conservation (Bulgaria, Serbia, Montenegro and "the former Yugoslav Republic of Macedonia").

In six out of eight countries/regions, responsibility for the heritage is thus shared by at least two ministries. This means that interministerial co-operation must be established from the outset in order to facilitate the integrated management of the cultural and natural heritage, and especially of documentation systems.

## 3. Legal basis

The gathering of information on the cultural and natural heritage is a statutory obligation, provided for in the relevant laws in all the countries analysed. Quite often, the decrees implementing these laws stipulate the methodology to be used and the form and scope of this documentation. In "the former Yugoslav Republic of Macedonia", for example, the new law that came into force in January 2005 explicitly provides for the establishment of a "cultural heritage information system" (Section 115).

This statutory duty is one of the main activities of the ministries responsible and is carried out by skilled staff, such as historians, archaeologists, art historians, architects and botanists. Owing to the wealth of information provided, it plays a crucial role in the preparation of the two other main public service tasks, which are the protection and preservation (maintenance, restoration and enhancement) of the heritage.

## 4. Identification of the heritage

The nature of the identification data collected when inventories and registers of protected properties are compiled is very similar from one country to another. Each property has its own identification card with the following data:

- general identification: registration number and date of entry in the register or inventory, name of the property;
- location: address, land registry parcels, boundaries;
- statutory bases for protection: formal protection decision (and its category), official publication;
- descriptions: appearance and significance of the property, specific observations;
- technical documentation: various plans, old/recent and general/detailed photographs.

When work is done to preserve the protected heritage, these basic data are added to by drawing up a dossier comprising:

- the results of (archaeological, historical, architectural and technical) investigations and studies carried out before the nature and extent of the measures needed are determined;
- identification of the owners and occupiers of the property and the use to which it is put;
- documents, plans and photographs supplementing the identification card;
- survey of the various works already carried out or planned, and list of those responsible (architects, companies etc.), with an indication of the relevant budgets.

## 5. Characterisation of the heritage and its context

While the competent authorities are thorough when it comes to gathering identification data, the same does not always apply to data characterising the heritage and its surroundings. The characterisation does much more than identify the property. It also covers the economic, social and environmental aspects of the heritage concerned, and it analyses the economic, social, cultural and environmental characteristics of the various elements in the surrounding area.

It is all the more important, and all the more difficult, to take account of all the parameters that characterise the heritage in the case of architectural ensembles (urban and rural historic centres), (natural and archaeological) sites and cultural landscapes (which combine architectural, archaeological and natural heritage) – in other words, "heritage" in the broad sense of the word.

This is, however, a prerequisite for taking decisions on strategies, programmes and plans for the preservation, rehabilitation and enhancement of the properties concerned. By analysing the elements of the heritage and its context, the characterisation makes it possible to engage in a long-term process of managing the space (a specific property or environment).

For instance, the description refers to management documents drawn up by other public authorities operating in the area, such as the Ministry of the Environment, the ministries responsible for nature conservation, water resources, forests and agriculture, and the ministries of Spatial and Urban Planning, Redevelopment and Housing.

The obstacles encountered by individual countries are considerable. Apart from the lack of funds and time to carry out this type of in-depth analysis, the main problems are the lack of staff skilled in this type of multidisciplinary approach (economists, sociologists, town planners, landscape gardeners, lawyers, etc.) and the absence of any mention of this type of analysis in the remit of the ministries concerned. However, the solutions to these problems, which mainly depend on the provision of information, are within reach.

## 6. Provision of information

The ministries responsible for cultural and natural heritage documentation are not the only ones that have to analyse the various features of an area before taking a decision on its management. The Environment and Spatial Planning ministries also have the task of collecting cross-sectoral data on all aspects of the area (of which heritage constitutes only a small part). They clearly have more human and financial resources at their disposal for this purpose than do ministries of culture.

Communication and the exchange of information among these three ministries is accordingly important for the integrated and sustainable management of the various elements that make up the territory. Each of the ministries benefits from this, because it saves paying a second time for studies that have already been financed and carried out by authorities more directly responsible.

For example, when it comes to preserving the protected historic centre of a town, the Ministry of Culture will benefit from a cross-sectoral study of the entire town carried out by the Ministry of Spatial Planning as part of a development plan, while the Ministry of Spatial Planning will not have to pay for an analysis of the heritage of the town (which it is obliged to take into account in its development plan), thanks to the first-hand information provided by the Ministry of Culture. Specific examples of the sharing of information in computer databases are given in section 7 below.

Communication with the general public is also extremely important for the preservation of heritage, since the public form its leading champion if they are well informed about its role and importance.

Whether the information is communicated from one institution to another or to the general public, it will be necessary to employ the best means of disseminating it. The use of the new information technologies and, in particular, the computerisation of databases should be a priority in the management of documentation systems in all countries.

## 7. Current state of documentation systems

All countries report computer systems, of varying degrees of sophistication, integrated to a greater or lesser extent. Here follows a summary of the present situation in each country analysed.

### *Albania*

Information on cultural assets is gathered together at the National Centre for the Inventory of Cultural Property attached to the Ministry of Culture. This information, which is being computerised and is not yet accessible to the public, relates only to the property itself and not its context. No computerised mapping system is currently attached to the database.

The Ministry of the Environment's ACESS database relating to "protected areas" is very interesting because it links the natural to the cultural environment. Since 2004, it has, with the help of the European Environment Agency, included national monuments and protected countryside in its six categories of protected area (archaeological sites, caves, churches, etc.), an example being the Butrinti National Park. These data are accessible to the public.

### *Bosnia and Herzegovina*

Only "national monuments" and their surroundings have the benefit of a proper information database and protection measures. The data are divided into three categories, of which only the first (relating to the protocol) is currently accessible. The data are also used for drawing up spatial and urban planning schemes. A link with a computerised mapping system (such as MapInfo) is planned, but has not yet been established.

The Spatial Planning Act requires the setting up of a "Uniform Territorial Information System". This means that all the public authorities concerned are obliged to collect, classify and transmit their information in the same format so that it can be co-ordinated by a single body. In addition to data on spatial planning, land use, infrastructure, buildings and so on, the cultural and natural heritage is to be included in this integrated information system.

## Bulgaria

The 40 000 or so items in the register of cultural monuments are documented, but not their context. The data are not computerised or linked to a digital mapping system and are not easily accessible to the public.

Studies and computerised maps have been made of the heritage and its context in connection with development plans for historic towns (for example, Sofia and Plovdiv), tourism development plans (PHARE programme) and regional development plans. Some data are computerised and linked to a geographical information system (GIS). Other specific computerisation initiatives have been launched on an *ad hoc* basis, an example being the archaeological map of Bulgaria.

Since 2005, Bulgaria has had a new multimedia laboratory for the cultural heritage, which was set up as a collaborative venture by the University of Architecture and Civil Engineering and the British Council with the aim of digitising information on the cultural heritage and making the heritage known to as many members of the public as possible.

As in the case of the Ministry of Environment in Albania, the National Nature Conservation Service has a database relating to six categories of area (including national parks, nature parks, reserves and protected zones) that are protected on account of their biological diversity and ecosystems. These protected areas are shown on digital maps.

Finally, there is an information exchange mechanism linked to the global network for the exchange of information on biological diversity (Clearing House Mechanism – CHM) established by the Convention on Biological Diversity. This system employs cutting-edge technology and involves several partners (institutions, a foundation, a university and an association among them).

## Croatia

In autumn 2002, the Ministry of Culture established a digital cultural heritage database (with about 8 400 items) called TEUTA. It conforms to European standards and is mainly based on the British, French and Slovenian models. It contains five types of information, taken from:

- the central cultural heritage inventory (immoveable and moveable property);
- administrative databases (register, conservation work);
- collections of documentation (photos, CD photos, plans, microfilms, press articles);
- databases relating to heritage damaged by the 1990-95 war;
- auxiliary databases (Croatian place names, contacts, thesaurus).

This database is not yet linked to a digital mapping system (such a project is under consideration). It should soon be incorporated into another digital database (BREUH) that is also concerned with the heritage. Broad public access is currently guaranteed by the Internet.

## Montenegro

The general situation is the same as in Serbia with regard to the organisation of registers and information on cultural properties. There are as yet no computerised databases or digital mapping facilities.

The authorities responsible for nature conservation have at their disposal more comprehensive documentation than in the case of the heritage (17.2% of the territory enjoys international protection). They draw up very detailed analytical files on natural assets for the purpose of protecting them and drawing up development plans, local land use plans or (annual and operational) programmes for the protection and development of the national parks. With the exception of the scanning of partial maps in connection with specific files, this information is not computerised or entered into a digital mapping system.

## Serbia

There is no systematised digital database for the cultural heritage. Nevertheless, a digital mapping system and database for the Danube Region are currently being set up as part of the Interreg IIIC Argedonau European project.

On the other hand, there are several computerised databases in the field of nature conservation, but they are not co-ordinated, which poses a management problem. They are not connected to a GIS.

## Romania

The Ministry of Culture has no computerised database or link to a digital mapping system containing documentation on the cultural heritage. Work on a national digital mapping system is under way.

Since 2004, the Spatial and Urban Planning and Housing Department, as the body responsible for protected urban areas, has had a computerised database known as the "National documentation and information resource for construction, architecture, spatial and urban planning and housing". It is the result of a co-operation agreement between the Romanian ministry and France. For example, some fifteen towns and the county of Valcea currently have general urban plans with a computerised mapping system, but other towns have problems with land registry plans.

## "The former Yugoslav Republic of Macedonia"

The existing data have not yet been computerised and there is no digital mapping. However, work is under way to set up such a system as part of a community development and culture project financed by the World Bank. It so happens that a national report is accessible to the public on the Internet via the Council of Europe's HEREIN website. In addition, some architectural documents and recent reports have been digitised since 2002.

## Conclusion

A good computerised database and a geographical information system are essential in order to be able to integrate the heritage with other land management tools (environmental assessments, spatial and urban planning schemes and regulations) and into heritage management instruments (planning permission, inspections and penalties). The various authorities responsible must, therefore, be urged to make a greater effort to work together to ensure a more comprehensive and integrated approach to the different components of the territory.

# Examples of good practice in documentation

## 1. Identification and characterisation in the United Kingdom

*Graham Fairclough*

### 1.1. Identification: inventories and records

Understanding the inherited resource is the starting point for heritage management. One of the simplest forms of understanding is an inventory of what is known, and inventories – or registers, lists and records – are the origins of heritage management in most European countries. Very often (as in the United Kingdom with the first Ancient Monuments law of 1882) inventorisation began with the selection of sites considered to be of special importance. The connection between inventories and designation was and remains strong, although most countries moved rapidly to attempts at more comprehensive records. In the United Kingdom, for example, the schedule was followed quite early by the establishment of royal commissions to identify and record archaeological and historic monuments and by the 'antiquities' mapping of the state cartographic survey, the Ordnance Survey.

English records (and similar systems operate elsewhere in the UK) are held at two main levels. The National Monuments Record (NMR) is held by English Heritage, the state agency for archaeology and historic buildings. There are also county council Sites and Monuments Records (SMRs) – now called Historic Environment Records (HERs), as they start to take a broader view of the historic environment – which are part of the local government land-use planning system. Both the NMR and SMRs are publicly accessible, and starting to be available via websites. Records are also kept by other bodies, such as the National Trust (for its own landholdings) or the agriculture ministry (for the administration of EU farming support schemes).

Records are now always computerised, map-based and increasingly GIS-based. The data they contain are mainly standardised, covering such essential information as location, identification, interpretation, description, condition and use, ownership and occupancy, legal status (if any), management recommendations and bibliographic references. There is an important element of signposting, that is, of guiding users to more detailed information and reports kept elsewhere. The difficulties of maintaining such records include technical problems (e.g. standardisation and inter-operability), access to historic maps, resources (of course!) and the difficulties of revision, updating and enhancement.

SMRs are increasingly coming to contain (digital) historic mapping and new data sets such as historic landscape characterisation, air photographic interpretation and urban archaeological surveys. As a result of taking a much more comprehensive view of the historic environment, new attitudes towards documentation and its accessibility are beginning to emerge; spatial data are becoming increasingly important, and the increase in digital data sets from other sectors (e.g. ecology) is also changing the character of SMRs.

Despite the proven long-term effectiveness of these systems, which are the bedrock of successful heritage protection, the traditional approach has been seen in recent years to have limitations:

– it is site-based: it (obviously) includes only known sites and is unsuited to predicting where new sites might be (it tells us where we found things, not where they exist);

– it works best for traditional monument types, and less well for other records – non-site archaeology, for example;

– we risk seeking more and more detail about fewer sites, losing the larger picture;

– it rarely extends to landscape scale, nor to historic patterning or general character; at most, a concept of setting is included;

– it focuses on the individual component, not on the relationship between components nor on the general character of an area: that is, it mainly concerns 'things' not the idea of 'place'.

Heritage as defined in traditional inventories usually reflects a limited range of factors, notably expert-led ones such as archaeological evidential value or architectural beauty. These are undoubtedly important, and cannot be overlooked. However, the increasing demand for public access and 'ownership' of the heritage, combined with the changing cultural and ethnic composition of society and a recognition of the very broadest sense of the word 'heritage', requires a fuller range of social and other values to be recognised as a measure of common heritage (cf. the European Landscape Convention).

## 1.2. Characterisation: a broader context for integrated management

Characterisation is a tool designed to take the broader view required by the considerations set out above. It is leading us away from entirely site-based approaches and it draws together ideas from sustainable development about multiple ways of valuing a place, the desirability of wider participation and inclusion, and the benefits of taking a larger view in terms of scale and inter-relationships. It broadens the concept of heritage to include locally distinctive as well nationally important sites and buildings; and these may be recent as well as ancient, and semi-natural as well as built.

It also creates a broader, generalised understanding of places, putting objects in their context. Context can be seen to be as valuable as fabric: what does a building (irrespective of its special value) contribute to the area around it? How does the character of that area frame the building and give additional meaning and value to it? The characterisation process assumes that everywhere – every place – has a historical character of some description, whether that is seen as being weak or strong, much or little valued, in need of protection or of enhancement. It goes hand-in-hand with the aims of the European Landscape Convention (the ELC) by providing a tool to capture the common heritage of a place's landscape in a way that site-based records cannot easily do.

Landscape is central to characterisation. As in the ELC, landscape is taken to refer to urban as well as rural areas, everyday as well as outstanding places. Particularly important is the core meaning of landscape as being "an area, as perceived by people" – it is how people give meaning and value to the environment where they live and work (or just remember). This overall, perceived character can be more important than its individual components. Characterisation tries to capture as many as possible of the aspects (material and physical, intangible and experiential) that make landscape.

Characterisation also assumes that as a matter of course all aspects of an area or a place's historical character will as far as practicable be taken into account when designing new development, regeneration or landscape change, irrespective of the presence or not of protected monuments. It does not, of course, assume that "taking into account" means preservation of everything. It takes a step towards sustainable development by integrating an understanding of an area's historically-derived character into spatial planning and land management, so that it becomes one of the factors in designing and planning change and new development. As the concept of heritage is broadened, it becomes more evident that not everything can be preserved; the result is a recognition of varying levels of preservation and of varying ways in which a heritage object can contribute to the future landscape. Between total preservation and total loss, there are many options for a building's or a site's contribution, if it is viewed in terms of character and context as well as fabric.

Characterisation is based on three linked ideas: integrated decision making, landscape as unifying concept and spatial planning.

### Integrated decision making

Any piece of land can have not only multiple values attached to it, but also multiple land uses and demands. Conflict between them can best be resolved by integrating our understanding and by balancing different needs. This is especially so of cultural and natural values, and particularly important when institutional structures are fragmented. In the UK, for instance, cultural and natural heritage are controlled by different government ministries, different (and sometimes overlapping) state agencies and often different departments in local authorities. Spatial planning is controlled by a different ministry again. The "map" is completed by the delegation of many roles to different tiers of government, or to the private sector, whilst universities and museums also have roles of various sorts as well.

## *Landscape as unifying concept*

The ELC defines landscape as perception – and as something that is everywhere, that has multiple values and that is a general common heritage. In the sense that it belongs to everyone, and because landscape is much more than the sum of its parts, landscape brings together different viewpoints. In the traditional system, landscape features would be placed in separate compartments – for example, the list of monuments, the list of buildings, the list of habitats, the list of amenity sites and so on. Using the concept of landscape can allow all these ways of seeing (potentially at least, though not always easily) to be integrated into a single perception. Landscape also acts as the meeting place for many disciplines, so it is a first step towards integrated management.

## *Spatial planning*

This is the practical forum in which integrated management through landscape can be achieved (in conjunction, where appropriate, with legal protection through designation). In the UK, SMRs already work as part of the planning system, and consultative practices allow a wider heritage voice to be heard. Because spatial planning aims to be strategic, forward-looking and positive, it aims to treat all aspects of the cultural and natural heritage as opportunities, as potential contributions to future landscape, rather than see them only as constraints.

Several principles support characterisation as a tool for achieving a positive and heritage-friendly use of spatial planning:

- a concern for areas, not only sites – landscape-scale;
- understanding character (general inter-relationships of the heritage), not just its components;
- the importance of context and localness;
- the concept of place;
- present-day landscape (the past sits within the present: it is not separate);
- the definition of benefits and uses, as well as values;
- the recognition of multiple ways of valuing, ownership and participation;
- identifying past (and thus future) directions of change (trajectories).

In several countries, these ideas are beginning to create new ways of approaching heritage conservation that are based on the management of change, not just on the protection of fabric and objects. This approach requires new types of documentation systems such as spatial, map-based, comprehensive, character-based GIS; such new techniques are starting to change the objectives and methods of conservation and heritage management.

Finally, one further idea that emerges from characterisation is that change can be seen not just as an impact upon landscape, but more constructively as an attribute of the landscape. The results of changes in the past are very often some of the very qualities that make a place's historical character and which are appreciated by inhabitants and visitors. Working with characterisation, therefore, tells us that the effects of very recent, current and future change need to be managed so that they sustain the historic character that we have inherited, and in order that our successors can "read" and enjoy the past in their present. Sometimes change needs to be encouraged as well, and that is when the concept of trajectory – the direction of (past) change – can be used to inform new change so that it sustains the inherited historical environment and the historical land-scape as much as possible.

## 1.3. Methods and uses: examples

Characterisation in the UK is most advanced in its application to the rural landscape, partic-ularly through English Heritage's Historic Landscape Characterisation (HLC) programme. There are national frameworks: in England, landscape characterisation at a very general level is used to distinguish 159 Countryside Character Areas, and the Settlement Atlas describes regional variations in long-standing settlement patterns. Both have strategic uses for research, monitoring and land management. Landscape characterisation is recorded in more detail at county level, where the English Heritage programme of HLC also operates.

HLC is also used in urban areas. It complements and improves traditional urban archae-ological surveys and is used alongside Conservation Area Appraisal. LARA (Lincoln Archaeological Research Assessment) uses characterisation to create new understanding of a 2 000-year-old city as it is redeveloped. Areas are characterised (in several period layers) in terms of our knowledge of their past, and a research agenda is drawn up for each area to identify how best to target efforts to extend our understanding. New techniques are also being developed to characterise dense urban areas: the big cities and their most recent suburbs, areas that are often overlooked as heritage, but places where the majority of the urban population have their lives. These projects are starting to explore how to engage the local community in the process.

HLC is also starting to be used on a smaller, more local scale for large complexes of heritage land, such as disused military airfields, historic towns and nineteenth-century hospital sites at the edge of cities.

Finally, HLC is being used to start to define the sensitivity of landscape to major changes (its capacity to absorb change without complete alteration of its historical character). These are still experimental methods, but they are being used in planning large-scale developments (such as London's Thames Gateway and other expansion areas), the sort of place where heritage in the past has been confined to a few special buildings protected by being left out of the planning process. The process of considering sensitivity alone is creating better dialogue between planners and developers.

More detailed examples of using HLC and characterisation in England can be found in:

- "Characterisation", an issue of *Conservation Bulletin* (issue 47, Winter 2004-05) devoted to English Heritage's work in characterisation.

- J. Clark, J. Darlington and G. Fairclough, *Using Historic Landscape Characterisation* (English Heritage 2004).

Both can be read at (or downloaded from) www.english-heritage.org.uk/characterisation/.

## 2. Cultural heritage documentation systems in France

*Geneviève Pinçon*

The Ministry for Culture and Communication is currently giving priority to technological innovations and the renewal of information systems. Several innovative instruments bear witness to this, among them the computerised archaeological map (with the Patriarche application available from 2001) and the Renabl electronic file (file production in XML format for the general inventory).

These projects combine a traditional relational database with a geographical database, enabling archaeological sites, protected monuments, monuments under study, protection boundaries and protected areas to be placed in their relationship with their environment. These instruments for recording locations are useful not only in terms of scientific knowledge, but also for heritage management. Geographical information systems (GIS) are playing a growing part in the ministry's range of IT tools.

Localised heritage data vary widely and exist in large quantities. They must be comparable with one another so that a more coherent geographical analysis may be made. The ministry is working on data consistency and interoperability. The first step was to develop management tools to move towards applications incorporating a geographical approach. The second was to develop an XML data schema for heritage.

## 2.1. Development of management tools: the Patriarche application for archaeology as an example

This database encompasses all the archaeological heritage known to exist in the whole of French territory. By law, the Ministry for Culture has to monitor all archaeological research anywhere in the country and is, therefore, aware of every archaeological site discovered, so it can be recorded.

The aim is to obtain the fullest possible documentation of archaeological sites, with quantitative and administrative management data. Patriarche makes possible an archaeological inventory, management of development and protection issues, management of documentation, research administration, and research assistance and guidance. It also helps in drawing up the national archaeological map, including the inventorying and mapping of archaeological sites.

Patriarche was designed in the Ministry for Culture in 1998 and made available in May 2002. After further work recently, mainly on ergonomic aspects, version 2.3.2. was released to *départements*. It combines an Oracle database with the geographical information system known as ArcView 3.3. recommended by the ministry's own IT department. BusinessObjects is the tool used for searches. Patriarche is a national database generated through consolidation of the 26 regional databases. Only the island of La Réunion is not represented. Underwater archaeology is brought together in a single regional database.

Patriarche enables localised archaeological information to be used. In order to combine the information from regional and national departments, a common core has been created, comprising:

- four geo-referenced sets of archaeological entities, archaeological operations, protection and geo-administrative data;

- two non-geo-referenced sets of documentary sources and a directory of researchers' and operators' addresses.

This application enables geo-referenced data to be produced, directly recording site co-ordinates according to period, as well as cartographic retrieval (results of analyses, overviews) and cartographic navigation within the geo-referenced data.

Maps are drawn up at regional level, on the basis of cartographic holdings at varying scales (large, medium or small). The geographical database, comprising map references and the exact mapping of items, continues to be stored on local servers in the regions. Some of the many maps produced by departments provide information for use in local development plans, architectural, urban and landscape heritage protection areas (ZPPAUPs) and the like, or show zones where it is assumed that archaeology will be necessary. They are also used to help programme archaeological research, highlighting continuing investigations or gaps.

The central authority has no direct access to regions' cartography at the moment. Only attribute data can be consulted on the database. The centroid method is used for the mapping of items for data processing at national level.

This application is highly efficient (with potentially over 300 multivariate fields to fill in) and complex, but it should enable data to be communicated as set out in the new regulations. And the Patriarche application was initially designed specifically for the archaeology departments of the Ministry for Culture and Communication. A data export and import module is now needed, to facilitate exchanges between departments and institutions.

## 2.2. Production of the general inventory electronic file

The general inventory, which is being drawn up systematically using a territorial approach, produces files on architecture and other items with the assistance of another application, which also combines a relational database and a geographical information system.

The finding and subsequent examination of works is based on documentary tools that help to organise their analysis and to structure the results so as to facilitate retrieval. The heritage may be broken down into units of study: individuals, sets and families, to which two distinct approaches may be taken, sometimes simultaneously: recording and study. The aim is, by the end of the study, to obtain documentation in the form of a file. This file is an organised compilation of all the different documentary elements, texts and images (photographs, graphics, maps).

This application was produced by Pierrick Brihaye, from the Brittany region's general inventory department. His tool is based on DTD (Document Type Definition), enabling such files to be produced in XML format. This DTD comprises a model of the general structuring of the information present in the files. It is based on the tagging of the different documentary elements according to their function, organising them among themselves, independently of any form of retrieval. It enables them to be retained in the memory in a standardised and structured form suitable for automatic processing, *inter alia* for retrieval in various forms and on various media (paper, screen, disk).

These new tools now make possible the creation of a wholly digital document production chain, referred to as the "electronic file". This chain facilitates or makes feasible methodological innovations either impossible or unreasonable in a chain using paper sources. The electronic file, for instance, enables works linked to one another in various ways (typology, history, topography, etc.) to be matched *a priori*, whereas paper records could not associate them unless very time-consuming cross-referencing or manual duplication systems were used. These digital files are stored at regional level.

At national level, priority has been given to databases for documenting works: the Mérimée database for architecture, the Palissy database for movable items and the

Mémoire database to index illustrations of the works. These databases are designed as a way of indexing the file, an entry point enabling the main information to be provided in controlled form. The notice at an entry point thus indicates the existence of a file; in the case of simple works with little documentation, the notice often contains all the textual information on the work.

The electronic file may thus be directly accessed via the national databases, which act as identity cards providing access to the full file, in paper or electronic format. In the latter case, on-line availability already exists for some electronic files.

The topographical inventory run in the context of the general inventory is intended to "locate and identify" those works of such interest that "the opening of a file and the collection of essential information about them is justified". The heritage map, while rationalising and going further in both content and form than the map showing the location of selected works and those showing the works found, was intended to restore its original importance to the prime task of the topographical inventory. If the protection arrangements for buildings or parts of buildings (classified or listed), the areas of Conservation and Enhancement Plans (PSMVs) and the areas covered by Architectural, Urban and Landscape Heritage Protection Areas (ZPPAUPs) are added to this document, it becomes a vector of integrated heritage information capable of simplifying dialogue with outside agencies.

The historic monuments departments and the architecture and heritage offices of the *départements* (the SDAPs) also have at their disposal a management tool linked to a GIS for the management of historical monuments and surrounding areas.

Gestauran, for instance, is a computerised system for managing the issue of permits under land law within the remit of the architecture and heritage offices of the *départements* and the *Architectes des bâtiments de France* (heritage and architecture authority). Opinions drawn up using Gestauran are based largely on the Town Planning Code, the monuments and open spaces protection guidelines, the Environment Code and the decree of 1979, which set up the SDAPs. About 600 000 cases are dealt with every year within the time limit, using a variety of procedures. The application operates on the basis of the creation of "section-zones" encompassing restrictions on property imposed in the public interest and some details of spatial management policy, providing help with decision making and the drawing up of opinions. This approach clearly fosters the inclusion in the application of a cartographic view to be used for locating protection arrangements and town planning regulations, and offering qualitative evaluation criteria for open and built spaces.

Thus, a cartographic tool is available to the *Architectes des bâtiments de France* with which they can produce graphic records of the heritage entities they are responsible for managing. These graphic records may be linked to their Gestauran database.

## 2.3. An XML schema for heritage data

The Directorate of Architecture and Heritage decided to create an XML schema for all heritage data, and this work has been done in conjunction with a company called AJLSM. The aim is to allow different departments (archaeology, historical monuments, general inventory) to co-operate in the standardised processing of information, so the schema will by definition be usable by all partners.

With AJSLM's help, the schema was produced in January 2005. The outcome of the work done can be seen at http://projets.ajlsm.com/sdapa/. We would advise anyone seeking their first introduction to the subject to visit http://projets.ajlsm.com/sdapa/schema/guidelines/index.html.

The schema currently covers the transcription of documents relating to:

– archaeology (Patriarche, regional scientific overviews),

– the general inventory (file),

– historic monuments (files), and

– protected areas (ZPPAUP database).

Architecture is being tackled now, with a database being set up for cultural establishments. In the near future, the schema should be opened to ethnological data.

The aim of the DAPA schema is to offer a structuring model for architecture and heritage-related information, enabling all the documents produced by the various heritage departments on a single heritage item to be shared and recovered.

The language selected is XML (Extensible Mark-Up Language), the international standard for the Internet adopted by W3C (a consortium producing free and open standards and protocols with a view to maximum interoperability). This format is independent of software editors, is used for storage irrespective of retrieval methods chosen and is pivotal to exchanges between heterogeneous systems, as well as being recommended by the ADAE (the French e-government agency).

The DAPA XML schema fits in with departments' current working methods and offers for each category a drafting method appropriate to its subject, both compatible with and complementary to existing systems.

The schema redefines the data (structures and attributes) in each base in XML exchange standard, and documents their meaning and therefore their use. The schema does not validate an XML document as such. Instead, it defines in advance the elements, which then receive the corresponding content from each base. For example, the DAPA XML schema's "place" tag – metadata relating to the place described – will be able to contain the descriptive attributes of a city or just one street in that city, or the land register geo-referencing attributes, or geo-referencing attributes in either.

As well as the data derived from specific aspects of heritage trades, the DAPA schema also defines transverse elements common to all DAPA trades, bibliographic references, descriptions of illustrations, locations – using geolocation-geocoding in XML or geo-referencing in GML (Geographical Mark-up Language), biographical information and relationships within a document (in the form of hyperlinks).

In order to provide a practical illustration of this, a document in DAPA XML schema format is currently being created, through the compiling of scattered data, using the various heritage data produced by the *départements* in the Rhône-Alpes region.

This XML schema can potentially create a file on a heritage element containing all observations from the individual specialisms (protection, architectural study, archaeological study, etc.), *inter alia* through XML exports of different departments' applications. A single schema and a single structure are shared by people using their own language.

The Directorate of Architecture and Heritage wishes to set up technical architectures and interfaces enabling data to be located. The aim is to offer a portal placing all sources of heritage data in a single network. This is a need particularly felt when one of the links in the heritage chain, the general inventory, is going out to the regions. For this study, the ministry is drawing on the experience of the Aquitaine region, which is building up its own knowledge bank. A portal gives access to various data sources on the different partners' servers. The different sources are indexed in a standard metadata format (Dublin Core). They are integrated into the portal through automatic collection of metadata using the OAI (Open Archive Initiative) protocol for metadata harvesting.

## 2.4. Conclusion

It has now become normal for departments to create maps showing the precise location of the heritage elements that they deal with. These ought to be harmonised, producing as full and accurate as possible a map of the documented heritage entities. At the moment, however, it is difficult to achieve this nationwide. This is because the data are dispersed, there is no tradition of work among different heritage departments, the staff are often under pressure, departments lack appropriate equipment and hardware, and significant and time-consuming efforts are required.

The creation of the architecture and heritage atlas, in particular, should help with the production of such maps. The atlas project was begun by the Directorate of Architecture and Heritage of the Ministry for Culture and Communication in order to meet the need for information retrieval: of knowledge of the heritage (archaeological, architectural, urban and landscape), of heritage potential and of protected status in a given area. The need for such retrieval very much stems from ever-increasing demands by the ministry's various partners.

The heritage units described by the inventory (archaeological, classified or listed as historical monuments, sited in conservation areas or in ZPPAUPs) all have at least one location attribute. This criterion is vital to indexing them and viewing them on maps or plans, which is a straightforward way of apprehending them, but is absolutely essential if we are to look beyond typology or classification to the spatial dimension.

The prime aim is to make available to departments the information derived from the specific work each of them does, to make data comparisons possible and thus to embark on a fuller interdisciplinary approach necessitating collaboration between departments.

The usefulness of this atlas was emphasised when the archaeological map was drawn up, to warn both developers selecting building sites and local elected representatives preparing town planning documents. During discussions on preventive archaeology, it was pointed out that this archaeological mapping needed to be supplemented by an inventory of buildings, historical monuments and protected spaces and sites. In several kinds of area, such as towns and conurbations, elected local representatives are already calling for the structured and geo-referenced heritage information they need to take into account for spatial planning purposes.

## 3. GIS systems in Germany

*Friedrich Lüth*

The Federal Republic of Germany is based on 16 separate states, each of which has legal responsibility for its cultural heritage. There is no legal responsibility at federal level and consequently no federal agency active in cultural heritage.

Within their legal responsibility each of the 16 states has set up a legal framework to manage the cultural heritage, and consequently each state has its own system, both legal and administrative.

### 3.1. Beginnings

Ever since the early nineteenth century, people living in the area now covered by the 16 states have been collecting information about their entire past. This information has been assembled in (paper) archives, which are organised and kept by the different states. Although Germany has undergone rough times in its history, a lot of archive material has survived, even through several war periods.

Since the mid-1970s, projects have been launched to transfer the existing information into electronic archives. None of these first attempts was ever completed and all of them were stopped halfway, leaving a new collection of partly transferred material.

From the 1980s, attempts were made in the former federal Republic of (western) Germany to create electronic databases. The State Agencies for the protection of the Archaeological Sites and Monuments of the Rhineland and Baden-Württemberg were the leading agencies. These attempts were very successful and they are still running in modified ways with modernised techniques.

In the former German Democratic Republic, no attempts were made to create electronic databases, most probably due to the lack of adequate equipment. Archaeological investigations and scientific research have produced huge amounts of evidence and a vast amount of data; all this information was entered into the paper archives. The organisation was centralised through the Academy of Sciences and regional offices for the management of the archaeological heritage.

After the fall of the iron curtain the administration was re-organised, following major changes in the legal framework. The former eastern GDR was divided into five "new" states and the legal responsibility was devolved from the central government down to state level.

Immediately there was a need for new "regional" archives within the eastern German states and the need for precise information was enormous, since there was a concerted effort to develop the eastern part of Germany in order to raise standards there and reach the quality of organisation in the western parts. This was the moment when it seemed urgent to move to a modern system.

## 3.2. The stage now reached

In order to bring about the new digital age, the federal government launched a programme to reclassify the listed archaeological sites and monuments as well as listed buildings and protected areas. Since every existing entry had to undergo an immediate check, sufficient electronic equipment (hardware and software) was provided and from 1991 to 1994 generous support was handed out to the governments in the accession states in order for this work to proceed fast enough.

In the archaeological records, the information from the traditional paper archives was transferred into a very basic database of dBase type. The information was taken 1:1 into a simple spreadsheet with all administrative data; co-ordinates were taken from a map to mark the centre of a site.

Scientific information was categorised only by type and date of site, whether any finds were known or excavation had been carried out, the date of discovery of the site and the latest date of inspection by the state agency or the volunteers.

Any other information about finds and inventory numbers, possible publications or anything else, was re-typed into a free-access field. This work was carried out by three or four archaeologists and an assistant between 1994 and 2004. The number of entries for sites and monuments (many of them lost over past centuries) has reached 91 000.

In the year 2000, the first attempt was made to transfer the database into a GIS-system. This was successfully completed at the beginning of 2001. The next step, from 2001 to 2004, was an extensive site-management project that aimed to visit all the visible sites and monuments, to check the co-ordinates with a portable GIS-connected laptop, to describe the status of each monument and to take photographs.

## 3.3. Handling the system

Sites are shown up to a scale of 1:2 000. The state agency for surveying provides different maps and these can be used as a background through the menu. There is even a historical map from the middle of the nineteenth century provided, which is useful when using old recordings and descriptions of the sites from those days.

The system is very easy to handle: to locate a site, you can go either from the map through zooming down or you can search for a site through the menu.

Sites were mapped in the first phase by a spot in the centre of the site; the second phase showed their real size on the map. Pointing at the map opens the site register with all entered information. And here starts the modern approach of electronic government, so-called e-government: any action taken is recorded directly into the system, even in the field. There is no need to take paper notes and transfer them later. Even digital photographs can immediately be entered in the system.

When connecting the laptop to the mainframe system in the agency, a printout of every new entry is automatically produced and this goes to the paper archive. A supervisor checks when there is a double entry for the same site.

Through the main menu a selection of criteria is possible. Through this selection process, any kind of distribution map can be produced. Examples are shown for megalithic graves, bronze-age tumuli, mediaeval castles, hill forts and submerged sites in the Baltic Sea. Different maps can be produced for specific uses, such as landscape mapping, tourist planning or scientific research.

ARCHAEO-GIS is shown under ATKIS data, using vector-based digital maps provided by the State Agency for Surveying. The Software used is an ArcVIEW format, in ESRI standard. The outcome is shape-files that can easily be transferred as overlays onto other maps.

The system can immediately react to a request for maps needed in planning or any pre-investment phase. By creating a shape-file, overlays can be produced and can be laid over other files, such as forestry maps, agricultural maps, land-use maps, or geological and hydrographical maps.

Finally, the database has to be as easy to use as possible, with all the relevant administrative data and the necessary scientific information. Any further details can easily be added at any time later.

## 4. Documentation of the cultural heritage of the historic centre of Riga

*Juris Dambis*

In 1997 the Historic Centre of Riga was added to the UNESCO World Heritage List, which is evidence of the site's universal cultural value that should be preserved for the sake of all humanity.

### 4.1. The aims

There are three aims associated with documenting the Historic Centre of Riga:

- to create an information system for planning with the aim of ensuring sustainable development;
- to create an information database capable of performing management and monitoring of changes and development;
- to record the current situation in detail, in order to have a point of reference for the future.

The territory of the Historic Centre of Riga covers 1.4% of the total territory of Riga (435 ha), it contains 193 blocks of buildings and 4 500 buildings. The Historic Centre of Riga has four elements that deserve to be protected:

- its historic urban structure;
- panoramic views, silhouettes and street perspectives;
- its historic building pattern, including medieval buildings, *art nouveau* architecture and wooden buildings;
- public open spaces, together with a green zone.

## 4.2. Action plan

These three aims were pursued through an action plan to:

- draft a documentation system, on the basis of examples from other European countries in order to create the system adapted for local needs;

- draft a digital map at a scale that allows viewing of separate buildings in comparison with historical plans;

- train experts for inspection work and purchase necessary technical equipment;

- develop the inventory content (through fieldwork) by recording:
  a) address
  b) owner
  c) status (listed building or not)
  d) period of construction
  e) original use of the building
  f) architectural style
  g) actual use of the building
  h) number of storeys (above the ground),
  i) material(s) and type of construction
  j) windows of the main facade (authentic to the construction period or changed)
  k) windows of the main facade, by predominant material (wood, metal, plastic)
  l) outer doors of the main facade (authentic to the construction period or changed)
  m) outer doors of the main facade, by predominant material (wood, metal, plastic)
  n) transoms [lintels] of the outer doorways of the main facade (authentic to the construction period or changed)
  o) transoms [lintels] of the outer doorways of the main facade, by predominant material (wood, metal, plastic)
  p) finish or rendering of the facade
  q) interior decoration of the rooms open to public access
  r) evaluation of the building's technical condition (on a 10-point scale)
  s) work necessary for stabilisation, renovation or repair
  t) the role of the building in the historic centre (on a 5-degree system)
  u) an up-to-date photograph of the building
  v) information on whether recent repairs are visible (yes or no)

w) information on whether there is visible damage caused by reconstruction and/or building elements degrading the environment of the historic centre (yes or no).

## 4.3. Review of the information and digitalisation

Following the fieldwork, the information gathered has been used to:

- determine the comparative cultural and historical value of each building (on a 10-point scale, each building evaluated by five independent experts),
- evaluate blocks of buildings and parts of the city,
- draft thematic maps showing:
  - date of construction of the buildings
  - technical condition of the buildings
  - construction material of the buildings
  - number of storeys
  - cultural assets of the buildings
  - evaluation of public open spaces
  - evaluation of blocks of buildings
  - sites of lost buildings and development possibilities.
- match the database with the daily monitoring and management work on site.

## 4.4. Conclusions

Evaluation should be complex, and based on definite, adopted criteria; it should regard the city as a whole, not just as separate buildings, and it should reflect:

- the value of building pattern in the planning structure,
- the value of blocks in the town plan,
- the value of parts of historical centre with different building patterns.

It is important to create one's own user-friendly database for certain circumstances, which can be utilised by all interested and responsible institutions involved in site management.

Databases should contain enough information for daily use in managing separate buildings, but the most important aspect is to use them for managing the whole city. Collection of information should be performed so that it is easy to classify it. One should avoid collecting information that is not of use – the database should not become a scientific study, but be the basic tool for planning and site management.

# PART 3

## ENVIRONMENTAL ASSESSMENT

# Comparative summary of environmental assessments – RPSEE countries

*Myriam Goblet*

## 1. Environmental impact assessment

Environmental impact assessments are a key stage in the decision-making process and form part of the "technical documentation" that is a precondition for the adoption of major projects by public policymakers. As a result of the light they shed, they constitute a decision support tool.

Environmental impact assessments have a direct bearing on the cultural and natural heritage, since they analyse the impact of large projects on the environment, of which the heritage is an integral part.

All the countries analysed possess this tool. This in itself is very positive and provides a good working basis.

## 2. Competent authorities

The authority responsible for following up and adopting environmental impact assessments may be:

- the Ministry of the Environment (Albania, Bosnia and Herzegovina, Bulgaria, Croatia, Romania),
- or the Ministry of Spatial Planning (Serbia),
- or the Ministry of the Environment and Spatial Planning (Montenegro and "the former Yugoslav Republic of Macedonia").

These ministries often work in collaboration with their regional/ supra-local departments.

There is nothing surprising about this, since environmental impact assessments are at the very intersection of the heritage, the environment and spatial planning: the impact on the environment (of which the heritage is part) is studied before granting environmental permits or planning permission (for construction, renovation or demolition, or for change of use) and before adopting spatial planning schemes.

Environmental impact assessments thus constitute the first integrated management tool analysed and recommended by the Regional Programme for Cultural and Natural Heritage in South-East Europe.

## 3. Study authors

The production of environmental impact assessments is usually assigned to private experts (individuals or legal entities). It is sometimes the responsibility of public institutions or other public bodies when the work to be assessed has been proposed by a public body. This applies, for example, in Romania to measures initiated by the Ministry of Transport, Construction and Tourism in natural areas at risk and in Serbia in the case of spatial and urban planning schemes. In Montenegro, the initiators of projects can enlist the aid of both the private and public sectors (scientific or research institutions).

The authors of these studies are responsible for the data and the recommendations they make, which they must issue in compliance with current laws and regulations. They must not have any personal interest in the execution of the project to be assessed.

These experts are usually listed in a special register of experts certified by the ministry responsible (Bulgaria, Croatia, Romania, Serbia and "the former Yugoslav Republic of Macedonia"). In some countries, such as "the former Yugoslav Republic of Macedonia", they must meet a range of criteria and sit an examination to acquire the status of impact-assessment experts.

Experts are always paid by the project initiator, whether the latter be a private individual or entity (investor/ developer) or a public body (ministry, local authority).

## 4. Legal basis

The production of environmental impact assessments is a statutory obligation in all the countries studied (in most cases this has been so since the year 2000). The environment or spatial planning laws provide for this obligation, while orders, regulations, decrees, directives or sets of rules (which vary from one country to another) elaborate on it, specifying the procedures and conditions for, and scope of, impact assessments. A list of the types of project subject to these assessments is often attached to these documents. These are of two types of assessment: they involve either development work (construction, infrastructure, etc.) (generally known as environmental impact assessment) or plans and programmes (development, management, etc.) that may have an impact on the environment in the broad sense of the word (generally known as strategic environmental assessment).

## 5. Types of projects assessed

In all the countries, impact assessments are required for projects involving work relating to:

- industry (energy, chemicals, textiles, paper, copper, other metals, resource extraction and food);
- water and waste treatment;

- agriculture and forestry;
- transport infrastructure (railways, tramways, airports, roads and ports);
- tourism and entertainment projects (hotel complexes, camp sites, theme parks).

In some countries, impact assessments are also required for projects involving work relating to:
- fishing and hunting (Serbia, Montenegro);
- telecommunications and new technologies (Serbia, Montenegro);
- sports facilities (Croatia);
- building complexes (Croatia, Montenegro);
- rural rehabilitation projects and the construction of shopping arcades and car parks (Albania).

In Bulgaria, the legislation requires the developer to carry out not only an Environmental Impact Assessment for any development project, but also an Ecological Assessment (a kind of sectoral EIA) for all plans and programmes relating to agriculture, forestry, transport, energy, waste management, water management, tourism and development. The same applies to urban and spatial planning programmes and flora and fauna protection schemes in Serbia and Montenegro.

## 6. Categories of impact assessment

Given that these various projects are likely to have different levels of impact on the environment, in most cases (Albania, Bosnia and Herzegovina, Bulgaria, Romania, Montenegro) the legislation wisely provides for two categories of assessment:
- compulsory in-depth assessments for projects the environmental impact of which is thought to be "large" owing to their nature, size or location;
- less detailed assessments for projects the environmental impact of which could be merely "significant".

The second category of assessment is sometimes included in a list of measures provided for by law (Albania), but is more often left to the discretion of the ministry responsible, following a case-by-case examination (Bulgaria, Romania, "the former Yugoslav Republic of Macedonia"). In Bosnia and Herzegovina, the Ministry of the Environment decides whether to carry out a more detailed examination (first category) on the basis of the results of a preliminary study (second category).

In Montenegro, the regulations do not distinguish between projects on the basis of their potential environmental impact. This absence of a threshold beyond which an impact assessment is required acts as a disincentive to carry out assessments and affects their actual quality. New regulations are being drawn up to solve this problem.

## 7. Types of environmental impact

Environmental impact assessments must identify, describe and assess, in an appropriate manner, in each individual case, the direct and indirect impact of the project on the environment, specifically on:

- health and human living conditions,
- flora and fauna,
- the soil, territory and countryside,
- water,
- the air and the climate,
- material values and the cultural heritage.

They also analyse the interaction between these different types of impact as well as between the project examined and other planned projects when there could be a cumulative impact on the environment under consideration.

In Romania, particular attention is paid to certain sensitive or environmentally important geographical areas such as parks and nature reserves, protected areas and countryside of special historical, cultural or archaeological significance. It often happens that environmental impact assessments are carried out in the case of the siting of new buildings in the historical context of a protected area. In Bucharest, for example, an impact study was carried out to decide whether to build new, higher buildings, including skyscrapers, in the historic districts of the city and where to site them.

In Montenegro, all measures planned in protected natural areas are subject to an impact assessment.

In Croatia, impact assessments concerning the cultural and historical heritage are based on documentation from the competent institutions (ministries, museums, etc.) and on information from the relevant literature and visits to the site where the measure is planned. They assess the existence (or otherwise) of cultural and historical assets and potential threats to them and conclude by recommending the appropriate protection measures and a programme to monitor the state of the environment.

It is, however, difficult to determine from the national reports whether environmental impact assessments cover underground archaeological heritage in the case of large construction or infrastructure projects.

## 8. Content of impact assessments

Impact assessments usually consist of the following elements:

- description of the project;

- description and analysis of the elements of the environment that could be put at risk by the project;
- description and assessment of the likely major impacts on the environment;
- description of the measures/alternatives envisaged to lessen the adverse effects of the project;
- conclusions and possibly an outline of the alternatives, in compliance with current legislation.

In Bosnia and Herzegovina, a non-technical summary is made of impact assessments.

## 9. Decision-making process

Once the assessment report has been completed, the decision-making process involves several more stages:

- taking advice from the authorities affected by the project and already involved in preparing the study: the ministries of the Environment, Spatial Planning, Tourism, Agriculture and Forestry, Transport, Economic Affairs, Energy, Culture and so on, as well as regional/local authorities;
- gathering opinions from the public affected and of organisations specialising in environmental affairs. Organising public information campaigns in the national and local press and perhaps on radio and television may be the job of the competent ministry (Bosnia and Herzegovina, Croatia, "the former Yugoslav Republic of Macedonia") or of the project initiator (Romania);

  N.B: In Montenegro, public consultation is not compulsory, but the ministry can organise this in the case of projects that have a major negative impact;

- preparation of the report containing the results of this public consultation and the opinions of the authorities concerned; only reasoned opinions submitted by the deadlines specified are considered;
- an assessment of the study by the competent ministry, which may enlist the help of an outside expert (Montenegro) or a commission (Croatia) consisting of members of national and local administrative authorities (in the locality affected by the project), the scientific community and professional circles;
- final approval by the ministry responsible, in the form of an official document called an "environment permit" (Bosnia and Herzegovina), a "resolution" (Bulgaria), "official approval" (Serbia), "ecological authorisation" (Montenegro) or a "decision" approving or refusing permission, valid for two years ("the former Yugoslav Republic of Macedonia");
- the grant of other permits necessary to carry out the project (operating permits, planning permission, etc.).

## 10. Influence on the heritage

The national reports do not enable us to clearly establish the influence of impact assessments and environment permits on preservation of the heritage, although such an influence does exist. As emphasised by Serbia, the fact that impact assessments are carried out does not automatically result in the impacts concerned being taken into account at the decision making and operational levels.

Moreover, it is difficult to assess to what extent the authorities responsible for the heritage are actually involved in drawing up and approving impact assessments and acting on their recommendations. In "the former Yugoslav Republic of Macedonia", for example, the new law on the heritage states that it is compulsory to obtain the opinion of the Office for the Protection of the Cultural Heritage when the study is being drawn up and that this body is empowered to monitor the impact of pollution on buildings forming part of the cultural heritage and their immediate surroundings. However, this measure is not yet being implemented.

Strategic environmental assessment (SEA) for plans and programmes has been introduced in some countries (Albania, Bulgaria, Serbia). However, it is also not clear whether heritage considerations are being fully recognised through this process. The development of SEA procedures should help to ensure a more integrated approach through the consideration of heritage interests in spatial and urban plans and development programmes and strateges such as for regional tourism strategies (cf example of good practice: Albania's southern coast, heritage and tourism impact assessment).

# Examples of good practice in environmental assessment

## 1. Environmental impact assessment for the landscape of Tåkern-Omberg, Sweden

*Ann Mari Westerlind*

The Swedish National Road Administration has used Environmental Impact Assessments (EIAs) in parts of their processes since 1981. In the beginning, cultural heritage was not well treated. With the Council Directive 97/11EC of 3 March 1997 and new Swedish legislation of 1999, it became obvious that cultural heritage should be part of an EIA. Since 1993, the Swedish National Heritage Board has produced several reports and recommendations on EIA and there has been much co-operation with the National Road Administration. The procedures for deciding on new main roads are often very long. The process of upgrading part of main road 50 – Rv50, which crosses an open historic landscape in the eastern part of Sweden – is one example.

The important parts of an EIA-process are the character of the project, the character of the place, the steps in the process and the participation of different actors. This chapter follows the process.

### 1.1. The preliminary investigation, 1994

Rv50 was made part of the national road network in 1993. It was important for national heavy transport from the southern interior through the middle and to the north of Sweden, as well as for regional traffic. Part of Rv50 goes from Ödeshög to Motala, past Omberg Hill and Lake Tåkern, where the standard of the existing road varies. The road passes through towns and villages, causing noise, pollutions and accidents, even in the countryside.

The intention in 1994 was to give the road a higher standard in order to benefit national and regional transport, increase traffic safety and decrease pollution, noise and barriers. There should be due regard for areas of national interest of heritage, nature, recreation and agriculture. The standard road width was 13 m, which meant a "road area" corridor about 25 m wide. The existing roads were 6-7 m wide, but without protection areas.

The interests of heritage and nature of the landscape were presented on a map where areas of five classes of protection values were marked in different colours. The map was a summary of all registered objects in the area. There was practically no ground without some such interest marked.

Four possible routes were discussed: West (following the existing Rv50), Middle and East (two new roads) and Rv32 (in parts new and in part following an existing regional road). The impacts on heritage and nature were high in every case, as were the impacts on agriculture, water, recreational and residential areas.

People living in the area did not want any of the routes. Different NGO groups were formed. Private heritage experts acted. They claimed that the area of national heritage interest – with a collection of valuable heritage from prehistoric to mediaeval epochs – was comparable with only a few other areas in Sweden. The road authorities used an external expert to comment on the investigation.

### The heritage expert

The view of the heritage expert was that the reasons for building a new road through the Omberg–Tåkern area must be very strong, in view of the following:

- the Omberg–Tåkern area, the old agricultural area of Östergötland with its special natural and geographical features, must be seen as an entirety.

- lake Tåkern was the basis for the oldest culture.

- the area has been in constant use since the Stone Age.

- this was also a highly valued and rich district during the Iron Age.

- the area was of great importance in mediaeval times.

- it was characterised by great farming villages in the sixteenth and seventeenth centuries.

- its character shifted during the nineteenth century and became a landscape of big farms.

- there are few visible archaeological remains left.

The heritage expert's conclusion was that the values of national interest in the area needed to be better described.


## 1.2. The second investigation, 1995

The Road Administration for the South-East District decided to continue with investigations of the East, Rv50 and Rv32 routes. The standard for building new roads was 13 m and for rebuilding 9 m. Compared to the existing road, there was less flexibility in the form of the road and the number of private entrances had to be reduced. The aim was to make as little impact as possible on heritage areas of national and Class I regional interest. Two possibilities were studied: new roads and improvements of existing roads.

As the basis for the EIA, the authorities ordered a complementary study of heritage within two very narrow corridors. The study was to include the pattern of the old buildings as structures of cultivation, ownerships and communications, as well as individual monuments in the form of villages, farms, buildings and archaeological remains. The study was required to include an analysis of the need to remove objects and a description and judgement of the consequences.

These studies on patterns of colonisation were academic texts without conclusions and were not used in the EIA. The register of protected archaeological remains was produced to suit the Swedish legislation about archaeology and not to be part of the EIA judgements.

### Analysis of the Omberg–Tåkern landscape

The National Heritage Board produced an analysis of the values of the Omberg–Tåkern area. This study presented three important epochs and three important themes that, between them, had given the landscape its present character:

- the structure of the mediaeval central district is still clear in the landscape.

- since large-scale agriculture was introduced in the nineteenth century, there have been few changes: towns and other urban areas have grown, but there have been no new settlements.

- the agricultural district of Omberg–Tåkern is obviously uniform and characteristic of a plain.

- the churches and the great farms, with the roads between farms and fields, form a large-scale pattern all over the plain and show the growth of a district of rich farmers.

- the borders of the cultivated district are based on natural conditions; all the fertile soil has been cultivated, so there has been no need for new structures or communications.

### The epochs that have shaped the Omberg–Tåkern landscape

In prehistoric times, the rich soil encouraged settlement, and people have cultivated the plain around the lake from the Stone Age until today. The plain was densely populated, with settlements in all parts. Settlements are known mainly near the former shores of the lake, but maybe the higher parts of the area were also populated. Magnates controlled the area: graves and heaps from the Bronze Age show that there was a governing society in the area, of higher importance than in other parts of the county of Östergötland.

Imported goods were found in the material from both the Stone and Bronze Ages. Trade developed during the Iron Age.

Mediaeval times were the period of the royal dynasties. The western part of the plain in Östergötland, around Lake Vättern, was a centre for national politics in the Viking Age and the Middle Ages. The Sverker dynasty owned an estate in Alvastra; the Bjälbo dynasty owned one in Bjälbo and one in Vadstena. The Monastery of Alvastra was an international and cultural centre. Together with the monasteries in Vadstena and Skänninge, this area had the greatest concentration of monasteries in Sweden. They owned many farms and introduced new means of cultivation and crafts. Skänninge was a Hanseatic town as important as Kalmar and Visby. The port of Hästholmen was a trading place until the fifteenth century, when Vadstena took over that role.

In the nineteenth century, large-scale capitalistic agriculture brought improvements in the structure of agriculture and a spirit of enterprise amongst big farmers. New infrastructure – the Göta Channel and the railway – enabled Hästholmen and Borghamn to develop.

### The themes that have shaped the Omberg–Tåkern landscape

National history has shaped the district. The fertile soil, the good local climate and its situation at the crossing-point of east–west trading communications made it a centre of power and a place for kings.

The mediaeval network of roads is the frame of the network of roads today. Many roads still follow the ancient riding paths along the higher ground and the borders of the landscape.

The agricultural landscape remains a major influence. There are remains of mediaeval villages connected to the churches, but the area is today characterised by the social and economic reforms of the eighteenth and nineteenth centuries, with some very large farms and some small, landless plots.

### Opinions and advice

The regional museum made written comments on the consequences of the suggested alternatives:

- the integrity of the landscape would be split.
- the entire area of national heritage interest would be vulnerable.
- the major widening of roads would be negative for the urban areas concerned.
- there would be a huge impact on heritage values in all cases.

The material presented in the EIA was one map showing the areas of national interest for nature, heritage and recreation. These areas were to be protected from obvious damage in line with Swedish law. The areas were presented with short texts and photos. Other heritage areas were presented as sites of different values within narrow corridors: Class I – highest protection value, high value for understanding continuity; Class II - very high protection value, with representative or unique items of value; Class III – high protection value, including archaeological remains not contributing to understanding continuity; and Class IV – possible site of archaeological remains.

The descriptions of impact were based on the inventories, studies of maps and photos, and visits to the area. The consequences for heritage were presented in the EIA in text that was difficult to understand along with clear pictures, but without text analysis, and maps. The consequences for heritage were items removed, barriers erected, visual impacts and loss of experiences. The map showed different small sites with numbers, listed in tables. The text could for instance say: "Site O10 (III) old house of a teacher – no impact" or "Site 13 (III) stone for road maintenance, old bridge, old farmers shop and small farm – no physical impact". The summary said that broadening the existing road would not cause a great impact as it followed the old structures.

The suggestions for reducing noise and accidents in villages along the road were illustrated by, for example, a photo showing the situation today compared to a drawing of the road with high fences. The result in this case was that the line of a new road was drawn outside the village. The best descriptions of the impacts were those concerning impacts on "the view of landscape", which wrote about the form of the new roads not being adapted to the old patterns, the road passing the villages instead of serving them and the impact of mounds and fences to avoid noise.

The summary of the consequences was: "A new road in a landscape without earlier roads will damage heritage. Improving the existing roads is better as long as the existing buildings are not densely situated next to each other or close to the road." This conclusion could have been reached without any heritage investigations.

The regional authority announced that the two main roads ought to be improved as soon as possible. The importance of care and protection of valuable buildings and archaeological objects was stressed. As part of its formal opinion on the National Plan for Road Investigations 1998, the National Heritage Board proposed to the government that Rv50 should become a Cultural Route.

The process and findings were presented in the 1999 TemaNord report "Heritage in Environmental Impact Assessments – a collection of examples", which suggested several lessons for the future:

- linking the project's aims and the objectives for the area would strengthen the investigation.
- a programme for the investigation was needed that would identify the critical and most relevant questions, avoiding a huge investigation with work leading nowhere.

- developing methods of analysing impacts on landscapes at a structural level and ordering them early in the process would avoid large amounts of work on registrations and inventories.

- the use of indicators and clear judgements of heritage values would improve the process.

- maps were needed that would present heritage values.

## 1.3. An overall analysis of the landscape, 2001

The National Road Administration was ordered by the government to produce a new investigation into the "design" of better communications across the Omberg–Tåkern area. The values of nature and heritage should be considered, the National Heritage Board and National Board of Environment were invited to co-operate, and a landscape architect was engaged as a consultant. The task was to produce a better presentation of the entire landscape in such a way that it could be understood and used by the road authorities. This is what part of the summary said:

> "The landscape around Omberg and Tåkern, between Motala in the north and road E4 in the south, is really a landscape of national importance. It is an area of great importance in Swedish history. In the important area, communications on land and water crossed each other from south to north and east to west. The network of roads of today is mainly the same as on the maps from the eighteenth century. Many of them have certainly been there since prehistoric and mediaeval times. The flat plain has been cultivated and has been producing wealth for thousands of years. The area is rich in remains of human activities from all epochs since the last ice period. The area is probably one of the most important heritage areas in the country."

The aim of the report was to clarify the heritage context of the landscape and to inform decision-makers of the objectives from a heritage point of view that should be fulfilled by a new traffic system. The regional road administration intended the new heritage investigation to include an environmental impact assessment (EIA).

The process began with experts from different disciplines gathering with maps for several round-the-table discussions. The consultant listened, asked questions and put the material together between meetings. The first meetings were used to "tell the story of the landscape" and the later meetings were to formulate the objectives, which were related to various heritage values: of knowledge, of experience and of function.

The presentation of different areas was based on the earlier report from the National Heritage Board. The three epochs – prehistory, the mediaeval age and the nineteenth century – and the themes of communications, national history and agricultural history were used – together with the geography – to define characteristic smaller districts within the larger area.

The smaller areas were: the Border District in the South – between the forests and the plain with many archaeological remains; the District of Powerful People – the area around Lake Tåkern with fertile soil, many roads, churches and farms; the Districts of Forests in the East – with old roads, archaeological remains but less cultivated land; Vadstena – a town from the fifteenth century; and Skänninge – a town from the twelfth century.

There was a discussion about the functions of a new, fast national road. It would pass most farms and villages, so local traffic would not be able to use it. It would be broader and straighter than the old, with crossings on different levels, the light poles and signs placed up high and so on.

## Heritage Objectives

Representatives of the road administration, regional authorities, museum and national heritage authorities co-operated to formulate heritage objectives for the future road system, using a method introduced by the National Road Administration as a result of a project called Objectives and Indicators. The objectives were presented through illustrations.

The overall objective was defined thus: "It shall be possible for future generations to experience the historical diversity and character of the area. That means that the characteristic cultivated landscape, buildings and communications shall be preserved."

Objectives for the entire landscape:

- any new road shall follow and strengthen the forms of the terrain.
- it must still be possible to use the cultivated ground rationally even in the future.
- the existing network of roads shall be used for local and regional transport and tourist traffic.
- the system of roads must make it possible to visit and show heritage treasures.

Objectives for appointed heritage areas of high value:

- areas of great importance for their history shall be preserved.
- important historic connections and structures shall be preserved.
- important connections in villages shall be preserved and developed.
- the system of roads must improve the experience of heritage areas and remains.

Objectives for urban areas:

- the silhouettes of the towns must be visible from the roads.
- the boundaries between town and countryside shall continue to be distinct.
- traffic through Vadstena should be reduced.

Future questions to be used in the EIA:

- will the heritage characteristics of the area be improved or reduced?
- will the possibilities of preserving valuable heritage sites be increased or decreased?
- will conditions for people living or working in the area be better or worse?
- will it be more possible or less possible to experience and enjoy the heritage qualities of the area?
- will the damage to heritage caused by pollution, noise and vibration increase or decrease?

The background was presented as the last chapter, which presented the forms of the landscape today, the natural structures, the history of the people and the roads.

## 1.4. The third investigation, 2003

Four possibilities were presented: Zero (no improvements), Zeroplus (improvements of existing roads), Rv50 and Rv 32. In two of them, Zeroplus and Rv50, different improvements were suggested, but both had Rv50 as the national road and Rv32 as a regional road. In the fourth option, Rv32, that road was to be the national road of a high standard, with Rv50 as a low-standard road for local traffic.

The conclusion of the EIA was that the Rv32 option was best for nature, heritage and recreation; it could run near the railway, which would reduce its impact on the landscape. The government later decided to accept that solution. The road has not been built yet because of lack of money.

In the EIA, the material from the heritage analysis was used in different ways. The description of the natural values of the landscape stressed the importance of historical myths and the cultivated areas, as well as the strong connections between Omberg Hill and Lake Tåkern. In the description of heritage, photos and maps illustrated the valued features pointed out in the heritage report.

The text about the road in the landscape discussed the history and connections between the road and the natural and cultural landscape. The visual problems were the proportions and scale of the road, its close proximity to buildings and the management of side areas. The functional problems were to connect roads of different importance and function to existing buildings and roads. The visitor problems were opportunities to stop, drive slowly, get good views and reach sights and monuments.

The heritage objectives from the report were used in the EIA summary:

- the overall objective – "It shall be possible for future generations to experience the historical diversity and character of the area. That means that the characteristic cultivated landscape, buildings and communications shall be preserved" – would not be met by Zeroplus and Rv50.

- the objectives for the entire landscape – "The road shall follow the character of the landscape, existing forms must not be broken and new dominating forms must not be created. The road must not become a barrier and fragment the cultivated landscape which must be used in the future. The existing net of roads is important for the landscape and for the people living there" – would not be met by any of the four options.
- the objectives about preservation – "Concerning areas of historical values as archaeological remains, the monasteries, the churches, towns and villages and the structure of settlements and roads" – would not be met by Zeroplus and Rv50.
- the objectives for towns – "Concerning silhouettes and the distinct borders of the towns and the reduction of traffic in Vadstena" – would be met by any of the options.

## 1.5. Summary

Rv50 will become a road for people living and working in the area, and for tourists. The actions of NGOs, heritage authorities and experts have been successful, even though it took a long time.

The advice from the National Heritage Board is to:

- try to understand the type and scale of project,
- describe clearly the heritage values visible in the landscape of today,
- formulate distinct heritage objectives in co-operation with the project leader,
- be active in the process from the beginning and do not give up.

## 2. Albania's southern coast, heritage and tourism: impact assessments

*Jacques Rémy*

## 2.1. Local context: heritage, a collateral damage of development or an asset to valorise?

Any southbound visitor traversing the Llogara Pass is struck by the beauty of the landscape and the authentic character of the traditional villages. The thought immediately comes to mind that one has just discovered one of the very last pristine coastlines on this side of the Mediterranean. Called "the Mediterranean's best-kept secret", the Albanian southern coast has steep mountains and cliffs falling into the sea, ravines, coves and long open beaches, but the landscape is also endowed with remarkable man-made features – terraced plantations and century-old olive groves around villages that seem almost unchanged. This unique region gives Albania its best opportunity to capture part of the fast growth in the tourism sector, an industry for which the Mediterranean area is and will remain the first destination in the world. The region has been identified by successive Albanian governments as a priority area for tourism development, with the latest Government Programme for Development of Environmental and Cultural Tourism 2006-2010 approved in February 2006.

However, the situation on the southern coast of Albania exemplifies the challenges and conflicts that transition countries today face. Heritage-rich rural regions, such as coastal or mountain areas, often suffer from under-development due to the dismantling of collectivist production and land ownership structures. Combined with this lack of economic perspective, the freedom of movement re-established in the early 1990s has led to severe depopulation of traditional settlements and under-exploitation of the land.

Both natural and cultural heritage are affected by this state of affairs, and the conflicting challenges of local development and preservation are often met by short-sighted responses causing severe degradation to the heritage, landscape and environmental assets. These responses consist primarily of illegal development and building projects for housing and tourism.

Housing supply is inadequate, especially in areas of perceived economic opportunities, such as from Saranda to Ksamili, and to a lesser extent all along the coast. Families and local investors alike are rushing to position themselves, either to grab their share of the existing rudimentary tourism activities through employment or to take part directly in the tourism offer by construction of hotels and rental flats. Both approaches are rational in their assumptions about the tourism potential of the coast, and property investments are correctly perceived as the most promising revenue-making sector.

It turns out, however, that the lack of planning and land use regulations, or disrespect for those that exist – combined with the absence of a tourism development strategy that would spell out what is needed for maximum sustainable profitability – has allowed chaotic and substandard development to take place. Local people's reaction – to the diminishing revenues from agriculture, the lack of a clear mid- to long-term economic outlook and the availability of investment capital – has shown a real dynamism. However, their ignorance of tourism demands and standards and their misconception of what precisely are the assets of the coast are entailing very serious damage to its development value: not only is actual tourism income less than what the coast could yield, but the area's attractiveness for future high-quality/high-return tourism development is already dented. This "coast rush" has created severe disparities within the narrow strip (5 to 6 km wide) between the coastal settlements and inland villages such as old Himara, Kudhes, Qeparo, Borsh or Lukova, where up to half the houses may be unoccupied.

## 2.2. Why impact assessments?

The concept of Impact assessments stems from awareness of the intrinsic value of natural and cultural heritage, both in immediate economic terms and for future developments. Impact assessments are a response to widespread concern for the preservation of threatened heritage assets and they contribute to the integrated management of these assets. Impact assessments complement, and, ideally, influence land use and urban planning regulations, by taking into account firstly the effects of a given project or activity in a given area and secondly the capacity of the area to accommodate and sustain this project or activity without significant alteration or damage. Impact assessments provide an essential tool for decision makers, local authorities and investors to design the most appropriate projects.

They are particularly relevant for tourism development: as we will see, tourism is at the same time a "consumer" of natural resources and dependent on their quality for its profitability and sustainability.

## 2.3. What are impact assessments?

Many negative impacts of poorly planned tourism development can already be seen along the Albanian coast. The impacts arise from uncontrolled urbanisation and insufficient infrastructure, and they include alteration of traditional settlements, conversion of natural and agricultural land for tourism use, poor water quality, discharges of untreated waste water to the sea and pollution on land caused by inappropriate disposal of solid waste.

Setting capacity limits for sustainable tourism and other development on the Ionian Coast. It involves shaping a vision about the region's development as well as specific decisions on land use, preservation and infrastructure investment. In order to produce an integrated, forward-looking assessment that will inform the planning decision-making process, those involved need territorial, environmental and tourism assessments of carrying capacity.

Territorial capacity is the widest in scope. It concerns the level of population and development that can be sustained in an area without social, cultural, environmental or economic impacts beyond an acceptable level. The territory in this definition is the coherent spatial unit within which (current and planned) human activities take place; it reacts negatively or positively to them, according to its capacity.

Environmental capacity concerns the level of population or development that can be sustained in an area without environmental impacts beyond acceptable levels. In this definition, environmental capacity is one component of territorial capacity. Impact is ranked from no impact (rank 0) to severe (rank 5).

Tourism capacity can be defined as the level of tourism development (often measured in number of tourists) that can be sustained in an area without social, cultural, environmental or other adverse impacts beyond an acceptable level. For tourism, the concept of capacity is more complex, because a wide range of environmental and socio-economic factors interact at tourism destinations, and their importance in many cases is measured in terms of the perceptions of host communities and tourists. Tourism capacity translates into planning guidelines. We will focus now on tourism capacity.

## 2.4. Assessment of territorial and tourism capacity

For tourism on the Ionian Coast, capacity depends on five factors: environment, infrastructure, management, population and the territorial unit in question.

### Environmental capacity

Ecological and physical factors or hazards limit the numbers that can be accommodated. These limitations include the capacity of land for development because of steep slopes or geological risks, the capacity of species to withstand disturbance or the capacity of coastal seas to absorb pollutants. The following subsystems are included in the environmental capacity assessment:

- spring water
- underground water
- coastal seawater
- soil
- air
- habitat and biodiversity
- coastal landscapes

It is not always reasonable to estimate the capacity of an environmental subsystem numerically. The value and vulnerability of habitats and landscapes are more aptly assessed qualitatively. Air conditions (gaseous pollution and dust generation) are considered at the detailed planning stage.

### Infrastructure capacity

Existing infrastructure – especially water-supply systems, sewage systems, the transport network and power supplies – is the short- to medium-term limitation on tourist numbers.

### Management capacity

This relates to the numbers of tourists (with the associated impact) that can be realistically managed. The key constraints here are the available institutional and human resources, as well as the division of roles and responsibilities between public authorities and the private sector.

## Population capacity

This is based on registered inhabitants and forecast increases in population, including seasonal, detailed demographic data and trends, including age groups and migration in and out, and existing and planned tourist numbers. Capacity is then expressed as acceptable population numbers for given environmental subsystems.

## Territorial or landscape units

The region of study was divided first into Landscape Units, then into Tourism Development Areas (TDAs) through a qualitative assessment, reading of the territory (see boxed text, below). This exercise identified 11 TDAs, based on a number of criteria: geomorphology, quality of environment, landscape and views, presence of traditional villages, other notable cultural heritage assets, extent of damage from illegal or unsuitable construction, ease of access and other factors. Based on this assessment of their suitability for tourism, the most appropriate type of development has been identified for each TDA, ranked in one of the following categories: strategic site, major site, ecotourism site, preserved site, other development site.

---

**Description of a landscape unit: Logara to Himara**

**The natural landscape**

The Mount Cikes ridge is higher to the north-east of the pass and includes the Llogara National Park. Since the park is on the higher ridge, it has a visual connection to the sea, both directly to the south and over the Karaburun peninsula to the west. The character of the coast from the Logara Pass to just north of Himara is defined by the considerable height of the Mount Cikes ridge, running parallel to the shoreline, with its steep slopes close to the sea. The seaward slopes are eroded into ridges and valleys, producing a series of coves and mixed sand/pebble beaches between transverse ridges that sometimes end in promontory cliffs at the seashore. These cliffs are occasionally broken and/or eroded by spring-fed streams, creating ravines and caves. The beaches themselves have rocky fingers extending into the sea. The views of the sea from the slopes and the ridge itself are immediate and dramatic, as are the views of the slopes and ridge from the sea. The Llogara National Park, near the Logara Pass, includes a National Natural Monument in its stands of pine trees, *Pishe Flamuri*. Natural *maquis* mixed with pine is making a comeback on the steeper sections of the slopes between exposed limestone outcrops. Watercourses are rich with riparian flora, sometimes in stark contrast to the sparse *maquis* nearby.

---

## The cultural landscape

Lacking large arable plains, the agricultural character of the landscape is of scattered orchards in areas of more gentle slopes of the ridge, creating a patchwork pattern with the *maquis* and natural limestone outcrops. The area includes random plantings of Italian cypress, some of which may have been planted as systems of windbreaks. Traditional villages are set on hillsides in typically defensible positions and blend well with natural forms.

## Detracting features

New building along the coast often sits in conflict with the natural forms, creating a disharmony of site and scale. The landscape alongside roads is degraded by land spill and garbage.

Finally, in judging tourism capacity, Table 1 shows the typical ratios used in estimating the need for services and land. Tables 2 to 6 show examples of summarised results for Albania's southern coast.

## Table 1 – Tourism needs and consumption ratios

| Power supply | Water supply | Waste water* (g per capita/day) | | | | Land (m²) | |
|---|---|---|---|---|---|---|---|
| | | $BOD_5$ | TKN | P | SS | Bed (resort) | Villa |
| 1.1 kW/bed 0.3 kW/inhabitant | 0.3m³ /bed/day 0.2m³ /bed/day | 70-80 | 15 | 2-4 | 20-40 | 400 | 300 |

*Mitigation scenario corresponds to the implementation of EU waste water directive 91/271 for reduction by 70% of pollution loads for Biological Oxygen ($BOD_5$), Nitrogen total (TKN), Phosphorus total (P) and total suspended solids (SS).

In addition to the technical procedures of the assessment, stakeholders' participation is an essential part of the process, aided by information presentations and public consultation in each community. Typically, stakeholders include representatives of local and regional authorities, NGOs, professional associations, and members of civil society including entrepreneurs. Participation in any kind of capacity assessment is crucial if projects are to be seen as locally acceptable and relevant. In a local development perspective, local consultations ensure that communities will directly benefit from investment in their area, in the form of income generation, regeneration of idle rural and fishing activities and enhancement of public services.

## Table 2 – Environmental capacities identified by SEA at commune level

| Commune | Population registered (2004) | Population forecast (2015) | Environmental capacity (persons) | | | |
| | | | Spring water and tapped groundwater | Coastal seawater | Coastal seawater for mitigation scenario | Soils[†] |
|---|---|---|---|---|---|---|
| Himara | 10 697 | 12 100 | 412 000 | 72 000 | 240 000 | 20 000 |
| Lukova | 8 911 | 9 700 | 118 100 | 52 500 | 175 000 | 31 300 |
| Saranda | 34 226 | 50 400 | 59 000 | 17 000 | 90 000 | |
| Aliko | 8 066 | 7 647 | 10 800 | See Saranda | See Saranda | |
| Ksamili | 7 124 | 10 500 | 0 | 16 300 | 54 000 | |
| Xara | 6 811 | 9 500 | 1 100 | 9 000 | 30 000 | |
| Total | 75 835 | 99 847 | 601 000 | 166 800 | 589 500 | 51 300 |

[†]Solid waste carrying capacity. Impact of construction activities must be assessed though a site- and project-specific SEA.

## Table 3 – Tourist capacities related to coastal seawater environment (2004)

| Commune | Environmental capacity (coastal seawater) | Population registered 2004 | Tourist capacity |
|---|---|---|---|
| Himara | 72 000 | 10 697 | 61 303 |
| Lukova | 52 500 | 8 911 | 43 589 |
| Saranda | 17 000 | 34 226 | 0 |
| Aliko | See Saranda | 8 066 | 0 |
| Ksamili | 16 300 | 7 124 | 9 176 |
| Xara | 9 000 | 6 811 | 2 189 |
| Total | 166 800 | 75 835 | 116 257 |

## Table 4 – Carrying capacities and wastewater impacts – summary for coastal communes

| Commune | Carrying capacity | Population registered 2004 | Population peak season 2004 | Impact ranking relative to wastewater |
|---|---|---|---|---|
| Himara | 72 000 | 10 697 | 14 335 | − 3 |
| Lukova | 52 500 | 8 911 | 10 467 | − 1 |
| Saranda + Aliko | 17 000 | 42 292 | 46 816 | − 5 |
| Ksamili | 16 300 | 7 124 | 11 761 | − 3 |
| Xara | 9 000 | 6 811 | 6 824 | − 1 |
| Total | 166 800 | 75 835 | 90 203 | |

## Table 5 – Numbers of tourists (peak season 2004) compared with tourist capacities

| Commune | Tourists in peak season 2004 (daily average) | Tourist capacity |
|---|---|---|
| Himara | 3 638 | 61 303 |
| Lukova | 1 556 | 43 589 |
| Saranda | 4 524 | 0 |
| Aliko | 13 | 0 |
| Ksamili | 4 637 | 9 176 |
| Xara | 13 | 2 189 |
| Total | 14 381 | 116 257 |

## Table 6 – Tourist capacities for coastal seawater mitigation scenario*

| Commune | Environmental capacity (coastal seawater) | Population forecast (2015) | Tourist capacity for mitigation scenario |
|---|---|---|---|
| Himara | 240 000 | 12 100 | 227 900 |
| Lukova | 175 000 | 9 700 | 165 300 |
| Saranda [1] | 90 000 | 50 400 | 39 600 |
| Aliko | See Saranda | 7 647 | See Saranda |
| Ksamili | 54 000 | 10 500 | 43 500 |
| Xara | 30 000 | 9 500 | 20 500 |
| Total | 589 500 | 99 847 | 496 800 |

*Mitigation scenario corresponds to the implementation of EU waste water directive 91/271 for reduction by 70% of pollution loads for Biological Oxygen (BOD$_5$), Nitrogen total (TKN), Phosphorus total (P) and Total suspended solids (SS).

## Table 7 – Numbers of tourists (peak season 2004) compared with tourist capacities for coastal seawater mitigation scenario

| Commune | Tourists in peak season 2004 (daily average) | Tourist capacity for mitigation scenario |
|---|---|---|
| Himara | 3 638 | 227 900 |
| Lukova | 1 556 | 165 300 |
| Saranda | 4 524 | 39 600 |
| Aliko | 13 | See Saranda |
| Ksamili | 4 637 | 43 500 |
| Xara | 13 | 20 500 |
| Total | 14 381 | 496 800 |

As a result of the assessment and consultation exercises described above, a number of scenarios and recommendations were presented to decision makers and investors. For the Albanian Southern Coast, five options or scenarios were devised, based on each site's capacity and tourism suitability, combined.

At that point, other factors also had to be considered, including: (i) competition from other tourist destinations set against Albania's comparative strengths and weaknesses in view of existing and forecast demand in the tourism sector in the Mediterranean; (ii) regional balance; (iii) contribution of tourism to local development; (iv) planned large investments in infrastructure, such as an airport at Saranda and/or Vlora, ferry terminals at Saranda and Vlora, and road improvements; (v) existing protected areas such as the Butrint National Park; (vi) land ownership, the land restitution process and the planned land compensation scheme.

The scenarios were:

- No action (estimated number of new beds: 8 400),

- concentrated development, 1 anchor at Saranda/Ksamil/Butrint (est. no. of new beds: 9 500),

- concentrated development, 2 anchors at Palasa, Saranda/Ksamil/Butrint (est. no. of new beds: 14 500),

- concentrated development, 3 anchors at Palasa, Porto Palermo, Saranda/ Ksamil/ Butrint (est. no. of new beds: 17 000),

- ribbon development (est. no. of new beds: 23 100).

## 2.5. Conclusion

The Southern Coast of Albania is an asset of national importance for the country. It is, however, an asset under threat, whose tourist potential is being reduced by uncontrolled property development. Capacity assessments are a proven tool in establishing limits to development. They are, however, only one factor to be taken into account in the integrated management of natural and cultural heritage assets. We can see that their results differ, depending on the criteria considered. Limited to water issues, the tourist capacity assessment allows for 116 257 visitors if no mitigation scenario is in place and 496 800 with mitigation scenarios; whereas, when the soil is taken into consideration, this figure is reduced to 51 300. Impact assessments must include landscapes, viewpoints and cultural heritage, with quantitative assessments, to provide the bases for integrated management of cultural and heritage assets through spatial planning and land-use regulations, including heritage preservation, zoning designation and design standards.

# PART 4

# SPATIAL AND URBAN PLANNING SCHEMES AND REGULATIONS

# Comparative summary of spatial and urban planning systems – RPSEE countries

*Myriam Goblet*

## 1. Spatial and urban plans and regulations

Although environmental impact assessments are important decision-support tools, it is the various spatial planning schemes and urban planning regulations that are the medium-term or long-term planning instruments for a particular territory, with cultural and natural heritage as a key element.

The various strategic spatial plans outline the economic, social and environmental development objectives of a specific territory and the limitations to be observed. In addition, the land use plans lay down the "use" permitted by law for all buildings, green spaces and infrastructure in the territory concerned.

They are supplemented by urban planning regulations, which cover the physical planning of buildings, including siting, building lines, design, size, materials, shape, colour and so on. In some countries, these rules also apply to advertising signs, road signs, street lighting, street furniture and the felling of trees – in short, anything that forms part of the surroundings.

## 2. Competent authorities

Responsibility for plans and regulations at national level or equivalent (i.e. regional or local, but of national importance) may lie with:

- the Ministry of Spatial Planning (Albania, Serbia, Romania);
- the Ministry of Spatial Planning and the Environment (Bosnia and Herzegovina, Croatia, "the former Yugoslav Republic of Macedonia");
- the Ministry of the Environment (Montenegro);
- the Ministry of Regional Development and the Ministry of the Environment (Bulgaria).

The actual adoption of these documents is the responsibility of the national political authorities: the Parliament (Bosnia and Herzegovina, Romania, Montenegro), the Parliament and the Government (Croatia, Serbia), or the Minister of Regional Development (Bulgaria).

Responsibility for plans and regulations at the regional and local levels lies with the competent regional and local authorities. The adoption of these documents and their implementation are accordingly the task of the political authorities: governors or councils of cantons (counties, provinces, regions), mayors or municipal councils.

It should be noted that in the territory of the autonomous provinces of Serbia, plans to develop areas of special significance (national level) and regional development schemes are adopted by the Serbian government and the Assembly of the autonomous province concerned.

These authorities co-operate with the other institutions concerned with land management, such as the Ministry of Culture (in the case of data and provisions relating to the cultural heritage), the Ministry of the Environment or Nature Conservation (in the case of the natural heritage), the Ministry of Public Works (in the case of public buildings and infrastructure) and the Ministry of Justice (in the case of legal aspects).

It is worth pointing out that in Bosnia and Herzegovina a "council" is set up, tasked with horizontal and vertical co-ordination, as soon as the decision has been taken to carry out a plan. This body is made up of representatives of the authorities operating at the different levels concerned as well as of the representatives of the various sectors, experts, NGOs and others.

Although this cross-sectoral co-operation is often a statutory obligation, some countries regret that it is not as effective as it might be, especially co-operation with the authorities responsible for cultural heritage.

## 3. Project authors

The authorities responsible give the task of drawing up these documents to outside independent experts – individuals or legal entities – who have the skills for this type of work and whose names are listed in a special register (Bosnia and Herzegovina, Bulgaria, Croatia, Serbia, Montenegro and "the former Yugoslav Republic of Macedonia"). The conditions and criteria for registering these experts and organising public invitations to tender are laid down by law.

Quite often, the preparation of these documents is assigned to public institutions: local authority officials (Bosnia and Herzegovina, Bulgaria), the Institute of Urban Studies and Urban Planning attached to the Ministry of Spatial Planning (Albania), the Spatial Planning Institute attached to the Ministry of the Environment and Spatial Planning (Croatia), the Spatial Planning Agency, which includes public and private entities ("the former Yugoslav Republic of Macedonia") or registered public companies, in competition with private companies (Serbia and Montenegro).

Spatial and urban planning schemes are always financed by the project initiators, that is, the public authorities responsible. In most countries, national legislation automatically provides for the national co-funding of regional and local plans. In Croatia, local authorities with insufficient income can request additional funding from the national authority to help them honour their statutory obligations.

## 4. Legal basis

The statutory obligation to draw up these plans and regulations is in the general laws on spatial planning and construction (or urban planning). In Bulgaria, it is in the law on territorial development.

This obligation is often detailed in subordinate documents (sub-laws), such as the "decree on standard methods for drawing up spatial planning documents" in Bosnia and Herzegovina, or in regional and local regulations.

## 5. Types and levels of documents

It may be observed that there are two types of spatial and urban planning documents in all the countries analysed: non-binding strategic documents (studies, strategies, development plans) and binding regulatory documents (spatial plans, land use plans, urban planning regulations etc.). This second category of document is necessary to guarantee and secure a framework for practical action in the medium and long term, along with the public and private investments associated with it.

These documents are adopted at three main territorial levels: national, regional/cantonal and local. However, the geographical boundaries of these plans do not always correspond to administrative boundaries: several regions or municipalities can participate in a single plan according to their mutual interests and regional management responsibilities.

Moreover, specific plans are drawn up for "areas of special significance" or "protected areas/territories", opening up interesting management opportunities for areas with a large number of cultural and natural assets (cf. the examples in section 7 below).

Under current legislation, there is a hierarchical order for these documents, ranging from the national (highest) to the local (lowest) level. There is a wide range of legal instruments peculiar to each country. Here is a summary:

*Albania*

> Strategic plan (local level)
> Master plan (for an area of more than 10 hectares matching administrative boundaries)
> General adjustment plan (local level)
> Operational plan (to implement general land-use plans)
> Partial spatial planning study (to implement general and operational plans in towns)
> Regional land use plan

There are also specific provisions relating to urban planning in heritage or ecologically sensitive areas, designed to protect these areas.

*Bosnia and Herzegovina*

Spatial plan of the Republika Srpska

Spatial plan of the Federation and the measures provided for in it

Spatial plan of the Canton (in the case of the ten cantons)

Spatial plan of the City (in the case of the old parts of Mostar, Sarajevo and Banja Luka)

Spatial plan of an area with special features

Urban development plan (urban area or municipality that is administrative capital of a canton)

Urban development plan of a town (other urban areas)

Regulatory plan and urban development project (in the case of an urban district mentioned in an urban development plan)

*Bulgaria*

National comprehensive development scheme (for the entire national territory)

Regional development scheme (for one or more cantons or a group of municipalities)

General development plan (for the territory of one or more municipalities)

Detailed development plan (setting out the general development plan in specific terms, especially in terms of the protection of heritage and the environment)

*Croatia*

*Spatial planning*

Strategy and programme of the spatial regulations of the state

Spatial plan of a district or spatial plan of the city of Zagreb (which has the status of a county)

Spatial plan of a territory with specific attributes

Spatial regulatory plan of a municipality and/or town/city

*Urban planning*

Urban regulatory plan

Detailed regulatory plan

The law also specifies the urban planning requirements to be complied with when using any land prior to the grant of building permit.

## Romania

### Spatial planning

Spatial plan of national territory

Spatial plan of county territory

Spatial plan of zonal territory (inter-municipal, inter-county, regional, boundary, urban or suburban)

### Urban planning

General urban planning regulations

General urban plan + local urban planning regulations

Zonal urban plan + local urban planning regulations (there are different regulations for different parts of a district and for its urban core)

Urban plan for protected built areas + local urban planning regulations

Detailed urban plan

## Serbia

### Spatial planning

Spatial Development Strategy for the Republic of Serbia

Spatial Development Schemes (nine sector schemes for the entire Serbian territory)

Spatial plan for a special purpose area

Regional spatial plan (for the territory of an autonomous province, a region with between 100 000 and 4 million inhabitants, and the City of Belgrade)

Municipal spatial plan (for the territory of one or more municipalities)

### Urban planning

General urban plans: a general plan and a plan of general arrangement (local)

Regulatory plans: a general regulation plan and detailed regulation plans (local)

## Montenegro

### Spatial planning

Spatial plan of the Republic

Spatial planning for areas of special treatment (national parks, coastal areas)

Spatial plan of the municipality

*Urban planning*

General town plan (for all or part of a town)

Detailed town plan (for part of the area covered by a general urban planning scheme)

Town plan for a specific entity (such as the historical centre of a town or buildings entered in the Register of Cultural Monuments)

*"The former Yugoslav Republic of Macedonia"*

*Spatial planning*

National spatial plan

Regional spatial plan

Spatial plan for national parks (of national importance)

Municipal spatial plan

*Urban planning*

General urban plan

Detailed urban plan

Urban planning documentation (for a populated area)

## 6. Decision-making process

Generally speaking, the decision-making process for spatial plans is as follows:

- decision by the competent authority to prepare the plan;

- preparation of the programme of activities with a view to drawing up the plan, with public involvement;

- establishment of horizontal and vertical co-operation with the various institutions concerned;

- gathering of relevant information in the various fields (including cultural and natural heritage) and presentation of the preliminary draft of the plan or basic details to the public and the competent authorities for an opinion and/or approval;

- drawing up the draft plan incorporating comments made and holding a new public consultation;

- incorporation into the final proposed plan of the relevant comments and suggestions made during the public debate (summary report);

- final adoption by the competent authorities.

Public consultation is not organised in the same way in all countries. In some, such as Bosnia and Herzegovina, Bulgaria and Serbia, the law states that the public must be consulted on the various draft plans and that the opinion of a committee of experts must be obtained. In other countries, the public consultation is held only once, at the draft stage. It should be noted that in Croatia the public is informed a second time, by the local press, when the plan is finally adopted. After the period stipulated by law has expired, the plan comes into effect.

## 7. Influence on the heritage

Documentation of the heritage, in particular using databases and digital mapping, is one of the best guarantees that the heritage will be taken into account in spatial and urban planning schemes and regulations. This is particularly so in Bosnia and Herzegovina and Croatia. On the other hand, lack of computerised information explains the shortage of measures to protect the heritage in these schemes and regulations (Romania, Serbia, "the former Yugoslav Republic of Macedonia", etc.).

Nevertheless, a range of good practices has already been successfully tried out for the benefit of the cultural and natural heritage of the countries analysed. Here are a few examples.

In Albania, the law states that spatial and urban planning documents must take account of the requests and opinions of specialised heritage institutions. For example, any building is prohibited within a radius of 200 metres of a protected archaeological site. Similarly, any building in a protected town and its protection zone must comply with legislation on the heritage and take account of the opinion of the Ministry of Culture.

In Serbia, too, there are cases where the heritage has been systematically taken into account in spatial and urban planning documents. For example, before work starts on an urban project, the initiators of the project must obtain documentation on the current state of the protected assets (monuments, ensembles, sites) and the conditions for their use. Moreover, the Serb government adopts plans only after obtaining a favourable opinion from the Minister of Culture and the Minister of Nature Conservation. Finally, under the new regulations, heritage conservation measures are included in the plan itself and are accordingly binding on investors.

In "the former Yugoslav Republic of Macedonia", the new law on spatial and urban planning (in force since 30 June 2005) aims to solve the problem of the failure in planning documents to take account of heritage by laying down new obligations, on prior documentation, specific heritage conservation measures and the need to involve the competent authorities in expert discussions on draft plans.

In Bosnia and Herzegovina, "areas of special significance" (national parks, nature reserves, protected landscapes, cultural and historical heritage sites) benefit from preferential treatment at various levels: specific theme-based studies are carried out when the draft plan is drawn up, special preservation measures are included in the decision to implement plans, and funding is provided for their restoration or reconstruction by the state. This has been the case with the old part of the town of Pocitelj. There, the buildings have been placed at the disposal of artists, and urban management is along the same lines as in the case of a tourist area. The same applies to the old bridge in Mostar and the country's many castles, fortresses and historical towns.

In spite of the many obstacles encountered when it has attempted to have the heritage taken into account in spatial planning documents, Bulgaria has practices similar to those in Bosnia and Herzegovina, which benefit the cultural and natural heritage in "protected areas". Considered to be of special importance in the urban development plans and programmes adopted at the various levels of authority, these protected areas can benefit both from environmental impact assessments and from special regulations that deviate from the general rules (for example, the development plans for Koprivshtitsa, Melnik and old Plovdiv).

Like Bosnia and Herzegovina and Bulgaria, Romania affords preferential treatment to its "protected built-up areas". As a result of co-operation with the French Ministry of Culture (following an agreement signed in 2002), considerable progress has been achieved in this respect. For example, 98 protected areas of Bucharest and the protected area of the fortress of Alba Lulia benefit from special regulations, which relate to conditions for land use, traffic, car parks, urban amenities, types of advertising allowed, conservation of vegetation, the external appearance of buildings and landscaping. Attention should also be drawn to the establishment in 2002 of a new Department for Protected Landscapes and Areas at the Ministry of Transport and Construction. In particular, this department has adopted two regulations based on the Council of Europe's European Landscape Convention and participated in European work in this area.

# Examples of good practice in planning systems

## 1. A common development programme: Slovenia

*Tatjana Rener*

The Pilot Project Kras was a joint project by the Government of the Republic of Slovenia and the Council of Europe. It was designed to define strategies and a programme for sustainable development of the Kras (*karst*) region by incorporating the conservation of exceptional cultural and natural heritage into development efforts. The Pilot Project Kras (PPK) expressed a willingness to conduct a European debate on regional development conditions and share experiences contributing to an institutional and capacity-building effort launched by the Slovenian authorities. The adoption of a regional policy was considered one of the major reforms in the process of integrating Slovenia into the European Union.

### 1.1. Legal foundations

The legal basis for creating a Common Development Programme (CDP) for the Divača, Hrpelje-Kozina, Komen, Sežana and Karst areas of the Koper and Miren-Kostanjevica municipalities consists of:

- decision No. 630-06/96-16/1-8 adopted by the Government of the Republic of Slovenia, dated 15 November 1996, and decision No. 636-00/98-1, dated 5 February 1998, on the appointment of an Interministerial Commission for the Pilot Project Kras and supplementary statements by the Interministerial Commission on new impetus for the Pilot Project Kras, dated 15 February 1999;

- the co-operation agreement on the founding of the Karst Regional Park, dated 11 July 2000, signed by the Minister for the Environment and Spatial Planning, the President of the Interministerial Commission for the Karst, and the mayors of all six municipalities included in the project. The purpose of this co-operation is to preserve an area rich in cultural heritage and valuable natural assets for present and future generations. These internationally-recognised assets would be used to encourage social and economic development in the area of the Karst sub-region, thus facilitating greater development opportunities for local communities;

- the basic document on the implementation of the PPK signed in November 1999, which also determined the organisational structure responsible for the carrying out of project activities. The Secretariat is based at the Regional Office in Štanjel, a branch office of the National Agency for Regional Development of the Republic of Slovenia, and it has taken on the role of leading and co-ordinating all activities. With this, PPK became an instrument we have made use of to initiate the planning process aimed at meeting the development challenges of the Karst region over the next few years. It is a joint project, involving six municipalities, seven ministries and the Council of Europe;

- the Promotion of Balanced Regional Development Act (Official Gazette of the Republic of Slovenia, No. 60/99), Article 13, which enables two or more munici-palities to draw up a Common Development Programme (CDP).

## 1.2. Why is a common development programme needed?

The Common Development Programme (CDP), which is being developed as an intermu-nicipal interest integration, is needed because of:

- the characteristics, advantages and weaknesses of the Karst region (its natural and cultural heritage, unique in the world; the specific aquatic vulnerability of the Karst underground waters; its being a border region with low population density, unfa-vourable demographic structure and bordering on the rich area of the province of Trieste (with a large population);

- the limited funds available: so the co-ordinating and combining of financial, human and material resources will be improved by integration;

- the need for the co-ordination of different activities in the region towards a long-term development policy adopted by all partners;

- this forming a starting-point for negotiation on development priorities and finan-cial requirements at the regional (Regional Development Programme), national and international levels; the need for creating a powerful entity capable of asserting the region's interests in relation to other regions, on the basis of a social contract;

- greater expectations in respect of the standard of the provision of public services;

- new economic, political, social and spatial challenges that result from Slovenia's entry to the European Union.

## 1.3. The importance of the Common Development Programme at local level

No community can risk simply guessing about its future. Municipal councils and the state need programmes and direction in respect of the impact of today's decisions on the future.

The CDP is a map, which shows the path to be followed by the Karst region in order to go from the existing situation towards the future envisaged by its inhabitants. Its guidance is meant to consolidate the Karst as a remarkable region with its own identity, based on the richness of its landscape and on the rediscovery of heritage as an asset. The CDP is a tool for the local level that will:

– enable the different activities and resources of the various partners to be co-ordinated within a stable set of criteria and in line with a long-term policy designed and approved by the signatory partners, and

– provide a common yardstick for negotiations on development priorities and funding needs at regional, national and international level.

## 1.4. How is a CDP different? What is the added value of a pilot project?

The project has been co-ordinated by the National Agency for Regional Development; it is important at national level, especially from the methodological point of view. The approach in the Kras region will be a valuable experiment in the process of introducing regional policy, since the principles employed in the Kras region will make it possible to put forward legislative solutions that correspond to Slovenia's particular needs.

In this sense, the Pilot Project Kras contributes to furthering knowledge on:

– integrated approaches in regional planning methodology and integration of the conservation of cultural and natural heritage in the development process;

– public participation and consultation in the planning process;

– the concept of sustainability and conditions for ensuring it.

## 1.5. Formulation of the strategic part of the CDP

The Common Development Programme is based on the following principles:

– a joint political will by local authorities and ministries. Adoption of the analytical part of the CDP ensures the political validation of the process.

– a long-term perspective and partnership. Partners have committed themselves to co-operating within the framework of their competencies and to do their utmost on a long-term basis.

– an integrated approach to development issues, which assumes that handling of the region's social, economic, environmental and cultural challenges will be joint and co-ordinated, along with regular verification that the many activities affecting land use are consistent.

- a bottom-up approach to project planning and management, with concerted action. This presupposes public debate and direct involvement of local people throughout the preparation and implementation phases. The integrated approach aims at reconciling objectives of different sectoral policies at local/regional, national and international levels, in the public and private sectors, as well as trends in development and protection.

- opening up to the outside world and developing partnerships outside the region for effective co-operation, exchange of skills, information and experience.

The CDP was drafted in three phases, over a period of three years; each phase presupposed extensive co-operation with the public. To ensure political validation of the process and strengthen the commitment of all signatory partners, each phase concluded with formal adoption of a specially prepared document.

- shared view: The analysis is a collective evaluation of the region and the key issues that will guide the development programme;

- shared horizon: The development strategy is based on a long-term vision, indicating the development directions and expressing the regional players' intended strategic choices;

- shared course: The operative programme comprises priority projects for a certain time frame that are the steps necessary to implement the vision.

The working groups verified different development possibilities and reached a consensus on strategic choices and priorities following several meetings. They summed up expectations in their vision of development for their region, best conveyed by its principal idea "The people of the Karst balancing clean high technology and a revitalised Karst landscape without frontiers", rooted in the "development of activities in the economic, social, spatial and environmental fields, based on optimal use of resources and comparative advantages, which will ensure sustainable and balanced development of the whole region, and reinforced by co-operation between the border regions".

The common vision was a starting-point for the entire strategy. The vision expresses the hopes and wishes of local communities about the future of their region. The vision is, therefore, a description of what people would like to become in the future, in ten years' time, and is also a general objective at which the strategy as a whole is aiming.

The vision encompasses the basic principles of balanced and sustainable development applied to the specific features of the territory. They will be put into practice through the development strategy's four development axes, which are equal and interdependent:

- development of a dynamic rural area and competitive urban centres;

- preservation of the identity and attractiveness of the territory;

- creation of a high-quality, attractive living environment for inhabitants;

- protection of territorial integrity through co-operation.

Each development component typically brings to the fore one of the four functions (economic, environmental, social or spatial); all the components are nevertheless equal and co-dependent. If sustainable, harmonised development is to be achieved, all aspects should be as balanced as possible. The supremacy of economic development would mean taking heed only of economic mechanisms, which would have damaging effects on the other three components; a one-sided emphasis on protection would conceal the danger of stagnation; prevalence of the social element might slacken the competitiveness of the economy; and prioritising spatial balance might lead to excessive dependence of weaker areas and a loss of power in strong centres. For this reason, constant verification and harmonising, in all aspects, of a multitude of activities in the region is necessary.

The development components fall into different strategic fields, which are the nuclei of future development. After summarising the key findings of the analysis of the region – which stresses the dominant function of each component, but still takes into account connections with the remaining functions (an integral approach) – the report gives a schematic presentation of the global and specific objectives.

Global objectives indicate the direction of development and are, as a rule, of a medium- or long-term nature, which means that local communities would like to implement them in the next 5 to 10 years. Specific objectives are short-term goals and represent the path and steps by which the development vision will be implemented and the desired long-term state achieved. Finally, the priority tasks need to be identified, after which the strategy can be put into practice.

The objectives are linked vertically, as they are subject to the overall vision and development axes. They are also linked horizontally, as shown by the linkages between the objectives that are most directly co-dependent. No objective can be dealt with in isolation, as every objective sooner or later causes a chain reaction and influences realisation of another objective. This inter-relatedness enables verification of the strategy's internal consistency, as there can be no conflicts between objectives if they are to lead in the desired direction of development. Linkages also indicate possible positive mutual effects of objectives, so can serve as an important aid in the formulation of projects.

Thus, the strategy cannot be read in parts, but always as a whole. The vision and the development axes represent the framework, which guides the development activities in the agreed direction.

The development strategy was created on the basis of the needs of the region and its people. The envisaged objectives cannot all be realised at local level. Some will be realised in co-operation with neighbouring regions or cross-border partners, by the state or within wider forms of European integration. The fourth axis, which talks about preserving integrity by strengthening links, includes elements from the first three axes in the vertical perspective and indicates possible areas of co-operation.

## 1.6. Public participation

The Action Plan determines the communication strategy, whose goals are to keep the partners and local people informed about what is happening and to obtain feedback. It lists the target groups, objectives and communication tools, and defines how and when they will be used.

The main objective of the communication strategy is to create a shared developmental vision and sense of identity. It is important that other regional and local stakeholders agree with a certain vision and that all, in their respective areas, aspire to a common, over-arching vision, as only in this way will those involved create the right conditions for a balanced, high-quality development, acceptable to all.

Most of the work took place either in the Thematic Working Groups, which included all the region's users (except the international ones), or in the Management Group and the Interministerial Commission, which monitored and guided the work throughout.

Through the use of various tools of communication, our aim was to increase awareness about the project and to attract more partners to take part. Throughout the process, the public was informed about the course of the project via mass media, newspaper articles in municipal publications, special letters, meetings, public discussions, presentations at municipal committees and, last but not least, leaflets and brochures. These were originally created as part of the pilot activities, which not only guided future measures, but encouraged participation by local people in the development process.

## 1.7. Overview of the strategic part of the Common Development Programme

Throughout the development of the vision, the participants compared the Karst to, and placed it in relation to, other regions. At every stage, they realised that we cannot exist for others unless we first exist for ourselves; they, therefore, committed themselves to a search for a strong regional identity, an identity with the Karst landscape, and the desire to shape a common awareness of belonging to the same landscape, the same entity.

As a result, the creation of the strategy itself contributed to the formation of a common identity. The participants undoubtedly confirmed that the Karst landscape is something all local people can share, whether just by walking over it or by using it in different ways. Now that there is no sense of belonging to a rural farming society any more, it is the Karst landscape that really unites them. With the help of this landscape, a new sense of identity – in fact a new social bond – may be built on the basis of the place where they live and work, and which they share.

The strategy is based on the development of clean high technology in the centres of population, in co-operation with education and research institutions in neighbouring regions, and enhancement of the four pillars of Karst tourism in the rural area: Lipica as the cradle of Lipizzaners, Škocjan Caves as the home of *karst* phenomena and Štanjel as the area's architectural pearl, with Karst Edge and Glinščica as the route of castles and the place for active recreation in unspoilt nature. Linking these four pillars to other tourist features of note in the surrounding area will draw further attention to the Karst region, consolidate its identity and create additional sources of income for the population.

It is mostly the development of new technologies that has made this strategy possible, since the notion of physical distance is becoming increasingly obsolete. The economy is no longer dependent entirely on geographic factors; the possibility of access to various networks is increasingly important. Communications media allow us to spend more and more time in one place.

The development strategy of the CDP is a means of answering today's problems while responding to the risks of future development. Both strongly depend on the following:

- using the region's potential, which is one of its strengths compared to other regions (its geostrategic position, distinctive landscape with a high degree of biotic diversity, traditional activities and products derived from natural resources, and its cultural heritage);

- seizing external opportunities, particularly those resulting from Slovenia's accession to the European Union (high-tech corridor, the cross-border Karst Regional Park etc.);

- taking responsibility for development into one's own hands, and taking a long-term view: putting the vision into practice is not endangered by each change of authority, since it gains its true political power from everyone who agreed and voted for the development strategy;

- the public commitment of all participants, both local and foreign partners, to implementation of the development strategy over the next ten years, with targets being continually checked and revised before the end of this period;

- removing imbalance and inequality between areas of the region, between the towns and the countryside, through spatial solidarity;

- setting up the region's development structure to direct and co-ordinate planning activities.

Long-term development will be put into practice gradually by implementing the development strategy within the four development axes. In this respect, the strategic part gives a prominent place to the notion of a common interest promoting spatial solidarity, which means evaluating all the region's treasures and developing complementary functions, such as infrastructure and a network of services. The strategy integrates all parts of the region and ensures a balance between life and work in each area, by selective development that builds on the area's advantages. Intra-regional co-operation will be enforced through solidarity between urban junctions, the central Karst limestone landscape and the preserved landscape bordering on the Karst. Land use will be defined by upgrading the CDP with a regional spatial design that will be the basis for defining spatial and development measures.

## 1.8. Summary of the value of the strategy

The strategic part of the CDP will serve as a guideline for municipal councils in adopting decisions and in implementing their policies. It encompasses the essential strategic orientation, which will direct the region in the next 5 to 10 years. On the journey to the future we often find ourselves at a point where we have options; that is when we need tools with which we can evaluate the situation and the different possibilities correctly, so that we can make a reasoned and, hopefully, correct decision. This programme provides us with those tools.

The planning process is, therefore, not a one-off act but a continuing activity. The strategic part is the first step. The document will be changed, supplemented and upgraded on the basis of new findings, changes in conditions and common decisions. However, it lays the foundations that will orientate development; as it proceeds, the institutional structure must be adjusted to maintain the orientation. The last phase, an operational programme, was based on the priorities identified in the strategy. The programme determines the measures, partners and necessary finance for the next four years.

The commitments that the partners have made, to implement the shared measures, were the first step towards shouldering responsibility for self-development in the region. From the scope of the available local resources, public and private, it is possible to assess local investment capacities, on which the proposed development incentives, at state and European level, will depend. The attraction of financial developmental incentives will depend on the actual absorption capacity at local level.

The strategic part of the CDP, therefore, plays the role of a social contract between the local communities and elements of the social sphere and the state. The policy of spatial development reduces harmful competition between local authorities, which in turn has a positive effect on the investment climate. Private investing is among the most important factors for the acceleration of social, and, therefore, also spatial development. Together with the respective sector policies, the spatial development policy will help to increase the interest of municipalities and regions in private investment at regional and local levels, in a manner compatible with the public interest and with targets determined in the development strategy.

## 2. Preservation, development and planning of the historic centre of Riga

*Juris Dambis*

When a historic town centre is added to the list of protected heritage sites, there are mixed feelings in society – one group of people is usually pleased with the acknowledgment of its value, while the other is concerned about restrictions on development. No town can stagnate, if people want to live and work there, and it needs development; however, the quality of development is important. Cultural heritage is accumulated over many centuries, and degrading or destroying any part of it makes society poorer. In the management of a historic town it is not enough to look at separate monuments; the place must be regarded as a whole.

Only the original elements have the highest value. By losing original elements we lose a part of the heritage that is impossible to recover. Therefore, it is very important to study the treasures to be preserved, to look at problematic issues and then find a solution that ensures high-quality human living space.

## 2.1. Economic pressure

Besides the positive changes that economic development can bring to city centres, problems arise. These are caused by:

- transport,
- the loss of original substance and authenticity by destroying original buildings,
- buildings destroyed by fire,
- the use of new materials or technology, and thoughtless changes for comfort or convenience.

One fourth of cultural heritage losses are caused by delayed or unprofessional conservation efforts, whereas three fourths are caused by deliberate economic activity.

In order to gain immediate profits, construction activities become excessive, cheap and fast, usually resulting in buildings bigger than the site characteristics would normally support or erected in unsuitable places. Such buildings and structures represent a number of future problems, as aesthetic improvements to a degraded site require significant resources, which are much bigger than the margin gained through cheap and ill-considered construction effort instead of balanced, well-planned and even expensive activities. It means that we live today on investments to be made tomorrow – we take out a loan from our environment that will have to be repaid by coming generations.

Cultural heritage is an economic asset to be exploited sensibly, rather than destroyed to gain economic benefits. Destroying cultural heritage does not just mean tearing down cultural monuments, it is also related to building something bigger than the particular site demands, cheap construction in a worthy place or building in a place where it is not necessary. It is greed – the willingness to take quick profits.

Development is impossible without change, and time also leaves its footprints. Changes to the urban environment should serve as a contemporary contribution to future quality. In order to achieve that, it is important to obey ethical principles at various levels. Investors dealing in other countries have to obey overall ethical principles – for example, not doing something in another country that, in the interest of cultural heritage preservation, is forbidden in their own country, even if local laws allow it.

## 2.2. High-quality living environment

High-quality contemporary architecture does not degrade cultural heritage, and good cultural heritage policy does not hinder the development of modern architecture. Good contemporary architecture and design constitute future cultural heritage – they correspond to the predominant quality level in the particular environment, observe building scale and characteristics, respect traditional materials and respond to the atmosphere created by architecture. High-quality contemporary architecture and design add value to the environment.

## 2.3. Democratic planning

A town is a collective system – democracy is not permissiveness. Society should always place its common interests higher than those of individual groups. Land-use planning is one of the most efficient instruments in developing a balanced living environment. Planning is a democratic agreement on land development concluded by and between all groups of stakeholders, where each individual group is open to negotiations; it yields results in increased value with the use of rules on the preservation and development of historic town centres. Therefore, it is important to clarify the interests of society:

- what is the thing of value that we want to preserve?
- what is unnecessary or impeding, and should be removed?
- what do we lack that is new and necessary?

Open public space is important in the functioning of a city. The city's man-made environment also forms the person of the citizen. A good-quality, democratic environment fosters the intellectual, democratic and human values of society.

An architect or urban developer must not be a money-minded person, but rather an artistic individual responsible for creating a good-quality living environment in a long-term perspective. Not all elements may be preserved, but it is highly important to forecast and control the situation, to avoid losing the most valuable details, the special character and the atmosphere evoked by the cultural heritage. Any loss is permitted only if there is a corresponding gain in new and better quality.

First, we need good ideas and only then funding for spatial development; otherwise the money will only spoil the cultural heritage, if we say that preservation of the cultural heritage is short only of the financial resources it badly requires.

## 3. Integrated conservation in Bulgaria

*Todor Krestev*

### 3.1. Documentation methods and their relationship to spatial planning systems

The cultural heritage documentation systems in place in Bulgaria cover cultural monuments of all types and categories. They are governed by the State Archives Act and the Monuments of Culture and Museums Act. The main bodies involved are the Ministry of Culture, its dependent body, the National Institute for Cultural Monuments, various specialist public institutions and local authorities.

The National Institute maintains the National Register and the National Scientific Archives on Cultural Monuments and it co-ordinates the work of all the above-mentioned players. The National Archives hold some 800 000 documents on about 40 000 cultural monuments, along with the Archaeological Map of Bulgaria, which is (re)drawn and updated jointly with the Institute and the Museum of Archaeology. The local partners in the system at municipal and regional level also draw up and add to the local archives on cultural monuments.

In the light of the above, the following problems with documentation systems may be identified:

- there is a lack of advanced modern documentation systems and no national strategy for digitising the cultural heritage using GIS (geographic information system);

- one shortcoming shared by all existing documentation systems is the way they are closed off and difficult to access, especially for the general public. Moreover, the national archives and the national register are not accessible online;

- there is no permanent information system on endangered cultural heritage sites, those that require urgent conservation measures.

In recent years, most of these problems have been resolved as a result of several local initiatives. In connection with the preparation of spatial and urban development plans and the establishment of specific programmes, various land registers, regulation plans and digital maps of cultural monuments have been developed for certain regions and built-up areas, along with relevant databases, on the basis of GIS.

In this context, the following examples are worth noting:

- the Sofia Development Plan: a GIS database has been established, covering the entire municipality, which has a particularly rich cultural heritage, and the inner city;

- the Plovdiv Development Plan: comprehensive studies have been conducted in the vast area of cultural monuments, covering their development, different historical periods etc;

- under the PHARE programme for the development of cultural tourism (2003-5), the cultural heritage of the municipality of Assenovgrad has been studied in its cultural and natural context, as a potential factor in cultural and environmental tourism;

- in 2005, with financial assistance from the British Council in Bulgaria and the British Council Fund for South-East Europe, a multimedia cultural heritage laboratory was set up at the University of Architecture, Civil Engineering and Geodesy for the purpose of fostering digitisation of the cultural heritage and encouraging public dissemination. The laboratory has produced digital maps of the cultural heritage of South-East Europe in connection with the regional forum on Cultural Corridors in South-East Europe (Varna, May 2005).

In spite of these developments, there is still a need to adapt the various information systems as part of the long-awaited legislative reform and to utilise them in the context of integrated spatial planning systems.

## 3.2. Integrated management plans and regulations

As mentioned, spatial development plans also have an impact on the cultural heritage. In principle, they lay down the local/regional conditions for its protection and enhancement or development. In the case of spatial and town planning that takes account of historic, ethnographic and architectural factors, there are special rules and standards drawn up in line with its specific features.

Nevertheless, there is a general lack of effective, integrated conservation instruments for historic regions. In this connection, the following problems should be noted:

- there are still no regulations on specific protection plans, although such regulations are needed for the purpose of harmonising conservation policy with spatial and town planning policy;

- there is a lack of effective machinery for co-ordinating archaeological research policy with conservation policy. Archaeological excavations are carried out without taking account of the possibilities of conservation, and this poses a threat to the archaeological remains discovered;

- there is no complex management for the various conurbations. In some cases, development policy is divided into several partial urban planning proposals, which are put forward without consultation and cover individual urban areas and often underestimate public interest in integrated conservation of the urban cultural heritage as a whole. There are no rules on advertising, lighting or urban design in historical town centres;

– there is no effective legislation or management that protects landscape as an asset with recognised cultural dimensions in accordance with the European Landscape Convention – for instance, the Black Sea coast, which is suffering from rapid development compounded by management lacking in foresight, is showing signs of gradual degradation.

One thing is, therefore, clear: the state does not at present have effective machinery or relevant instruments for protecting the public interest via integrated conservation systems that relate to the cultural heritage or for striking and maintaining the necessary balance between public and private interests.

## 3.3. The historic city of Plovdiv

An example is offered by the historic part of the city of Plovdiv, which has a rich history covering very many different periods, dating from the second millennium BC to the present day. Plovdiv therefore has an outstanding urban archaeological system. Over the last 30 years, a whole series of significant projects have been carried out at the various archaeological sites in the city. However, as there is a lack of relevant instruments, integrated town planning in terms of the urban archaeological structure has not been possible. As a result, the condition of the latter has deteriorated significantly. In 1985, for instance, the area of the ancient forum was cut through by the new underground transport route. It was subsequently sold (in 2000) to a private firm, which announced its intention to build a six-storey business centre on it. The lesson we have learnt is as follows: if urban architecture is to function as a comprehensive system, it is absolutely vital to draw up and adopt legislative instruments for integrated conservation and effective management, while fostering the development of partnerships at different levels.

Various efforts have been made to overcome the existing problems in spite of the above-mentioned legislative shortcomings.

In 1985, the National Institute for Cultural Monuments put forward a pilot project to integrate town planning for the ancient heritage of Plovdiv, which was to be enhanced as an active component of the urban environment.

In 2003, a strategy was developed for the preservation and sustainable use of the "Ancient Plovdiv" site, supplementing the detailed spatial development plan with a whole series of measures aimed at integrated management. The strategy gave rise to analysis of the cultural heritage, assessment of its current state and the development of a Conservation Steering Plan, which provides for integrated conservation in successive stages. A strategy for the sustainable use and development of the site's resources and a comprehensive spatial management plan were also put forward. Following the project, the "Ancient Plovdiv" site was presented for inclusion on the World Heritage Site list. UNESCO and the Japan Trust Fund have provided financial assistance totalling $1 000 000 for the conservation of cultural monuments within the site and the management system has been duly upgraded.

## 3.4. Integration through authorisation

Apart from the spatial planning process, an integrated approach is applied by the Ministry of Culture through the system of permits and supervision by the National Institute for Cultural Monuments, local self-government and municipal councils. The institute's orders are binding on all authorities, organisations and individuals. The Monuments of Culture and Museums Act provides that projects involving cultural monuments and their environment are subject to prior consultation procedures from the outset of the investment project. If the relevant orders are not complied with, the institute is entitled to have any work affecting cultural monuments and their environment stopped. Any buildings built in breach of the above act must be demolished. The legislation also lays down penalties for individuals or legal entities in the event of non-compliance with the relevant regulations.

The above procedures demand a degree of co-ordination between central and local government and, in particular, the establishment of an effective partnership between the Ministry of Culture and the Ministry of Regional Development.

In this connection, the following problems may be identified:

- there are unacceptable contradictions between the Monuments of Culture and Museums Act and the Territorial Development Act. For instance, if only up to three neighbourhoods are affected, the latter Act dispenses with the need for public consultation in the case of town planning, conservation activities involving cultural monuments and the siting of advertising, information or other panels and suchlike, in protected areas, whereas the Act on Cultural Monuments requires prior consultation in all such cases.

- there is no effective supervision of the cultural heritage and there are no adequate penalties for offences committed. This is leading to increasing levels of illegal building, excavations by treasure hunters and neglect of cultural monuments. In this connection, archaeological monuments must be regarded as being particularly at risk: for example, a large proportion of the country's 10 000 burial mounds have recently been pillaged by treasure hunters who have partly or totally destroyed the various structures and wiped out valuable archaeological data.

As a consequence of the many problems mentioned above, valuable historical sites such as Old Nessebar, a World Heritage Site, have been put at risk to some extent.

Most of the problems are the result of outdated legislation, lack of effective co-ordination between the three relevant institutions, the highly centralised management system and the limited role of local authorities in the conservation process, especially against the background of the strong commercial pressures exerted in relation to historical sites.

# PART 5

## AUTHORISATION, CONSULTATION, SUPERVISION AND PENALTY PROCEDURES

# Comparative summary of permit, control and sanctions procedures – RPSEE countries

*Myriam Goblet*

## 1. Authorisation, supervision and penalties

Once the heritage documentation systems have been computerised (see above, Part 2: Comparative summary) and provision has been made for heritage in the various environment documents (see above, Part 3: Comparative summary) and spatial and urban planning documents (see above, Part 4: Comparative summary), it is necessary to introduce efficient systems for granting authorisations, carrying out supervision and imposing penalties in order to guarantee the quality of work done on the heritage and its surroundings.

It is important to match the granting of permits with inspections and penalties because, if no sanctions are applied, authorisation will lose its importance in the eyes of the public, who will no longer necessarily feel the need to apply for it or comply with it when doing renovation or building work.

It should be noted that this report relates only to measures taken with respect to the cultural and natural heritage that is listed or otherwise protected by law, and to its surroundings, and not to all the buildings located in a territory.

## 2. Competent authorities

The distribution of powers with regard to authorisation, supervision and penalties corresponds to that already mentioned in the case of documentation of the cultural and natural heritage (see above, Part 2: Comparative summary). Thus, the Ministry of Culture is the principal authority responsible for these matters, along with the Ministry of the Environment or the Ministry of Nature Conservation (Albania, Bulgaria, Montenegro, Serbia and "the former Yugoslav Republic of Macedonia") and the Ministry of Spatial Planning (Romania).

The provincial or supra-local agencies of these ministries are usually involved in this work for which a knowledge of the area concerned is crucial.

In some countries, such as Bosnia and Herzegovina, Croatia and Romania, these ministries have at their disposal an *ad hoc* inspection service whose inspectors have the exclusive power to carry out inspections and impose penalties.

When a system involving a single/integrated permit applies (as is the case with all the countries apart from Bosnia and Herzegovina), there is co-operation between the authorities responsible for the cultural and natural heritage and those responsible for spatial and urban planning and for granting planning permission.

On the other hand, there is little co-operation between these authorities on supervision and penalties except for the possibility of exchanging information on irregularities found. In some countries, such as Croatia, Montenegro and "the former Yugoslav Republic of Macedonia", there is, nonetheless, an apparent willingness to engage in horizontal co-operation and in vertical co-operation with the local authorities to establish a common strategy for solving heritage-related problems.

Finally, in some cases, such as Albania, Romania and Montenegro, there is co-operation with the police in the case of some inspection tasks in serious or high-risk situations.

## 3. Legal basis

The statutory basis for planning permission, inspection and penalties is sectoral legislation on:

- laws on cultural heritage;
- laws on the environment, nature conservation, nature parks, protected areas and biological diversity;
- laws on spatial/urban planning and construction.

The provisions specifying the scope of planning permission, inspections and penalties, along with the relevant procedures, are an integral part of the laws (and thus not subject to implementing decrees), unlike the documents relating to the environment and spatial/urban planning discussed above (see parts 3 and 4: comparative summary).

With regard to penalties, the Criminal Code supplements the administrative provisions in the sectoral legislation (especially in Albania, Bosnia and Herzegovina, Bulgaria, Serbia and Montenegro). These penalties apply to much more serious offences than those subject to administrative sanctions (see Section 6 below).

## 4. Conditions for granting authorisation

Strangely enough, there is no public consultation before a permit is granted in any of the countries considered. Only in Romania is there a statutory obligation to consult the public, but in practice this does not take place owing to a lack of funds, staff and time and because the actual procedure to be followed has not been laid down by law. It might be asked whether this omission is a legacy of the communist period.

Public consultation is standard practice in the countries of western Europe and takes place in the form of a public inquiry. An information board set up on the spot tells the public about the planned work or changes in use. The public can obtain details of the project from the administrative authority responsible and submit a written complaint, which will be considered when the decision is taken on whether or not to grant permit.

Complainants are sometimes asked to express their objections orally before the decision-makers make their final decisions.

This public consultation constitutes another decision-support tool in that it is a safeguard against certain abuses or errors on the part of the project initiators that go against the general interest. It also permits the community to keep checks on the work done – neighbours are often the best inspectors of work because they are always on the spot and have a good knowledge of the area.

This system of public consultation could thus usefully be applied in the Regional Programme partner countries in the same way as the public consultations they already hold in the context of their procedures for adopting environmental impact assessments, development strategies and plans, land use plans, urban plans, plans for the management of natural sites and, indeed, plans for the statutory protection of the heritage.

As regards the type of work that requires a permit, analysis of the national reports shows that all the countries require a planning permit for work involving the protected cultural and natural heritage.

By contrast, a change in use requires a permit only in Croatia, Serbia, Montenegro and "the former Yugoslav Republic of Macedonia", while archaeological excavations require one only in Bulgaria and "the former Yugoslav Republic of Macedonia".

The procedure for granting planning permit for work involving the protected heritage is similar in all the countries apart from Bosnia and Herzegovina, where the Ministry of Culture issues a permit but without issuing planning permission as such – in other words, there is only one permit, a heritage permit.

In all the other countries, the urban planning authorities issue a single permit (combined, integrated) for the work planned and its technical documentation, after obtaining prior approval (agreement, authorisation, permit) from the authorities responsible for the cultural and natural heritage.

This prior approval given by the Ministry of Culture and/or the Ministry of the Environment/ Nature Conservation specifies the conditions for preserving the protected property affected by the planned work – that is, what measures are authorised and prohibited, conditions for carrying out the work, specific technical measures to be implemented for the restoration or change in use or appearance of the protected property.

The organisation of this two-stage procedure varies from one country to another with regard to:

- the need for the prior approval of other ministries affected by the project;
- the prior issue of an urban planning certificate informing the applicant about the authorised use and about the prior approval to be obtained from various bodies (Romania);
- the authorities (national and/or local) responsible for granting permit;

- special procedures in an emergency or in the case of work of minor importance (e.g. shortened procedures in Croatia);

- the need to take account of ensembles and sites in addition to monuments (Albania, Romania, Montenegro and Serbia);

- the need to take account of protection zones around listed properties (Albania, Bulgaria, Croatia and Romania);

- the nature of work not requiring a permit (maintenance, conversions for the disabled, minor construction work, etc.);

- various possibilities for filing an administrative appeal against the final decision.

## 5. Organisation of supervision

Generally speaking, the work subject to supervision is work that affects protected cultural and natural assets and, sometimes, their surroundings.

In some countries, inspections are also made of:

- archaeological excavations or investigations (including work done under water);

- transactions concerning cultural assets or their import and export;

- other activities provided for by law.

Specialised inspectors or officials charged with monitoring work in progress check its compliance with the conditions laid down in the permit and by law.

In Croatia and Montenegro, inspections also involve checking the documents authorising individuals or institutions to carry out work on the heritage. Among those who may carry out such checks are restoration institutes, museums, galleries, archives and libraries, as well as experts and specialised companies carrying out protection, preservation and renovation work or dealing in cultural assets.

The authorities responsible for supervision are the same as those in charge of granting permits. At the Ministries of Culture and the Environment/Nature Conservation it is sometimes specialised inspectors who carry out checks (Albania, Bosnia and Herzegovina, Bulgaria, Croatia, "the former Yugoslav Republic of Macedonia") and sometimes officials whose job is to monitor work carried out (architects, engineers, archaeologists, botanists, etc.). In some countries, such as Romania, inspections are carried out by local officials from these ministries.

The Ministries of Spatial and Urban Planning also carry out checks in connection with the granting of permits. In Bulgaria and Romania, the authorities responsible for state buildings also check to ensure compliance with conditions of approval, authorisation and standards of work on state buildings.

## 6. Penalty mechanisms

In general, penalties are imposed in the case of work that destroys or causes damage to the heritage as well as for any breach of legal requirements or failure to comply with permit conditions. In particular, there are penalties for:

- illegal preservation or restoration work, or illegal excavations within a cultural monument (without a permit issued by the competent authority or in breach of the conditions laid down in such a permit);

- destruction of, or damage to, a monument owing to a lack of maintenance or neglect;

- inappropriate restoration or reconstruction;

- export of cultural or natural assets without a permit from the competent authorities;

- failure to return cultural or natural assets after the deadline laid down in the authorisation;

- archaeological excavations or investigations that may destroy or severely damage a monument or destroy the features that make it part of the heritage;

- taking possession of cultural or natural assets discovered during excavations or other work.

The penalties provided in the case of the cultural heritage are similar from one country to another:

- payment of a fine, the amount of which varies considerably from country to country: €8 000 to €40 000 in Albania, compared with €275 to €2 750 in Romania;

- imprisonment for serious offences, in Bosnia and Herzegovina, Montenegro and Serbia;

- discontinuation of restoration and new construction work, repair of damage done, demolition of illegal structures (Bulgaria, Croatia, Romania, "the former Yugoslav Republic of Macedonia");

- suspension of the work planned on the property for a period of six months up to two years ("the former Yugoslav Republic of Macedonia").

The penalties provided in the case of the natural heritage are quite similar:

- payment of a fine (€50 to €10 000 in Bulgaria, €80 to €8 000 in Albania, €500 to €5 000 in Bosnia and Herzegovina, and in Serbia);

- imprisonment for serious offences (Serbia);

- suspension or withdrawal of planning permission (Albania);

- confiscation of property or of pollutants that damage the environment (Albania, Serbia);

- banning/suspension of planned activities (Serbia and "the former Yugoslav Republic of Macedonia" up to five years).

It is worth noting that in Bulgaria, the Ministry of the Environment and Water also punishes civil servants who have allowed activities to be carried out in protected areas in breach of the law (or the order of designation, or the management plan of the particular protected area) or civil servants who have failed to punish those responsible for illegal activities in protected areas.

Finally, the main penalties provided in the case of spatial and urban planning are:

- payment of fines (Albania, Bulgaria);

- ordering work to be stopped and demolishing illegal structures (Albania, Bulgaria, Serbia).

## 7. Problems Encountered, and Solutions

It may be noted that, generally speaking, there is a lack of inspections and penalties, and there is difficulty in organising or applying those provided for. Penalties are often ineffective as they are too lenient, are lacking in substance and are applied rarely or too late. It is also difficult to establish clearly who is responsible for taking action, in what cases action must be taken and how.

Moreover, it would seem that inspections carried out and penalties imposed by the Ministry of Culture are less effective than those carried out or imposed by the ministries of the Environment and Spatial and Urban Planning.

The problems encountered by countries are to be found at various levels:

- institutions: permanent lack of staff, time and funds for carrying out inspections, applying penalties and (especially) destroying illegal constructions (Bosnia and Herzegovina, Bulgaria, Romania, Montenegro and "the former Yugoslav Republic of Macedonia"); over-centralised and over-concentrated heritage management systems, combined with the weak role of the local authorities in this area (Bulgaria); complexity and excessive red tape (Romania); impropriety among public employees and supervisory bodies (Romania);

- legislation: proliferation of laws on the heritage, frequent overlapping of legislation and powers (Bosnia and Herzegovina, Montenegro); legislative contradictions, especially in monument preservation work and the provision of information in protected areas (Bulgaria, Montenegro);

- politicians: lack of political will at all levels of authority genuinely to protect the heritage and support the imposition of penalties (Bosnia and Herzegovina, Romania);

- investors: sometimes intense pressure by investors, who want to maximise the return on their investment (Romania);

- owners and the general public: lack of information, failure to raise public awareness of the importance of the heritage and the need to preserve it; low levels of compliance with the law (Bosnia and Herzegovina, Montenegro)

- economic and social context: transition process still under way.

Consequently, the number of offences is still too high in the countries examined, in comparison with the situation in western Europe. Illegal construction, (archaeological) treasure hunting and the failure to maintain cultural monuments are placing the heritage at considerable risk. Sometimes the damage has become irreversible, even at exceptional heritage sites (such as the Nessebar reserve, a world heritage site in Bulgaria).

In order to find a comprehensive solution to this problem, it is necessary – as suggested by Romania and Montenegro – to address the various causes mentioned above by:

- strengthening the powers of the institutions responsible for cultural and natural heritage;

- reforming, harmonising and simplifying national legislation in line with international legislation;

- taking a political decision to establish sound and effective bodies to carry out inspections in the field and quickly impose severe, deterrent penalties on owners and investors;

- promoting schemes to inform and raise the awareness of owners and the general public of the key role played by the heritage in society and the importance of respecting and enhancing it.

This last solution is particularly important if we want to avoid more transgressions in the future and make it unnecessary to apply penalties – in other words, if we want the emphasis to be ultimately on prevention rather than punishment.

# Examples of good practice in authorisation and enforcement

## 1. Consultation, authorisation and enforcement in England: integration of heritage and planning, and comparisons with Ireland

*Robert Pickard*

### 1.1. Consultation and authorisation

Before explaining the consultation and authorisation procedures (and the proposals to change them), it is necessary to explain briefly how the cultural built heritage is integrated into the planning system in England. This chapter refers mainly to the system in England, as the legal provisions and planning systems are slightly different in each of the four parts of the United Kingdom – England, Scotland, Wales and Northern Ireland – though the situation in Wales is very similar to that of England.

There are three main forms of protection for the immovable cultural heritage:

1. Listed Buildings (buildings chosen for statutory protection because of their special architectural or historic interest); there about 500 000 listed buildings in the United Kingdom, over 400 000 of which are in England;

2. Conservation Areas (areas of special architectural or historic interest); there are about 10 000 of these in the United Kingdom, of which about half are in rural areas (small towns, villages or countryside) and half in urban areas (including historic centres of cities, and even suburbs);

3. Scheduled Monuments (archaeological sites and other "ancient monuments", including some buildings, for example, structures of the industrial heritage that are no longer in use); some buildings are both listed and scheduled (but the law for the latter is stricter and will apply first).

The legislation for listed buildings and conservation areas has been developed through planning law, and until the Town and Country Planning Act 1990 (here the TCP Act 1990) the provisions for them were contained in the main planning legislation. These designations remain integrated within the planning system, but were given separate legislation in 1990, namely the Planning (Listed Buildings and Conservation Areas) Act 1990 (here the P(LBCA) Act 1990). The TCP Act 1990 remains the principal planning Act but a new piece of legislation, the Planning and Compulsory Purchase Act 2004 (PCP Act 2004), has brought changes to the system of land use plans at strategic level (now based on regions) and local authority level as well as making "sustainable development" a statutory requirement of the land-use planning system.

The legislation for scheduled monuments – the Ancient Monuments and Archaeological Areas Act 1979 (AMAA Act 1979) – is not directly integrated with the planning system. However, since the late 1980s, when a number of significant archaeological discoveries were made in the course of new development, government policy on ancient monuments and archaeological remains, in the context of the planning system, has been strengthened. In 1990, Planning Policy Guidance Note 16: Archaeology And Planning (PPG 16) was issued to provide guidance for local planning authorities, property owners, developers, archaeologists, amenity societies and the general public, with particular reference to the handling of archaeological remains in the development plan and development control (planning consent) systems. Paragraphs 15 and 16 of PPG 16 specifically indicate that development plans should include policies for the protection, enhancement and preservation of sites of archaeological interest and their settings, including scheduled sites and other, unscheduled archaeological remains (those remains not directly protected by law) of more local importance. Paragraph 18 further indicates that the desirability of preserving an ancient monument and its setting is a material consideration in determining a planning application, whether the monument is scheduled (formally protected) or not. In fact, this follows a court ruling dating from 1975.

Another Planning Policy Note, PPG 15: Planning and the Historic Environment (issued in 1994 jointly by the two government departments responsible for cultural heritage and planning respectively – which reveals the level of consultation between government departments), further endorsed this view. Moreover, PPG 15 highlights the fact that any aspect of the "historic environment" is a material consideration in the determining of planning applications for new development. Thus, listed buildings and conservation areas are considered in this context. Moreover, the web extends further, as other aspects of the "historic environment" must be considered. (The term "historic environment" covers all elements of built heritage in the environment, whether protected individually or not.) These include some non-statutory designated sites, such as:

- sites included in the Register of Historic Parks and Gardens of Special Interest in England;

- sites included in the Register of Historic Battlefields;

- World Heritage Sites (the United Kingdom is a signatory to the UNESCO convention).

Both PPG 15 and PPG 16 are being reviewed and it has been proposed that the new planning statement will amalgamate the issues covered in these guidance documents following a review of the heritage protection system.

In fact, matters of more local heritage interest are now considered as being of material importance in land-use planning and for inclusion in development plan policies (such as a system of local listings of buildings by local planning authorities).

The key point about "material considerations" is that, under Section 38 (b) of the PCP Act 2004, there is a presumption in favour of the development plan for the determination of planning applications except if material considerations dictate otherwise. In simple terms this means that if a developer wishes to build new houses or shops, and the site being considered for this development meets the criteria for building new houses or shops, then planning permission should be given (unless material considerations dictate otherwise). However, if there are listed buildings adjoining the site or archaeological remains under the ground, for example, or the site is within a conservation area, then the impact of the proposed development on these issues is a material consideration in deciding the application for permission to develop. In this way heritage assets can be safeguarded.

Moreover, all aspects of the "historic environment" must be taken into consideration when development plan policies are being formulated. This process is being informed by characterisation and mapping studies for the "historic landscape", archaeological assessments of areas (such as whole urban areas), conservation area character appraisals, preservation and enhancement plans for such areas and other methods.

## 1.2. Consultation on the formulation of statutory plans

Since the PCP Act 2004, new forms of statutory development plan have been formulated:

- Regional Spatial Strategies (RSS) are strategic spatial plans covering nine regions in England. These inform the next level of plans at local authority level and have replaced the old system of county structure plans and strategic aspects of unitary plans. Regional planning guidance has been turned into spatial strategies, and these are being updated.

- Local Development Frameworks (LDF) include detailed planning policies and other documents, such as policies covering the "historic environment", which may be considered through Action Area Plans. They replace the old system of local plans and the detailed policies of unitary plans. All local planning authorities must have the new types of plan in place by spring 2007.

Since the European Directive 2001/42/EC on Strategic Environmental Assessment (SEA), the plan formulation process (for both RSS and LDF) must include a systematic process of identifying and assessing the likely effects on the environment of a plan or programme, or any proposed policy (which must specifically include the "historic environment"). The SEA process requires the production of an Environmental Report for these issues.

The SEA forms part of a "sustainability appraisal" of the proposed plan or policy, an appraisal which considers social, economic and environmental effects. This appraisal must set objectives for cultural heritage and landscape, such as:

– to preserve historic buildings, archaeological sites and other culturally important features;

– to create places, spaces and buildings that "work well, wear well and look well";

– to enhance countryside and townscape character;

– to value and protect diversity and local distinctiveness;

– to improve the quantity and quality of publicly accessible open space.

The appraisal must establish indicators – benchmarks and monitoring (so that plan policies can be reviewed according to progress in meeting indicator standards) – for example, by assessing the percentage of archaeological sites and listed buildings at risk (under threat) and monitoring this.

Planning authorities consult the public on issues and options as part of the process of preparing plan policies before the formal consultation stage. Moreover, since the PCP Act 2004, as a result of making "sustainable development" a legal requirement in the planning system, planning authorities must make a "Statement of Community Involvement" – which is a formal document describing how a local authority intends to involve local communities and other stakeholders in preparing the plan (and in deciding significant issues of development control in an adopted plan).

Planning authorities also consult relevant bodies with environmental responsibilities, such as English Heritage (the government's statutory adviser on the historic environment), on the scope of the Environmental Report. Public feedback at this stage may provide more information for the Environmental Report/sustainability appraisal.

A proposed (draft) plan is then published and full public consultation/participation begins. The Environmental Report on the draft plan is made available to the public and to environmental bodies. The consultation process includes an analysis of opinions on the draft plan. This means not only the views of the public and statutory consultees, but also – for the historic environment – various heritage groups. Heritage Link, an umbrella organisation, has produced "a guide for heritage groups", which emphasises how they are particularly well placed to "assist" planning authorities to build up a robust evidence base using their knowledge, skills and understanding of an area's history and important features. Consultation also involves negotiations with objectors to the proposals. The consultation process may have several stages, one being an independent public examination of the proposals.

Taking into account the representations and the opinions of statutory consultees, the draft plans can be amended and modified. The published plan must take account of the

Environmental Report and the opinions of consultees (such as English Heritage) because it is a requirement to publish information on how these were taken into account.

Heritage policies in LDFs (local-level plans) can be extensive and wide-ranging, because heritage is regarded as being integral to sustainability and the quality of life. These heritage policies then inform the process of considering any applications for development (or changes to designated assets) that may affect heritage interests. Such heritage policies may deal with:

- access and inclusion: the LDF should include a policy for improving access for disabled people to the historic environment in a way that is sensitive to its character;

- tourism: policies to promote tourism and associated facilities should recognise the importance of the historic environment and protect heritage assets;

- arts and culture: the historic environment is an important source of local identity and pride – policies should therefore enhance the cultural heritage;

- historic townscapes and landscapes: policies should not just protect listed buildings and conservation areas, but also put forward some aspect of the undesignated historic environment that respects local distinctiveness (such as landscape, local listing of buildings or retention of distinctive local features, or through good design);

- heritage-led regeneration and development: policies should maximise the environmental, economic and community benefits of heritage-led regeneration, supporting the restoration, repair and sympathetic reuse of historic buildings and areas;

- archaeology: apart from protected sites, policies should also cover the many undiscovered archaeological sites and this may require prior evaluation of an area's archaeological potential;

- design: policies should require the design of new development to be sympathetic to its context;

- characterisation: LDFs should include policies that recognise the value of characterisation studies and their role in guiding decisions about the location, form and type of development.

### 1.3. Consultation on development proposals and works affecting designated heritage assets: current authorisation systems

The background to development plans and policies, outlined above, is a sound basis for considering applications for development that may affect the historic environment in its widest sense. Apart from specific policies on safeguarding or enhancing heritage, the fact that preservation of heritage assets is a material consideration in deciding development applications reveals a high level of integration between planning and heritage law. Nonetheless, consultation and public participation form an essential part of the decision-making procedure for consent applications.

### i. Planning applications

In a general sense, any application for permission to develop (which includes change of use of buildings, including listed buildings, or development within the "setting" of a listed building) will be subject to a publication process to allow representations and objections; these, if deemed relevant in planning terms, will be taken into account in coming to a decision. Under Section 65 of the TCP Act 1990, developers must publish a notice in a local newspaper and put up a site notice on the land in question announcing the application for planning permission. In determining the application, the local planning authority must take into account any representations received within 21 days of the date of the application.

Furthermore, as part of the new sustainable agenda, the national guidance in Planning Policy Statement 1: Delivering Sustainable Development (published in 2005) is that the planning service should strive to ensure "openness, customer service and stakeholder satisfaction" when dealing with development consents. It stresses the importance of pre-application discussions with developers to ensure a better mutual understanding of the issues and constraints. In the course of these discussions, the proposals can be adapted to better reflect community aspirations as well as policies.

For example, in the context of conservation areas, the objective is to preserve and enhance their character and appearance. Thus, the design of new development is a key issue – early discussions can enable developers to judge whether their plans are likely to meet these criteria or to harm the area. Moreover, the planning authorities may have a conservation area advisory committee, made up of a cross-section of community interests, which will consider policy on the area and comment on proposals. Similarly, PPG 16 emphasised the importance of developers having early discussions on development in an area with archaeological potential.

All proposals to develop, whether or not they might affect heritage assets, should follow these consultation and discussion principles. In relation to designated heritage, the rules lay down specific consultation processes with the public and statutory consultees, and pre-application discussions are a key issue for any one proposing works.

### ii. Listed building consent applications

"Listed building consent" (to alter, extend or demolish a listed building) is required for any works that affect the special character of a listed building. Specific types of notification are required by law:

- as with development, applications must be publicised in local papers and on site notices (so that the public can comment) if they affect the most protected buildings (grade I and II*) or the exterior of grade II listed buildings; and the local authority must not decide the application until 21 days have passed (giving time for objections).

- English Heritage must be notified of certain types of application (particularly for proposed works involving demolition).

- the National Amenity Societies must be notified of applications to demolish a listed building. They are the Ancient Monuments Society, the Council for British Archaeology, the Georgian Group, the Society for the Protection of Ancient Buildings and the Victorian Society.

- the relevant Secretary of State must be notified where a local planning authority wishes to grant consent for works "of any consequence" – this enables the Secretary of State to "call in" the application for determination instead of the local planning authority making the decision whether or not to grant consent.

As well as those that have to be consulted (by law), there are many others who may have a particular expertise and can make a valuable contribution to the consideration of a particular proposal. These include local amenity groups and the voluntary sector, architects, local historians and others and it is generally considered important to make sure local people are kept informed to ensure there is no loss of goodwill amongst the local community.

### iii. Conservation area consent applications

Conservation area consent is required for the demolition of an unlisted building in a conservation area. Normally, the application to demolish must be considered at the same time as an application for planning permission for replacement development (so that the new proposals can be considered in terms of whether it will "preserve and enhance the character or appearance of the area" – or whether in fact it could cause harm to the area.

The publicity requirements for an application for conservation consent are similar to those for normal planning applications. Within London, English Heritage must also be notified of certain types of applications. The local planning authority must take account of representations made by the public (and specifically English Heritage in London).

### iv. The role of Conservation Officers

The first move for anyone proposing works to a listed building, or proposing to demolish a building in a conservation area, should be to discuss ideas with the Conservation Officer in the local planning authority. In some cases it will be necessary to discuss the proposed works with English Heritage.

Conservation Officers can advise the applicant whether the proposal is likely to gain consent (or what conditions may be required in order to gain consent). If consent is granted, this officer will be responsible for ensuring that the works are carried out in a proper manner and according to the terms of the consent. Such officers can be town planners, architects, building surveyors or archaeologists by profession and usually have a specialist qualification in conservation. Since 1998 Conservation Officers have been supported by their own professional body, the Institute of Historic Building Conservation (which has 2 000 members), and advertised positions for Conservation Officers usually require applicants for the post to be members of the professional body or to have considerable experience in relevant work.

Conservation Officers are key people in the integrated system. Amongst other things, they:

- undertake characterisation appraisals and advise on conservation policies in development plans (so that heritage assets are properly considered);
- undertake surveys of historic buildings at risk (through vacancy or disrepair);
- advise applicants for consents on projects on listed buildings or in conservation areas and recommend whether a project should be approved – in fact all applications affecting the wider historic environment will probably be considered by the Conservation Officer;
- supervise the work (where such applications are approved) and ensure that it is carried out according to the consent;
- advise the decision-makers on the need to take coercive action on emergency repairs or other repairing obligations under the law (the action may include expropriation if requirements are not met) and advise on enforcement to stop unauthorised work and/or require reinstatement where changes have been made illegally; such action is backed up by penal provisions (fines and the possibility of imprisonment). Enforcement Officials may be separately employed to begin proceedings where unauthorised activity takes place;
- supervise (with officers from English Heritage) any conservation or restoration work that has been given financial assistance.

Moreover, the Conservation Officer may be a key person in heritage regeneration/rehabilitation strategies, which use the heritage as a basis for improving depressed areas, liaising with English Heritage, property owners, developers and investors.

### v. Other consultations

Consultations with other officials and consultees may be required for some applications that may have an impact on the historic environment. For example, investors wishing to develop in areas with "archaeological potential" (even though not scheduled sites) are normally required to discuss their proposals with county or local authority archaeologists; and, in the case of development that may affect a Registered (non-statutory designated) Historic Park or Garden, by law English Heritage and the Garden History Society must be consulted.

### vi. Scheduled monument consent applications

As ancient monuments and archaeological sites protected under the AMAA Act 1979 do not come directly under the planning system, consultations are carried in a different manner.

All applications for scheduled monument consent must be made directly to the relevant Secretary of State. In practice, English Heritage will consider the application (and will usually have preliminary discussions with applicants) and then make a recommendation to the Secretary of State for his/her decision. The Secretary of State must also take account of any representations made as a result of a notice given by the applicant to other owners of the land in question. In fact, the owners and local planning authorities are both given an opportunity to comment. The Secretary of State may also give publicity to an application "if it seems appropriate" and consider any representations made by the public or interested groups (but there is no formal requirement to publicise).

Before coming to a decision, the Secretary of State is obliged either to hold a public inquiry or at least to allow an opportunity for the applicant and "anyone else considered appropriate" to be heard before an Inspector. There is no right of appeal against the final decision (except on a point of law), which is a difference from all the other consent procedures discussed above.

However, in practice few inquiries are held under the terms of the AMAA Act 1979, since proposals for scheduled monument consent often involve planning applications as well. In this situation, the Secretary of State will generally make every attempt to ensure that both aspects are the subject of a single inquiry.

## 1.4. Authorisation procedures: a new way forward

In England, although planning and heritage protection have been well integrated for many years, the authorisation system remains somewhat complex. A number of different consents may be required:

- planning permission – for new development and the change of use of buildings;

- building regulations approval – for health and safety as aspects of new construction or change of use to existing buildings. Buildings of architectural or historic interest (whether listed or not) can be exempted from some regulations if standards such as for fire safety are met in other ways to prevent detrimental impact on the character of such buildings;

- listed building consent;

- conservation area consent;

- scheduled monument consent;

- miscellaneous consents, for example through
  - hedgerow regulations,
  - tree preservation orders, or
  - advertisement regulations.

Under an ongoing Review of Heritage Protection begun in 2004, a number of significant changes are being proposed. The aim is for simplification and greater integration between planning control and heritage protection (but not building regulation control).

The first of these changes is to create a unified Register of Historic Sites and Buildings in England, structured in two ways. The main section, compiled by English Heritage, will incorporate the existing regimes for listed buildings, scheduled archaeological sites and monuments, registered historic gardens, parks, battlefields and world heritage sites, so that sites with multiple designations can have these integrated into a single list entry where appropriate. The local section will contain a record of all conservation areas and other local designations and registers.

A second change is a proposal to review the present consent regimes. In 2003, the Office of the Deputy Prime Minister appointed researchers to examine the case for unifying a variety of planning and heritage consent regimes. In the report (Unification of Consent Regimes, Office of the Deputy Prime Minister, June 2004, Reference No. 04 SCG 02275 M) a number of different models have been considered. One proposal is the unification of planning permission, listed building consent and conservation area consent; another idea is to unify listed building consent and scheduled monument consent.

The report has recommended that the unification of authorisation systems should take place in two stages, the first being to merge listed building consent with scheduled monument consent to create a "heritage consent", and to merge planning applications with conservation area consent. The second stage – suggested for some later point in time – would be to unify the two first-stage changes into one consent regime, merging all the present regimes for planning permission and heritage consent.

One advantage of developing a unified consent system is that archaeology (scheduled sites in particular), presently outside the planning system, would become more integrated with other aspects of the historic environment already considered in the planning system.

These changes in consent regimes will require new legislation, which will take time to prepare. Moreover, it is likely that changes will be made gradually. One proposal being considered is to move in this direction by streamlining the planning application process, introducing a standard application form to provide essential information on the full range of planning permissions and associated planning consents. An interactive electronic application form would allow submissions to be made by e-mail. The initial idea is to have an application form for planning permission for householders that can also be used to obtain listed building and conservation area consents. This would be developed over time to include a full range of permissions for different types of development.

Another proposed change is to develop the use of "management agreements". With the creation of a new Register and a unified consent regime, it is thought that management agreements could be employed wherever that approach might work better than a particular consent approach.

Management agreements could be used for:

- large buildings, sites and landscapes;
- complex historic entities that comprise more than one type of heritage asset;
- heritage assets that could be better managed in association with other regimes, such as in the natural environment;
- single types of asset in single ownership but in dispersed locations.

It is considered that these types of agreements could offer a better approach to managing heritage assets through:

- elimination of the need for close regulation for defined types of change/alteration;
- effective partnerships between owners, managers, local authorities, English Heritage and other parties;
- greater certainty and clarity for owners, users and regulators;
- complementary management with other parallel regimes (such as between the historic environment and the natural environment, as well as the planning process);
- a better understanding of relevant heritage assets over time.

All these proposed changes are being subject to consultation exercises and it will be some time before the final choices for change are formulated and given legal force through new legislation.

## 1.5. Comparison with Ireland: authorisation systems

It is perhaps worth mentioning how Ireland has taken a lead in developing a unified approach to consents in the planning and heritage sphere. Ireland's legislation on "national monuments" originally derived from legislation in the United Kingdom, when Ireland was part of this. National monuments are similar to scheduled monuments in

England; however, until recently Ireland did not have a significant form of protection for post-1700 historic buildings. This was changed by legislation in 1999, consolidated by the Planning and Development Act 2000.

This planning legislation is used to designate "protected structures" (equivalent to listed buildings in England) and "architectural conservation areas". Furthermore, development plan objectives must be set down for:

- the conservation and protection of the environment, including in particular the archaeological and natural heritage,

- the protection of protected structures, and

- the preservation of the character of architectural conservation areas.

Whereas archaeological heritage is more specifically controlled through the National Monument Acts, there are also provisions (as above) for its protection as part of the planning system, which is generally the primary means of securing the protection of archaeological heritage in development, through the consideration of applications for planning permission.

But, in the case of protected structures and architectural conservation areas, works are directly controlled through one consent regime, namely planning permission. The definition of development in Ireland includes, in a general sense, any "works" – meaning "any act or operation of construction, excavation, demolition, extension, alteration, repair or renewal" and, in the context of protected structures, "any act or operation involving the application of plaster, paint, wall paper, tiles, or other material to or from the surfaces of the interior or exterior of the structure". So works that materially affect the character of a protected structure require planning permission.

The system in Ireland is quite similar to England, but it effectively works as if planning permission, listed building consent and conservation area consent were amalgamated into one consent regime. Thus authorisation of changes to the "built heritage" in Ireland is more directly integrated into the planning code than in England.

## 1.6. Sanctions and penalties

Sanction and enforcement procedures for the key forms of designated heritage asset in England may change. Bearing in mind proposals to review heritage asset categorisation, it is likely that new legislation will amalgamate procedures for such things as urgent repairs and compulsory purchase.

The supervision of works to scheduled monuments is carried out by English Heritage; works relating to listed building or conservation area consent will generally be supervised by Conservation Officers. English Heritage will have a role if it has subsidised the work, and may have a role in other cases. Otherwise, measures to prevent damage/unauthorised work can be checked by rights of entry for officials and through administrative remedies and criminal sanctions.

## Rights of entry

### a. Listed Buildings

The relevant Secretary of State may authorise a right of entry for the purpose of surveying listed buildings under section 88 of the P(LBCA) Act 1990. In practice, this power may be used by planning officers from an LPA, including conservation officers, as well as officials from English Heritage. The right of entry may be used for a wide range of matters, but it is most commonly used for inspecting buildings for the purpose of selecting new entries in the statutory list of protected buildings, reviewing the condition of a listed building for the purpose of seeking repair action or to see if an offence has been committed in relation to the legal protection regime. Under sections 88A and 88B, it is a criminal offence to obstruct officials in carrying out their duties under the rights of entry provisions.

In addition to the rights of entry provisions, a local planning authority can serve a Planning Contravention Notice for the purpose of obtaining information about activities carried out on land (including buildings) where a breach of planning control is suspected. This power is backed up by prosecution provisions as the failure to comply with such a notice within 21 days is a legal offence.

The listed building regime falls under planning legislation, but unauthorised works to protected buildings are treated more strictly than unauthorised development, which is merely a breach of planning control, subject to enforcement action or a "stop notice". By contrast, to carry out works to a listed building without listed building consent is a criminal offence (see section 1.7.a, below).

### b. Scheduled Monuments

The rights of entry provisions for protected ancient monuments and archaeological sites are more loosely drafted than the listed building entry provisions. Section 43 of the Ancient Monuments and Archaeological Areas Act 1979 provides a power of entry to land where a scheduled monument is located to any person authorised by the relevant Secretary of State for the purpose of surveying it, or estimating its value, in connection with any proposal to acquire the land or any other land (such as adjoining land where the extent of archaeological remains may not be precisely known) or assessing any damage to land (including the protected site) or any other land that may have a bearing on the site's safeguarding.

By obtaining access and determining where unauthorised work or damage has occurred to protected assets, action can be considered for administrative and criminal sanctions.

## 1.7. Sanctions and coercive measures

### a. Listed Buildings

#### i. Unauthorised work to listed buildings

Under sections 7 and 9(2) of the P(LBCA) Act 1990, it is a criminal offence to carry out unauthorised works to a listed building or to fail to comply with a condition attached to a listed building consent (hereafter LBC). This is an offence of strict liability: it is not necessary to prove *mens rea* (intention). Therefore, ignorance of the fact that the building was listed is insufficient. In one example from a court case, the owner of a listed building authorised a building contractor to remove from a building everything of value (by which was meant only furniture), but which the contractor interpreted as meaning architectural fixtures to the buildings. The contractor's defence was that he did not know that that the building was listed and therefore, did not realise he had committed an offence. This was insufficient.

There are many reported cases of successful prosecution. Criminal sanctions can apply for each item of unauthorised work, so a developer was fined on each of 14 unauthorised actions of stripping out panelling and other features from a listed building in Soho, London.

The maximum fine for each unauthorised action on summary conviction (in the magistrates' court) was £2 000 (about €3 000) with the possibility of imprisonment for up to three months, but these were found to be insufficient as a deterrent, so in 1991 the maximum fine was raised to £20 000 (about €30 000) and the maximum prison sentence to 6 months, by amending legislation. The relevant provisions, in section 9(4) of the P(LBCA) Act 1990, also provide for conviction through indictment in the Crown Court leading to imprisonment for up to two years (originally one year) or an unlimited fine, or both. Prosecutors are often reluctant to go down this route, because it is tried by a jury (rather than being decided by a magistrate) and they may be uncertain of obtaining a conviction.

Where magistrates convict a defendant, they may decide, in the light of the evidence heard, that the Crown Court should decide the sentence (though they can do this only in the case of a individual being prosecuted, rather than a company).

The level of fine can be significant when imposed by the Crown Court. For example, in a 1998 case, the partial demolition of a building, one day after it had been listed for protection was categorised by the judge as a "cynical commercial act". After pleading guilty, the owner was fined £200 000 (based on the likely profit from redevelopment of the site) plus £13 000 costs.

Custodial sentences are extremely rare and imposed only in extreme cases. One example dating from 1992 involved a plan to cause damage to a listed chapel by the use of explosives so as to render the building unsafe and thereby gaining grounds for obtaining consent to demolish the building for the purpose of redeveloping the site. However, instead of making a crack in the building as planned, the bungled explosion caused the front of the building to be completely blown out. This resulted in the developer being jailed for four months (and his accomplice, an explosives expert, got 28 days in prison)

In criminal prosecutions, it is usual to seek the recovery of costs arising from bringing the case. The costs can be a significant part of the overall penalty, in some cases exceeding the fine. In a 1997 case, the owner of a listed building who made major roof and internal alterations without consent was fined £6 000 plus costs of £19 720, and escaped imprisonment only because of a guilty plea and an agreement to reinstate features.

### ii. Contravention of the terms imposed by a Listed Building Enforcement Notice

Instead of taking criminal proceedings, the local planning authority (or the Secretary of State) may issue a Listed Building Enforcement Notice (LBEN) to deal with unauthorised works (i.e. works carried out without LBC or in contravention of any conditions attached to an LBC). LBENs can also be used in conjunction with criminal proceedings. Enforcement powers under section 38 of the P(LBCA) Act 1990 are discretionary, allowing the local planning authority to consider whether it is expedient to take such action bearing in mind the relative impact of any unauthorised works upon the character of a listed building (i.e. the special character for which it was deemed worthy of protection in the first place).

An LBEN can specify various forms of action that are required, including:

– to restore the building to its former state (i.e. immediately before the unauthorised works occurred – not to the original state);

– where such restoration would not be reasonably practicable, to execute other works necessary to alleviate the effect of the works being carried out without consent;

– to bring the building to the state in which it should have been if the terms and any conditions of any consent had been properly complied with.

The LBEN must specify the date when it is to take effect and a compliance period. The local planning authority can specify different time limits within which the various requirements of the LBEN must be carried out. It must be served on the owner or may be served on any other person with an interest in the building – this could be a building contractor, architect or surveyor, where unauthorised works are actually in progress.

If the notice is not complied with, prosecution can follow. The maximum fine is £20 000 on summary conviction in a magistrates' court or an unlimited fine on indictment in a Crown Court. In determining the fine, the court can take into account any benefit resulting from non-compliance with the notice.

Following conviction for non-compliance, if the works are still not carried out, the person convicted, or any subsequent owner, may be prosecuted again. If the necessary works are still not completed, the local planning authority can enter the land and premises, carry out the work and reclaim the costs from the current owner (a subsequent owner can also reclaim the costs from the original owner). It is also an offence to obstruct a local planning authority from carrying out the work.

### iii. Injunctions

The ordinary method of controlling unauthorised development that requires planning permission is to serve an Enforcement Notice (similar to an LBEN for unauthorised works to listed buildings). It is also possible in these circumstances to issue a Stop Notice, which brings the Enforcement Notice into effect within three days (or less if necessary). However, the "stop" procedure can be used only against unauthorised development, not to stop unauthorised works to listed buildings.

Where a local planning authority (or English Heritage) wishes to bring a swift halt to unauthorised works to a listed building, a legal injunction may be sought from the courts (under section 44A of the P(LBCA) Act 1990) to restrain the owner of a building (or anyone else, as appropriate) from carrying out, or continuing, any authorised works. It is sometimes necessary to take urgent action to prevent a listed building being demolished or substantially altered (possibly within 24 hours!) as the use of criminal proceedings will have little effect – even if offenders are successfully prosecuted it will usually be too late to stop the damaging works being completed. If an injunction is granted and its terms are not followed, a further action can be brought for "contempt of court". The courts consider actions for contempt very seriously and can impose severe penalties, including, in appropriate cases, imprisonment.

The effectiveness of this power is shown by a case from 1990, where a property development company started work on a listed building that it owned, coating the brick exterior with adhesive and cement render without consent. An injunction was obtained the next day to stop the work, but this was ignored by the company. Following an action for contempt of court, the director of the company was fined £25 000 for the offence. The defendants agreed to pay for restorative and repair works and were ordered to pay the local authority's legal costs in bringing the case. The local planning authority subsequently served an LBEN and a Repairs Notice under section 48 of the P(LBCA) Act 1990 to restore the building.

Indeed, apart from legal remedies for unauthorised work, local planning authorities can take criminal proceedings in the case of damage caused to a listed building, and they have two potential courses of legal action in the case of buildings in poor repair (see below).

### iv. Damage

Under section 59 (1) of the P(LBCA) Act 1990, a person who does, or permits, any act that causes (or is likely to result in) damage to a listed building, or has the intention of causing damage, may be prosecuted. This provision does not apply to ecclesiastical buildings (listed places of worship) so long as the building is used for religious purposes (though a person who does damage to a redundant listed church can be prosecuted), nor does it apply to listed buildings that are scheduled monuments (for which different procedures apply).

Causing damage in this context means any damage, including where works have been carried out without consent, but can include any damage that affects the character of the building as a protected building. Works likely to cause damage include work that is sufficiently substantial to harm the building and could result in its decay and eventual demolition. (It should be noted that "like-for-like" repairs to a listed building do not require consent. However, repairs that affect the character of a building could be classed as unauthorised work or could constitute damage.)

An offence relating to damage can only be tried in a magistrates' court (summarily). The maximum penalty is £1 000. However, if after being convicted a person fails to take steps to prevent any damage or further damage occurring as a result of the original act, a further offence is committed. In this case a guilty person is liable for each day that the failure continues and is subject to a daily fine.

There are no specific legal obligations placed on owners to keep listed buildings in good repair. However, if owners cannot be encouraged to take action to preserve listed buildings, then statutory powers may be utilised to enforce action.

### v. Urgent repairs notice

Under section 54 of the P(LBCA) Act 1990, a local planning authority (or English Heritage in London, or elsewhere if authorised by the relevant Secretary of State) may execute urgent repairs for the preservation of an unoccupied or partly occupied listed building. The works are limited to emergency repairs to protect the building from weather damage or vandals and other matters that are thought to be "urgently necessary for the preservation of a building" (for example, work to exclude water damage, to prevent damage from organisms, to ensure safety and the stability of the building or to prevent damage by fire).

An Urgent Repairs Notice gives the owner a minimum of seven days' warning of an intention to enter the premises and carry out the work described in the notice. This period enables the owner to discuss the proposals and consider the merits of undertaking the work or whether there would be grounds to appeal against the notice. The procedure allows for the recovery of the cost of the urgent works from the owner. There are also a number of grounds of appeal against such a notice, including hardship (inability to pay).

English Heritage maintains a Register of Historic Buildings at Risk (risk being measured in terms of occupancy, disrepair and priority actions) for grade I and II* listed buildings, which can obtain preferential treatment for grant aid for repairs. Some local authorities maintain their own registers for (ordinary) grade II listed buildings, but these are less able to benefit from subsidies unless it is a special grant-aid scheme (usually an area-based scheme such as a Townscape Heritage Initiative).

### vi. Repairs notice

A second procedure has greater significance, because it can be used with occupied listed buildings, there is no ground of appeal in the case of hardship and there are further consequences if the procedure is not complied with.

Under section 48 of the P(LBCA) Act 1990, a Repairs Notice may be served. The notice specifies a full schedule of works (not just safeguarding works, as in an Urgent Repairs Notice) that are deemed necessary for the proper preservation of the building (i.e. to return the building to its condition at the date of listing, not restoration to the original state: in the UK the approach is generally to conserve rather than to restore!). Failure to carry out the terms of the notice within two months can lead to a local authority making a Compulsory Purchase Order (CPO), a form of expropriation. Indeed, the Repairs Notice must explain this consequence.

In practice, there have been some perceived difficulties in using the Repairs Notice procedure for neglected listed buildings, because the possible consequence is compulsory purchase. Research has shown that local authorities are deterred from using this power for fear of the cost of purchase and subsequent repairs of potentially problematic buildings. Compulsory acquisition is assessed by an independent Lands Tribunal at the market value of the building, bearing in mind its condition and the protection regime, and generally assuming no redevelopment potential for the site. However, the research has also shown that this can be an effective means of promoting repair, rarely resulting in compulsory acquisition. The threat of serving a notice is often enough to induce action on a building.

### vii. Compulsory purchase powers

The compulsory acquisition of a listed building is generally regarded as the last resort. In general terms, a historic building owner can avoid CPO proceedings by taking reasonable steps to preserve a building subject to a Repairs Notice, and this is usually what happens. However, an owner should not rely on the fact that financially restricted local authorities will not be able to afford to buy the property; sometimes grant-aid is given to support the authority in its action; and official guidance on the historic environment has given encouragement to the use of "back-to-back" deals, whereby the authority identifies a suitable private individual or organisation such as a building preservation trust to repurchase the property once it has been acquired by the authority. This is usually done by legal agreement before the compulsory acquisition is finalised.

### viii. Minimum compensation orders

If the local planning authority considers that a building has been "deliberately neglected" – there should be clear evidence that the owner has deliberately allowed the building to fall into disrepair in order to justify its demolition, so as to develop or redevelop the site or any adjoining site – it may apply for a "direction of minimum compensation" to be paid on compulsory acquisition (rather than the market value of the property). However, it is often difficult to prove that the neglect has been deliberate: an owner who could not afford to do repairs would not be "deliberately" neglecting the property.

For example, a country mansion designed by a famous British architect was compulsorily acquired, along with associated land, for £1 (about €1.50). The owner had previously applied to demolish the building, in part through various unsuccessful court hearings, to clear space for residential development. Twelve years after the first application to demolish, the building was acquired subject to the minimum compensation provisions, confirmed by the Lands Tribunal. However, cases of minimum compensation are rare because of the difficulty of proving "deliberate" neglect.

### ix. Dangerous structures

Where a building is in a dangerous condition, a local authority may apply to the magistrates' court for a Dangerous Structures Order, which requires the owner to make the building safe, or else demolish all or part of it and remove the rubbish resulting from the demolition work. At first, this created a loophole in the listed building legislation that allowed an owner to demolish a neglected protected building. However, the relevant legislation (the Building Act 1984) was amended to make such orders subject to the listed building legislation.

National planning guidance on the "historic environment" (PPG 15) directs local authorities that they should not serve a Dangerous Structures Order on a listed building owner before considering repair action (using sections 48 and 54 of the P(LBCA)Act 1990). Moreover, an owner who demolishes a dangerous listed building without LBC on the grounds of health and safety (after an order is made) can only be prosecuted if they were actually notified of the need for such consent. The same rule applies to the demolition of unlisted buildings in conservation areas.

## b. Conservation areas

### i. Criminal sanctions for unauthorised demolition

The demolition of an unlisted building in a conservation area, except in limited circumstances, is a criminal offence under sections 9(1) and 74(3) of the P(LBCA) Act 1990, because conservation area consent (CAC) is required for demolition. This offence carries the same maximum penalties as the corresponding listed building offences.

### ii. Conservation area enforcement notice

As an alternative to prosecution, the local planning authority can issue a conservation area enforcement notice if it considers this is needed because of the effect of the unauthorised works on the character and appearance of the conservation area. (The main goal of conservation area designation is to preserve and enhance the character and appearance of the area.)

### iii. Injunctions

It is also possible to use injunctions to halt unauthorised demolition of an unlisted building in a conservation area, although it could be more difficult to persuade a court to issue an injunction to prevent demolition of an unlisted building, except in the case of a persistent offender.

### iv. Urgent repairs in conservation areas

The power to undertake urgent repairs to listed buildings (see above) can also be used on unlisted buildings in conservation areas. The relevant Secretary of State must first give a direction that the procedure can be used (by a local planning authority or English Heritage) on the grounds that the preservation of the building is important for maintaining the character or appearance of the area.

## c. Scheduled monuments

### i. Unauthorised works

Under section 2 of the AMAA Act 1979, any person who carries out works to a scheduled monument without first obtaining scheduled monument consent (SMC) is guilty of an offence. Unauthorised activity includes works that result in demolition, destruction or damage, works of removal, repair, alteration or addition, and flooding or tipping operations in, on, or under the land where a scheduled monument is located. The effects of scheduling are therefore more severe than those of listing, particularly as all repair work requires official consent.

The penalty for failing to obtain SMC, or failing to comply with a condition attached to SMC, is a fine up to £2 000 in the magistrates' court, or an unlimited fine on conviction on indictment through a trial by jury at the Crown Court. As an example, in a case dating from 1992, a guilty plea – to one charge of causing or permitting unauthorised works to the scheduled site of the former Winchester Palace and associated Roman remains – resulted in a fine of £75 000, with £1 000 costs, being imposed for removing major stone and chalk walls from the site.

There are four defences to the section 2 procedure. In broad terms, two of these are the defence of due diligence (all reasonable precautions were taken to avoid contravening the conditions of a SMC) and the defence of avoidance of destruction or damage. A third defence, in the case of a concealed monument, is that the defendant did not know, or had no reason to believe, that a monument was in the area affected by the works. The courts have considered a number of cases where the precise extent of a scheduled monument was in doubt and they have confirmed that it should be possible to ascertain its extent from the relevant documents, which should ordinarily include the notification of scheduling and a map. Thus, criminal liability under section 2 depends on the facts, not guesswork.

A fourth defence is allowed if works were urgently necessary in the interests of health and safety, similar to the provision for listed buildings that have become dangerous structures, though the defence is less restrictive, requiring notice in writing to the Secretary of State only as soon as is practicable.

Where unauthorised works constitute serious "damage" to a scheduled monument, it can be preferable to use a different form of offence (as below) that carries a higher maximum sentence, though it is then necessary to prove *mens rea* or intention. (This is different from the case of damage to listed buildings, as considered above.)

### ii. Damaging a protected monument

Under section 28 (1) of the AMAA Act 1979, there is an offence of destroying or damaging a protected monument, meaning a scheduled monument or a monument in public ownership or guardianship; in practice any monument that is sufficiently important to merit taking into public control will be scheduled. The offence is committed by anyone who knowingly destroys or damages, or intends to do so or is otherwise reckless (i.e. does not give due consideration whether an action will harm the protected monument), though in the latter cases intention or recklessness must be proved. This procedure is normally used to prosecute cases of vandalism. The penalty is:

- on summary conviction in a magistrates' court, a fine up to £2 000 or a prison sentence up to six months, or both;

- on conviction on indictment in the Crown Court, an unlimited fine or imprisonment for up to two years, or both.

For example, the eighth Marquess of Hereford was fined £10 000 on indictment for the ploughing of a field, which resulted in serious damage to Roman remains. The Court of Appeal reduced the fine to £3 000, the court taking the view that the original fine would have been more appropriate to flagrant disregard of a monument for the purpose of personal gain, rather than negligence or inadvertence as in this case.

English Heritage proposed an increase in the maximum fine on summary conviction to £20 000, which would equal the listed building fine, but this would require an amendment to the AMAA 1979 Act. Following the present review of policy and legislation on the "historic environment", changes in fine levels are expected.

English Heritage often take the main role in cases that lead to prosecution, by keeping a record of reported incidents affecting scheduled monuments and carrying out preliminary investigations with police assistance before the Crown Prosecution Service take over the proceedings.

### iii. Using a metal detector in a protected place

Use of a metal detector in a protected place (meaning the site of a scheduled monument) in a way that may damage the fabric of a scheduled monument, or its interpretation and understanding if artefacts are removed, is an offence under section 42 (5) of the AMAA Act 1979. The penalty for removing artefacts without consent is a fine up to £2 000 in a magistrates' court, or an unlimited fine on conviction at the Crown Court (the same as the section 2 procedure). The use of a metal detector without consent, but without removing artefacts, is subject to a fine of £200.

### iv. Injunctions

As with unauthorised works to listed buildings, a court injunction is sometimes necessary to restrain or stop unauthorised works from proceeding any further.

### v. Mandatory reporting for chance finds

Until 1996, chance finds of archaeological artefacts where covered by the common law concept of "treasure trove". The Treasure Act 1996 redefined treasure, removing the need to prove that the objects had been intentionally buried. The new, objective definition of treasure includes:

– objects other than coins must contain at least 10% gold or silver and must be at least 3 000 years old.

– all coins from the "same find" (such as a hoard or ritual deposit) are treasure if they are at least 300 years old when found, except that if the coins have less than 10% gold or silver there must be at least 10 coins.

– any object is classed as treasure if it was found in the same place as, or had previously been with, an object that is treasure.

– objects substantially made of gold or silver that do not fall into one of the above categories, but which would formerly have been treasure trove, are classed as treasure. These objects need not have been buried with the intention of recovery, but it must not be possible to trace their owners or heirs.

The Act also defines certain types of find that do not fall in the definition of treasure:

– objects whose owners can be traced,

– unworked natural objects, including animal and human remains, even if found with treasure,

– objects from the foreshore that are not "wreck" (so wrecked ships may be treasure).

The Treasure Act lays down reporting procedures as required by the Valletta Convention. Finds of treasure must be reported to the Coroner for the district where the find is made, either within 14 days of making the find or within 14 days of the realisation that the find may be treasure (for instance, by professional identification). It is an offence not to report a find without a reasonable excuse; the maximum penalty is three years' imprisonment or a fine of £5 000. The obligation to report lies with the finder and the duty to report applies equally to objects found by archaeologists during archaeological excavations.

## 1.8. Comparison with Ireland

Returning to Ireland for a comparison, the level of monetary sanctions in England seems low. Under Ireland's National Monuments Acts, offences can be subject to a maximum fine of €64 486 and five years' imprisonment on conviction on indictment. (The relevant minister can also prosecute summary offences.) Under the Planning and Development Acts, the "removal, alteration, or replacement" of any specified part of a protected structure has a maximum penalty on conviction on indictment of €1 269 738 or five years' imprisonment. Thus, carrying out work to "protected structures" without the required planning permission carries a significant penalty, which is clearly a major deterrent to anyone undertaking unauthorised work.

## 2. Permits, controls and sanctions: a case study from Germany

*Friedrich Lüth*

The Federal Republic of Germany is based on 16 separate states. Each of these states has the legal responsibility for its cultural heritage. According to the constitution, there is no legal responsibility for cultural heritage at the federal level and consequently there is no federal agency for cultural heritage.

The states have set up laws and regulations to protect their heritage. The cultural department of the Federal Foreign Office is responsible for negotiating international conventions and bi- or multi-lateral agreements outside Germany. International agreements that affect the legal responsibilities of the separate states can only be ratified after consultation with the states and a decision in the Bundesrat. Thereafter, the separate states have to adjust their legal systems accordingly.

Depending on the regulations in the individual states, there are cases where permits are given on the basis of other acts, such as the Building Act or the Act on Nature Protection, that contain the necessary measures to protect the heritage. These acts in the different states are based on federal framework acts and are therefore very similar. If an exception is not explicitly mentioned, the rules described below apply to all 16 states.

## 2.1. Permits

Permits are necessary for any substantial change to the cultural heritage. The owner of a scheduled site or monument has to apply for permission. This application has to contain a description with the necessary details explaining the quality and purpose of the change. If the desired changes require any other permission, such as a permit under the Building Act, there will only be one permit (issued by the competent authority), which will contain the *Auflagen* [authorisation] from the heritage agency.

Any other permission given by a non-heritage agency, for work that affects the cultural heritage, must be issued only with the full agreement of the competent authority for heritage protection.

If the applied changes require only the permission of the competent heritage agency (at the county or state level according to the system in that state), no other permit is needed.

For any archaeological investigations, or any activities aiming to discover archaeological heritage through the use of technical equipment, permits are necessary. They are issued by the competent authority only when the application and project design meet the requirements of the legislation in the respective state and if the qualification of the applicant is guaranteed.

## 2.2. Checks

If permits have been issued, the competent authority for heritage protection (at regional or state level as mentioned above) within that particular state takes action to monitor and check the work. This is also required for works that have permits from non-heritage agencies. The quality and quantity of checks depends on the resources of the institution in charge. Works should in any case be checked at the end, but continuous monitoring is required if the project design shows that decisions will have to be taken during the work or if the project designs were incomplete and the permit specifies that design is to be confirmed during the building process.

## 2.3. Sanctions

Sanctions can be based on different legal backgrounds. If the heritage is harmed, the sanctions applied will come from the Heritage Act of the relevant state. In Rhineland-Westphalia, Brandenburg and Mecklenburg-Western Pomerania, the ministry in charge of cultural heritage has issued a catalogue of fines.

It is necessary to prove whether other legislation is affected. If heritage is destroyed or badly harmed, it has to be checked whether the Criminal Code (§304, federal law) is relevant and, therefore, even if there is only a small indication that federal law is relevant, the case has to be handed over to the State Attorney for approval. If it is not relevant, the project will be given back to the competent authority for further processing.

In some instances, two legal systems might apply in the same case and then it has to be decided which laws the case should be based on. In cases of built heritage, this can be done through the Building Act or the Heritage Act.

There are different offences in the case of archaeological sites and monuments. If finds are violated, this could easily be a case for the criminal code in case of destruction (§ 304); if the finds are of scientific value under state ownership, it could be a case of theft. If the *unterschlagenes* [stolen] material is damaged or sold, the case will also be dealt with under the criminal code; if no income tax was reported to the competent tax authority, this will also be part of the case under the criminal code.

## 2.4. Enforcement

Although there are clear regulations on permits, checks and sanctions, the reality is slightly more difficult. To comply with legal procedures, the supervising authority has to very carefully record any failure and report this in due time to the competent authorities for enforcement. Although many cases have gone to court and been decided, many failures are not punished at the full possible scale. Often there are "misunderstandings" and incomplete reporting is a reason for milder punishment.

It would be better if enforcement was based on knowledge, rather than on the concept of punishment. Raising awareness at an early stage will help to create a better understanding of best practice in managing and handling the heritage; the better people's understanding, the fewer reasons there will be to enforce any punishments.

# PART 6

## CONCLUSIONS

# CONCLUSIONS

*Robert Pickard*

## 1. Characterisation and mapping systems

Characterisation studies and geographic information mapping systems provide a forward-planning tool to assist in the heritage management process. They can assist in explaining the importance of the heritage in relation to its local identity and context, and they can transfer heritage information to the planning process. The information they produce can be used to improve co-operation between different authorities – not just those responsible for heritage and for planning, but others such as highways and utility authorities responsible for infrastructure. For example, when proposals to build new roads are first being considered, they can provide important information about the heritage before a specific route is fixed (allowing alternative routes to be considered where there may be less impact on the heritage). Thus, they can assist the exchange and transfer of information for both horizontal and vertical co-operation between different competent authorities. The main goal of such systems is the provision of information to enable a more informed and integrated system of heritage management.

Such systems, when used for different management purposes, should have a degree of compatibility to allow the transfer of information to other local information systems. They should be structured in a simple manner, so that the information system can be developed as changes in areas or heritage information happen and opportunities occur to widen the scope of information to be recorded.

Digitalised systems require a certain amount of expertise in terms of knowledge of heritage and planning systems, as well as technical know-how. However, once the domains of information are determined, these systems should be reasonably straightforward to set up. Since the cost of information technology software reduces over time, the resources in terms of staffing to establish and maintain a map-based information system should not be extensive or a burden to public sector financial resources.

Once a system is established, the information fields can be widened in scope. Such information can be taken from a wide variety of sources including the local community, who may have wider knowledge of the heritage environment in which they live than the specialist competent authorities. Every point of contact in the assessment of the heritage in the field – with local people, heritage groups, investors and developers – can add new information to the resource base.

This form of information gathering not only informs directly the decision-making and management processes, but it can also inform the public: if such information is made generally available, it can educate people and raise their awareness of the heritage. If local people are more informed, they can make constructive representations about heritage protection and management, within the planning and development control sphere and otherwise. Access to such information through electronic heritage and planning portals is now an important aspect of this management process.

Bearing in mind the Council of Europe's Core Data Standards (for architectural and archaeological heritage) and Guidance on inventory and documentations systems, it is now relevant to consider whether such standards and guidance on recording methods should be updated – in particular, whether the traditional notions of the heritage have changed to include not just assets designated for protection, but also other elements of the cultural environment (as indicated by the Framework Convention on the Value of Cultural Heritage for the Society: the Faro Convention, 2005) that deserve recognition in the heritage management process.

## 2. Environmental assessment

A new awareness of managing change rather than simply protecting the heritage is a necessary step in the integrated process. Strategic environmental assessment (for plans and programmes) and environmental impact assessment (for projects) provide opportunities for instructive consideration in assessing, limiting or mitigating damage as a result of changes that development could bring.

At present, the main focus of such systems is the natural heritage. However, the cultural heritage makes an important contribution to, and is an essential part of, "the environment" in its widest sense. It is, therefore, relevant and necessary for heritage officials to have a role in environmental assessment processes. At present, there is little involvement in this context (and a lack of awareness by environmental assessment experts that cultural heritage is an aspect of the environment). It is, therefore, important for the responsible authorities – in the fields of heritage, environment/nature and spatial planning – to share information. There is also need for statutory consultation (i.e. by legal procedures) between all competent authorities in these related fields.

Awareness of particular heritage impact assessments may be drawn from the experience and methodology developed and used in Bosnia and Herzegovina – where environmental assessment expert groups include heritage officials – and there is horizontal and vertical co-operation between competent authorities. Characterisation and identification studies have an important role in this process. It is also necessary to develop and ensure "transparent" systems of environmental assessment, in which members of the local community can have the opportunity to make representations about, for example, a new road, which may have an impact on heritage assets.

## 3. Integration with spatial and urban planning systems

Drafting appropriate plans for safeguarding, preserving and enhancing areas recognised for their heritage quality and assets, and then developing them as statutory planning documents, can be assisted by characterisation and mapping studies. The latter could be produced by an appropriate service within one of the authorities competent in spatial/ urban planning and/or heritage, at local or other level – or they could be entrusted to private sector professional consultancies. Mapping of particular buildings, areas and features in the environment can be linked to reference documents and interpretation documents for such buildings, features, etc. Safeguarded or conservation areas, either urban or rural, can provide the opportunity for linking heritage management, landscape management, land use planning and development control.

It is necessary to develop procedures and effective communication, as well as laws and regulations, to ensure that the cultural heritage is more readily taken into account in the planning process. Some participants noted that natural heritage has greater considera-tion in the planning process than cultural heritage – and that there is a need for these issues to be considered on a more equal footing.

It is also important to develop a system of public awareness and participation so that the whole community is sufficiently informed about their heritage and all possible interested persons are able to raise issues about it – businesses, residents, visitors, the employed and unemployed, and so on. Local knowledge of heritage and features that create identity should be drawn from the community so that information can guide planning policies. New ways should be found to encourage public discussion of heritage issues, because too often owners and developers are the only voices and they seek to object to heritage protection. The value of information leaflets, design guides and other publications should be recognised in this context.

Spatial and urban plans – and the policies behind them – need to be adapted to make them accessible to the general public, to enable widespread comment and discussion, which should include local heritage considerations. There is also a need for greater public participation in the development control process, so the views of the public are consid-ered when decisions are made on applications for consent. It must be reiterated that public awareness and access to information are the keys to achieving this.

The capacity of the heritage should be scrutinised through the planning system to deter-mine the limits of acceptable change that will not unduly harm the area's character. Moreover, it should be recognised that new development and rehabilitation can enhance areas. Giving the heritage a function helps to keep it alive. It is, therefore, important to realise the economic and social potential of the heritage.

## 4. Consultation, authorisation, supervision and sanctions

The key issue arising from this theme is that the control of unauthorised and illegal activities affecting the heritage in South-East Europe generally does not work in practice, whether for political reasons (lack of political will to take action) or for other reasons.

There is a need for greater co-operation between administrative bodies with different competences, in authorisation, supervision and enforcement, not only horizontally (between ministries and between different local functions), but also vertically (between ministries and local authorities or between local authorities at different levels).

In general, the level of fines is insufficient to act as a deterrent. Also, action against unauthorised development needs to be taken immediately, rather than waiting until illegal work is well advanced. Swift, effective procedures, with co-operation between authorities, must be established for this purpose.

The long-term preservation of buildings can be aided by urgent assistance and technical protection. Protected buildings that have been abandoned or otherwise neglected, or only partly occupied in poor condition/repair, could be subject to emergency action to keep the building weather-tight, structurally stable and safe from vandalism or theft. "Mothballing" a building can protect it until it can be conserved or restored, found a new user or rehabilitated. Such urgent safeguarding procedures should allow the competent authority to reclaim the costs of emergency action if owners or occupiers are unwilling to undertake such action.

Furthermore, identifying which properties are at risk (by swift surveys of condition and occupancy) should enable priority action to be determined. More positive approaches are needed for heritage assets under threat or at risk. The competent authorities could be proactive in encouraging owners of buildings to maintain them, perhaps by helping to market them and find new owners who are prepared to take the necessary action. It is important to recognise that heritage buildings may have an inherent market value, so a small investment in maintenance and repair may realise a building with a high capital value, which can be used rather than being left neglected.

A positive approach should be taken to encourage owners of heritage assets to sell them to entities and organisations (public, private or non-government) that will accept the necessary works and take the required action. In extreme cases, it may be necessary to expropriate, but this can bring financial burdens to the acquiring authorities unless they can immediately sell to another organisation that is prepared to undertake and finance relevant works.

Revolving funds, and financial and fiscal incentives, should also be considered in this context.

The countries of South-East Europe should take all opportunities to obtain heritage finance from international sources, including pre-accession funds offered through various European Union programmes and other international funds. Heritage projects should be developed for submission to those bodies that may be able to offer assistance. There is an urgency to this type of opportunity and a need to be proactive – rather than waiting for assistance to be offered. This further necessitates active political support for such action.

## 5. Final observations

This publication is the culmination of reports and presentations concerning the development of integrated management tools in the countries taking part in the Regional Programme for Cultural and Natural Heritage in South-East Europe. It is important to disseminate the messages from this discussion to decision-makers in the different competent authorities in these countries and to remind them that policies for the heritage should be properly included in relevant spatial and urban planning mechanisms. Moreover, there is a need to improve regional co-operation and the regional exchange of information, including the possibility of exchanging experts or developing trans-border or other joint projects on integrated management and sustainable development.

# Appendix 1 – Questionnaire forming the basis for national reports

## A. Format of the national report

The working groups will submit a joint "national report" to the institutions concerned, divided into three parts corresponding to the three key themes. The report, which should be submitted in the form of a document ready for publication, should be 10 pages long at most (3 pages per theme) and written in English. The report should be laid out as follows:

Table of contents

1. Documentation systems

    1.1. Identification

    1.2. Characterisation

    1.3. Databases and computerised mapping

2. Integrated management plans and regulations

    2.1. Environment

    2.2. Spatial planning

    2.3. Town planning

3. Consultation procedures, authorisation, supervision and penalties

    3.1. Consultation procedures

    3.2. Authorisation

    3.3. Supervision and penalties

## B. Explanation

## 1. Documentation systems

The first aspect will be directed at documentation systems to characterise all aspects of the cultural environment. Particular consideration will be given to computerised mapping techniques and associated databases, and how these can inform the planning process.

## 1.1. Identification

### Questions

Describe your country's heritage inventory systems or conservation registers, in the broadest sense of the terms, covering monuments, groups of buildings, archaeological sites, cultural sites and landscapes, and any special protection areas around them.

- what information do these documentation systems contain? Addresses, land registry references, construction and conservation-order dates, descriptions, illustrations, plans, etc?

- what ministries, departments and services are responsible for these systems? Do they operate at national, regional and/or local level?

- to what extent are the various documents held by different departments co-ordinated (communication channels between different departments, combining and re-using information)? Give a specific example.

### Comments

The first stage in the integrated conservation process, therefore, implies the need for identification of heritage assets, including those specifically designated as well as other aspects of the "cultural environment" such as areas where archaeological remains are perceived, where aspects of the architectural heritage of more local and regional importance contribute to the common heritage and in the wider context of landscape and the cultural environment.

These questions concern particularly the recognised systems of inventory and registration of heritage assets to be protected.

## 1.2. Characterisation

### Questions

Describe any documentation systems "characterising" heritage in its context before work is carried out on it (consolidation, renovation, rehabilitation, restoration, or improvement work) and before any other environmental or spatial planning document is drawn up (development, land-use and management plans, etc.).

- what information do these characterisation systems contain (results of historical, architectural, archaeological, town-planning, environmental or social and economic surveys of the property in question and its surroundings)?

- what ministries, departments and services are responsible for these systems? Do they operate at national, regional and/or local level?

- to what extent is this information passed on and taken into account when spatial and environmental planning documents are prepared? Give a specific example.

## Comments

Apart from the recognised systems of inventory and registration of heritage, the opportunity should be taken to identify the character and values of the heritage in a wider context.

The process of "characterisation" involves bringing together as many aspects of a place as possible in order to appreciate and understand it better, and to understand the experience of inhabitants (and visitors) of being in it. Characterisation should have certain objectives:

- to define the context or place in relation to how buildings and monuments relate to each other and to other aspects of the built and natural environment;

- to understand the past, the process of change or continuity, which has brought the cultural environment to the present and which provides the basis for future change;

- to provide a wider picture of the cultural environment which recognises people's perceptions and views of the common heritage.

By mapping the path of evolution it is possible to chart future directions, with or without intervention. This then allows the opportunity to set out choices in terms of works of preservation and management.

Characterisation should also be a tool for participation by providing information to help not just the specialists, but also the public to consider the implications of proposed changes to the cultural environment and to help shape the future environment.

## 1.3. Databases and computerised mapping

### Questions

Describe the processes by which the data collected through the above-mentioned identification and characterisation systems is computerised, and any link to a geographic information system (GIS). Give details of the target groups concerned and how these processes can be used in practice in the integrated management of heritage and its surroundings.

- is the information you collect through your identification and characterisation systems entered into a computer database? If so, what information is entered (figures, text, illustrations) and how is it organised?

- are these databases linked to a computerised mapping system (or geographic information system)? If so, how?

- what do you consider to be the uses and advantages of these integrated documentation systems? Give a specific example.

- are these documentation systems accessible to other interested public authorities and the public (target groups)? If so, are they fully or only partly accessible?

- have you encountered difficulties or obstacles in setting up such systems? If so, do they stem from financial, technical, human or other factors? How did you, or are you planning to, tackle these problems?

## Comments

The systems of identification and characterisation of heritage assets in their environmental context can be can be developed through a set of special databases attached to geographic information systems (GIS). This process can be used as a practical tool:

- to guide a process of strategic environmental assessment of proposed policies to be identified in the development and approval of strategic spatial plans or other detailed land-use plans;

- to inform the preparation of such plans and specific conservation and enhancement-management plans;

- to document cultural and natural heritage features and values in a particular territory (including landscapes, townscapes etc.);

- to provide an enhanced form of inventory that can be available electronically;

- to inform the development of safeguard and re-use strategies concerning the heritage under threat (register and survey of "buildings at risk");

- to provide heritage impact analysis;

- to prepare revitalisation plans for the heritage;

- to provide information for the public;

- to guide the sustainable use of the heritage.

The debate will seek to explore some of the systems presently in use by several countries. Some examples, which could be presented, include the following.

### United Kingdom

Various systems based on geographic information systems have been developed in recent years. These include a national programme of Historic Landscape Categorisation, which is applied to landscape management, agricultural-environmental policy and spatial planning, and for research and information. It has been developed in the context of sustainability and integrated conservation to provide a character-based approach to managing the historic environment. Other programmes of characterisation have been developed to consider local character in rural areas and villages, to make urban archaeological assessments for major and smaller historic urban centres (and these have been taken into account in planning urban renewal) and to assist the planning of new strategic development projects.

*Denmark*

InterSAVE, the International Survey of Architectural Values in the Environment, has three stages:

- preliminary investigation: topographic investigation, historic analysis, architectural observation of developed structures and individual buildings;
- fieldwork: mapping and registration;
- development of municipal atlases: identifying the topography, history and architecture of the area though a topic map of architectural relationships and an assessment map of buildings.

*France*

Work has been done to make various inventories and databases of information systematically available, in particular to decision-makers and municipal authorities, in the form of a Heritage Atlas. Based on a geographic information system, the process combines all heritage data available in a given region.

*Czech Republic*

The lack of effective integrated conservation programmes and the particular problems arising from uncontrolled development have led to the development of a documentation system for small historic cities using a geographic information system to better inform the planning process of heritage values.

## 2. Integrated management plans and regulations

The second stage of the integrated process involves the integration of heritage within the urban and spatial planning and environment documents. This debate will seek to explore the experience of countries that have developed integrated systems and how they use the planning and environmental process to safeguard and enhance the cultural environment.

Particular attention will be given to how the identification and evaluation process, including characterisation and mapping techniques, can inform the assessment process for the formulation and approval of different levels of plan mechanisms. Specific examples at different levels will be considered.

## 2.1. Environment

### Questions

Describe any "environmental impact studies" conducted in your country prior to the adoption of plans for large-scale projects likely to have an impact on the environment in the broad sense of the term (including heritage items).

- for what kind of projects are environmental impact studies conducted (infrastructure, tourist development, urban rehabilitation, landscaping, new divisions of land into building plots, new use of industrial wasteland, establishment of new industrial estates, shopping districts, etc.)?

- what types of environmental impact are considered (water, air, land, subsoil, population, fauna, flora, climate, noise, etc.)? Do the impact studies cover both cultural and natural heritage? Do they include archaeological heritage and landscapes? If so, do they make use of the documentation systems referred to above (databases and computerised mapping)? If not, why not?

- which ministry (or department or service) is responsible for preparing environmental impact studies and what other ministries does it work with? Does it carry out studies itself or assign the work to an independent research consultancy in the private sector? Does it finance studies itself or is it up to the project developer to finance them? Are the public consulted?

- what effect do impact studies have on decisions taken by the authorities responsible and on systems for supervising or assessing the implementation of projects? What effect do they have on the heritage affected by the project or heritage polices in general? Give a specific example.

### Comments

The formulation of strategic plans within European Union member states is now required to go through a process of Strategic Environmental Assessment following European Directive 2001/42/EC.

This involves a number of stages:

- preparation of an environmental report;

- consultation with authorities with environmental responsibilities (including authorities responsible for the heritage) and the public;

- taking the environmental report and the results of the consultations into consideration in the formulation of plan policies;

- providing information on the decision made when the plan is adopted;

- monitoring the significant effects of the plan's implementation.

The environmental report must identify the likely effects on the environment, including such issues as biodiversity, population, fauna, flora, soil, water, air, climatic factors, material assets, cultural heritage including the architectural and archaeological heritage, landscape and the inter-relationship with these factors. It should also identify the secondary, cumulative, synergistic, short-, medium- and long-term, permanent and temporary, positive and negative effects.

The assessment process will also aim to address sustainability of the proposals through this and the monitoring process (allowing for the review of plans as relevant).

## 2.2. Spatial planning

### Questions

Describe the different types of spatial planning used in your country (strategic development plans and statutory land-use plans) and how they take account of the cultural and natural heritage.

- what types of spatial planning are used in your country? What are their aims and scope?

- at what level are plans adopted (national, regional and/or local)?

- which ministry or local authority department is responsible for devising such plans, and what other ministries or departments does it work with? Does it prepare the draft plan itself or assign the work to an independent research consultancy in the private sector? Does it finance plans itself or is it up to the project developer to finance them? Is the public consulted before plans are adopted?

- are heritage documentation systems (databases and computerised mapping) used when these plans are prepared? If so, how?

- how is heritage taken into account in such plans? Is it singled out for special treatment or "positive discrimination" in terms of protection, conservation, management or use? In other words, what is the effect of such plans on the heritage concerned or heritage policies in general? Give a specific example.

### Comments

Spatial plans are an important vehicle for ensuring that conservation policies are co-ordinated and integrated with other planning policies. Imaginative plan policies can not only reduce threats to the cultural environment but also increase its contribution to local amenity.

Strategic spatial plans set out the broad "development" objectives or constraints for a territory. This broad planning framework should guide the approach to be adopted on a more local level of plan. In relation to the cultural environment, it could consider the capacity of historic towns to sustain development, for example, or identify opportunities for growth elsewhere to relieve pressure on areas of heritage importance, or consider the provision of strategic development such as transport infrastructure that respects the cultural environment.

Local level plans should set out detailed policy on the preservation and enhancement of the cultural environment in the area and the factors that should be taken into account when assessing applications for consent for new construction, including the change of use of architectural monuments or development that would affect their setting (including in the sphere of any defined protection zones) or the impact of development proposals on sites of archaeological significance, for example.

These plans could also:

- consider specific policies for ensembles or areas of architectural or archaeological importance, or other aspects of amenity including historic gardens, views, historic street layouts and other issues of local distinctiveness which should be safeguarded;

- set out policies concerning the requirement of impact assessments on the cultural heritage and the obligations of developers in the context of preventative archaeology;

- identify other design guidance or development briefs for sites that have may be regarded as having a negative or neutral impact on the cultural environment as a means of enhancing the appearance and character of the area;

- include a strategy for the social and economic revitalisation of buildings and areas (to support the beneficial use of the heritage) and, therefore, identify opportunities that the historic fabric of the cultural environment can offer as a focus for regeneration;

- identify the need for formulating special plans for safeguarding and enhancing areas of recognised heritage importance.

Land-use plans play a part in protecting the heritage in that they control to what use it may be put. Such plans lay down the legally permitted use of all the buildings, green spaces and roads in a given territory. They include a map and regulations specific to each category of allocation shown on the map. Thus, they supplement heritage protection orders, which seldom set out the legally permitted uses of protected properties.

Whether they are general (covering a town or region) or particular (covering a neighbourhood or street), such plans, therefore, make it possible to protect the heritage by avoiding types of use or allocation which would be fatal to it.

For example, the land allocation plan could prevent such things as an old neighbourhood consisting of small houses being transformed into an administrative area requiring large office capacity, a natural site being divided into plots, car parks being built or roads widened in the middle of an historic centre, etc.

Another advantage of such plans is that they enable the immediate protection of property that as yet enjoys no legal protection as part of the cultural heritage, and this is currently the situation of many groups of buildings and natural sites.

## 2.3. Town planning

### Questions

Describe the town planning regulations that currently apply in your country (at national, regional and/or local levels) and what provisions they make for cultural and natural heritage.

- what types of regulations apply in your country (general regulations and/or regulations applying to specific areas)? What is the scope of each of these types of regulation? Do certain regulations relate specifically to areas with a high heritage value (historic urban and rural centres, cultural landscapes, nature reserves, archaeological sites, etc.)?

- which ministry or local authority department is responsible for drawing up regulations (at national, regional and/or local level)? Does it work with other departments, including that or those responsible for cultural and natural heritage?

- is use made, when drawing up these regulations, of heritage documentation systems (databases and computerised mapping)? If so, how?

- what approach is taken to heritage in these regulations? Is it singled out for special treatment or "positive discrimination" in terms of conservation and planning in the surrounding area? In other words, what is the effect of these regulations on heritage conservation? Give a specific example.

### Comments

In addition to the studies and plans drawn up in the framework of spatial planning and environment policies, urban planning regulations favour the conservation of heritage by legally determining building/renovation regulations (building line, size, materials, shapes, colours, etc.). In some countries, they also regulate advertising hoardings, signposting, street lighting and tree felling.

Like spatial plans, urban planning regulations apply either to the whole of the national or regional territory or to particular areas (a town, village or old neighbourhood). It is, therefore, useful for heritage officials to take part in the drafting or revision of urban planning regulations in order to ensure that heritage considerations are taken into account and will, therefore, be respected in work requiring planning permission (splitting up into parcels, building and demolition).

Where such regulations concern areas including important historic groups of buildings, sites or areas of archaeological interest, it is even legitimate for heritage officials to guide their drafting since what is at issue is more the heritage than town planning.

For example, in Belgium a partnership was established in the 1970s between Wallonia's town planning and cultural heritage departments and the History of Art Faculty of the University of Louvain, to draw up urban planning regulations for historic city centres. They did this by producing atlases of historic town centres, the maps identifying the monuments and architectural groups to be protected along with details of the planning regulations for each area, supplemented by text explaining the objective (overall strategy) and the heritage and planning characteristics of the buildings mentioned.

The success of these atlases has led to the production of atlases of old rural centres and of buried archaeological sites so that the whole regional heritage is now protected by planning instruments.

Similar principles have been applied in Brussels through regional planning regulations, in France through the ZPPAUP (zones of architectural, urban and landscape importance), in Denmark through the SAVE system (Survey of Architectural Values in the Environment) and in the UK (see examples in section 1.3. above).

## 3. Consultation, authorisation, supervision and penalties

The third stage of the integrated process involves integration through consultation and consent regimes (heritage consent and building/planning consent). The conditions for supervision and sanctions procedures are also analysed.

### 3.1. Consultation procedures

#### Questions

Describe public consultation procedures (for private individuals and organisations) that take place prior to statutory heritage conservation measures, the issuing of planning permission for work in conservation areas and the adoption of the spatial planning measures referred to above.

Describe both formal and informal arrangements for horizontal and vertical consultation between the various ministries and local authority departments responsible for taking such decisions.

- how is public consultation organised in terms of the type of project involved (protection, conservation work or spatial planning), time constraints and the sequence in which opinions are sought, communication tools (public notices, press announcements, etc.) and the type of people concerned (property owners, local inhabitants, private investors/developers, non-governmental organisations, research institutes, official advisory bodies, etc.)?

- which public authorities are responsible for organising these public consultations? What is the true impact of the opinions expressed? Do public decision-makers generally take account of them? If so, in what circumstances?

- how do consultation and co-ordination with other authorities involved in the decision operate, both horizontally (between different sectors) and between the different tiers of government?

- are the arrangements for these two types of consultation formal (based on statutory documents) or informal (based on established practice and the goodwill of the parties concerned)? Do they work well and what problems do they raise, if any? Give a specific example.

## Comments

The debate will seek to explore good consultation practice between individuals or organisations and relevant authorities prior to submitting applications for works that may have an impact on the cultural environment and particular heritage assets, and also consultation between relevant authorities (those with competences in planning and development, heritage and environmental protection).

Early consultation with relevant authorities on works proposals or other activity that could affect heritage (of all types) is an essential preliminary, especially for developers and investors.

The organisation of consultation with heritage institutions, planning authorities and other interested bodies (such as voluntary organisations) allows an opportunity for refinement and revision of development proposals. This type of practice requires clear procedures so that potential damaging activity is fully considered before proposals become firm and timescales become inflexible.

For example, in the particular case of development activity affecting sites of known or potential archaeological importance, the Europe Code of Good Practice (Archaeology and the Urban Project) – based on the British Archaeologists' and Developers' Liaison Group Code of Practice – provides good advice on consultative processes that can mitigate the impact of development on buried deposits and remains. This allows other measures to be considered, such as using specially designed foundations or not constructing basements, which may be preferable to excavation (often resulting in the destruction of remains) unless there are strong grounds for requiring excavation and such investigation is fully funded. The code is intended to facilitate co-operation between planners, developers and archaeologists. This approach can also be agreed through attaching conditions to permits (such as to allow investigation for a limited time period and to require a developer to pay the cost of such archaeological investigation).

## 3.2. Authorisation

### Questions

Describe the authorisation procedures that take place prior to official land-use changes or work on property forming part of the protected cultural and natural heritage and any protected areas around it.

– what kind of work on protected property requires prior permission? Are certain kinds of "minor" work exempt (e.g. carbon-copy restoration, maintenance of sites and gardens, archaeological digs, etc.)?

– are there two forms of authorisation (a heritage permit and a town planning permit) or is there a single, combined form? Whatever the case, briefly describe the procedures for consultation and co-ordination between the two authorities concerned before authorisation is granted.

– if these authorities' views differ, how is the final decision taken? Does the more exacting opinion take precedence? Is it possible to appeal? Give a specific example.

### Comments

Works for the change of use of an architectural monument, development in a protected zone or designated area and development that may impact on archaeological sites represent some examples where two types of consent will be required (heritage consent and urban planning consent). It is essential for proper management that these are co-ordinated (so, where consent for development is granted, work should not begin if a heritage consent is also required). In such circumstances, consent systems should be co-ordinated through legal and administrative measures, and they should avoid complexity.

There can be advantages to using a single authorisation system for this purpose, and a number of countries have now moved in this direction. Such systems rely on defined mechanics of operation, consultation requirements and time considerations (periods allowed for consultation and determining an application).

In the Walloon Region of Belgium, for example, the decree relating to monuments, sites and excavations is incorporated in the Walloon Spatial Planning and Town Planning and Heritage Code and a single building permit is required, subject to the prior consideration of proposals by the Heritage Division of the Regional Spatial Planning Department. This single-track procedure is regarded as the most successful in terms of applying the principle of integrated conservation. From January 2003 this single consent system has been widened to include environmental considerations (such as the control of works on trees and environmental assessment).

The planning system in the Republic of Ireland has seen a number of reforms in recent years, mainly through legislation in 1999 and 2000. Although development affecting "national monuments" (generally archaeological and ancient monuments) needs two consents, all work associated with protected structures (including buildings in architectural conservation areas and the placing of advertisements) comes under the planning legislation as these items form "Planning Objectives in Development Plans". Accordingly, all works are dealt with by the same consent procedure.

In 2004, the United Kingdom also announced proposals to unify some existing consent regimes.

In the Netherlands, the 1988 *Monumentwet* (Monuments Act) differentiates various types of "Protected Monuments" (architectural, archaeological and religious monuments) and Town and Village Conservation Areas. While there is a separation between planning, housing, building and cultural environment legislation, the systems are integrated to some extent because development control and building control are dealt with via one building/planning permission, through one municipal department: the building inspectorate (subject to relevant consultation requirements).

## 3.3. Supervision and penalties

### Questions

Describe your country's statutory systems of supervision and penalties in respect of heritage, spatial planning, town planning and the environment. To what extent do these apply to illegal work and poor upkeep jeopardising protected cultural and natural assets?

– what statutory supervision systems exist in respect of heritage, spatial planning, town planning and the environment (and other relevant areas)? Are they applied? If not, why not? Give a specific example.

– are there formal or informal co-operation arrangements between the authorities responsible for heritage and those responsible for spatial or environmental planning to ensure that there are people in the field checking for illegal work? If so, how do these arrangements operate?

– what administrative and criminal penalties are provided for by law in respect of heritage, spatial planning, town planning and the environment (and other relevant areas)? Are they applied? If not, why? Give a specific example.

- what are the main problems and obstacles you encounter in trying to implement these laws? Do they stem from financial, technical, human or other factors? How have you tackled, or are you planning to tackle, these problems?

## Comments

There is a need for supervision in many Council of Europe member states, especially in the nine countries participating in the Regional Programme currently adjusting to the economic and social context of transition.

Control mechanisms are required to prevent and remedy:

- illegal works of construction, maintenance and restoration;

- inadequate reconstruction;

- lack of maintenance;

- other sources of heritage damage.

It can be also useful to draw up a priority list of "outstanding and endangered heritage", which requires urgent action and on which current resources should be concentrated.

In many countries, the legislation on cultural heritage includes penalties and coercive procedures that combine administrative and criminal measures. In some cases, these are found in other legislation.

Administrative procedures include reparation – in the case of architectural heritage, reinstatement of the situation that existed before unauthorised work carried out (for example, in Belgium, Denmark, Ireland, Malta, the Netherlands and the United Kingdom). In some instances, the relevant authorities are permitted to enter premises to undertake necessary repair works (but they still have the difficulty of recovering costs).

Administrative measures can also be taken in relation to the archaeological heritage (for example, penalties exist for failing to report "finds" in France). However, it is less easy to identify specific measures in this context.

One problem that exists generally is that the evidence shows that sanctions and coercive measures are ineffective because they are not often applied. Another problem is the low level of fines or the fact that the level of fines is not sufficient to act as a deterrent. The largest fine possible – a penalty of €1 000 000 can be applied in Ireland for carrying out "development" without permission or for not carrying out specified work or taking protective measures – appears to be a significant deterrent.

Criminal sanctions can extend to imprisonment, though this appears to be a measure of last resort. The maximum period of imprisonment varies from six months to five years in the sample of countries.

# Appendix 2 – List of contributors

## 1. National reports

*Albania*

Florent Çeliku, RPSEE Programme Co-ordinator of Albania

Arlinda Kondi Toçi, Ministry of Culture and Youth of Albania

Ariana Koça, Nature Protection Directorate, Ministry of Environment of Albania

Shpresa Leka, Ministry of Territorial Adjustment and Tourism of Albania

*Bosnia and Herzegovina*

Amra Hadžimuhamedović, Commission for the Protection of National Monuments, Bosnia and Herzegovina

Vesna Karacic, Assistant Minister for Physical Planning, Federal Ministry of Physical Planning and Environment of Bosnia and Herzegovina

Azra Korac-Mehmedovic, Head of Nature Protection Department, Federal Ministry of Physical Planning and Environment of Bosnia and Herzegovina

*Bulgaria*

Hristo Bojinov, Director, National Protection Service, Ministry of Environment and Water of Bulgaria

Todor Krestev, Professor of Architectural Heritage Preservation, at the University of Architecture, Construction and Geodesy, Sofia

Peter Miladinov, Head of European Integration Department, International Cultural Policy Directorate, Ministry of Culture of Bulgaria

Lidya Stankova, specialist with the Ministry of Regional Development and Public Works

*Croatia*

Jasen Mesić, Assistant Minister in charge of the Directorate for the Protection of Cultural Heritage, Ministry of Culture of the Republic of Croatia

Nada Duic-Kowalsky, Ministry of Culture of the Republic of Croatia, Directorate for Protection of Cultural Heritage

Tamara Ganoci Frisch, Ministry of Culture of the Republic of Croatia, Directorate for Protection of Cultural Heritage

Marijana A. Mance, Head of International Relations Department, Ministry of Environmental Protection, Physical Planning and Construction of the Republic of Croatia

## Montenegro

Lidija Ljesar, Senior Adviser for Protection of Cultural Monuments in the Ministry of Culture and Media of Montenegro

Vasilije Buskovic, Associated Expert, Republic Institute for the Protection of Nature

## Romania

Mircea Angelescu, Director, Historical Monuments and Museums, Ministry of Culture of Romania

Adriana Baz, Director, Directorate of Biodiversity Conservation and Protected Areas, Ministry of Waters and Environmental Protection of Romania

## Serbia

Tijana Zivanovic, Agency for Spatial Planning of the Republic of Serbia

Milica Risojevic, Environment Directorate for the Protection of Environment, Ministry of Science of the Republic of Serbia

Bozidar Kovacevic, Environment Directorate for the Protection of Environment, Ministry of Science of the Republic of Serbia

Borislav Šurdić, Ministry of Culture of the Republic of Serbia

## "The former Yugoslav Republic of Macedonia"

Biljana Prentoska, Head of European Integration Department, Ministry of Culture and RPSEE Co-ordinator

Danica Pavlovska, Head of Sector of Spatial Planning, Ministry of Environment and Physical Planning

Robertina Brajanoska, Adviser in the Department for Biodiversity, Ministry of Environment and Physical Planning

Biljana Tanovska, Head of Sector of Cultural Heritage Protection, Ministry of Culture

Juilja Trickovska, Head of Department for Identification, Protection and Use of the Cultural Heritage, Cultural Heritage Protection Office

Snezana Gerasimova, Adviser in the Section of Immovable Cultural Heritage, Department for Identification, Protection and Use of the Cultural Heritage, Cultural Heritage Protection Office

Mirko Andovski, Architect, Head of Department for Urban Planning, Public Enterprise for Spatial and Urban Planning

Rada Filipovska, Adviser in the Rural Areas Department, Area Arrangement Sector, Ministry of Transport and Communications

Pene Penev, State Adviser in the Ministry of Local Self-Government

Valentina Cavdarova, Adviser in the Department of Spatial Planning, Ministry of Environment and Physical Planning

Daniela Stefkova, Head of European Co-operation Department, Ministry of Environment and Physical Planning

## 2. Other contributors

Todor Krestev, President of ICOMOS Bulgaria

Robert Pickard, Professor of Built Environment and Heritage Conservation, Northumbria University, United Kingdom and Co-ordinator of the Council of Europe's Legislative Support Task Force

Myriam Goblet, Consultant Expert and Member of the Council of Europe's Legislative Support Task Force

Graham Fairclough, English Heritage

Geneviève Pinçon, Co-ordinator of the Atlas of Architecture and Heritage, Directorate of Architecture and Heritage (DAPA), Ministry for Culture and Communication, France

Friedrich Lüth, Archäologisches Landesmuseum, Landesamt für Bodendenkmalpflege Mecklenburg-Vorpommern, Germany

Juris Dambis, Head of State Inspection for Heritage Protection, Latvia

Tatjana Rener, Regionalna pisarna Štanjel, Štanjel Regional Office, Agencija Republike Slovenije za regionalni razvoj (ARR), Slovenia

Ann-Mari Westerlind, Architect, National Heritage Board, Sweden

Jacques-Emmanuel Remy, Architect, Team Leader for Component C of the Regional Programme for Natural and Cultural Heritage in South-East Europe, France

Mikhäel de Thyse, Regional Co-operation Division, Department of Culture and Cultural Heritage, Directorate of Culture and Cultural and Natural Heritage, Council of Europe